Praise for

MINDFUL WORK

"Intriguing, timely, and enjoyable ... A fascinating account of the increasing adoption of these ancient [Eastern] disciplines by Western businesses as means of improving corporate efficiency, reducing employee stress, and, directly or indirectly, boosting the bottom line."

— *Financial Times*

"[An] adroit exploration. [Gelles] deftly describes what mindfulness is and what it isn't, presents the science behind it, and handily succeeds in convincing readers that the practice is worth exploring." — *Success*

"What the corporate crowd may find most interesting [here] is that executives at several blue chip companies, like Ford and Google, practice mindfulness and even encourage their employees to do so ... Here's hoping this book influences many more corporations." — *Forbes*

"Readers curious about the benefits of mindfulness at work or in their personal lives will appreciate this book." — *Booklist*

"Brimming with insights and backed up with solid research, *Mindful Work* takes us to the front lines of a revolution that is transforming the business world." — **Arianna Huffington**

"A delightful, authoritative, and provocative guide to the new world of mindfulness at work. David Gelles covers the story from the inside out, giving readers exactly what they need to assess whether mindfulness is for them — and, if so, how to forge ahead. Give this book your full attention." — **Daniel Goleman, author of** *Focus* **and** *Emotional Intelligence*

"Gelles has done a masterful job of capturing the 'mindfulness movement.' His candid analysis and his dialogue with people from all facets of this movement paint a wonderfully clear view of a potent proposition for living and working in better ways."

— Scott Kriens, chairman, Juniper Networks,
and director, 1440 Foundation

"In this compelling book, Gelles describes how apparent paradoxes can resolve into a business culture where taking a breath is part of making a buck."

— Sherry Turkle, author of *Alone Together*

"In this wise and revealing work, David Gelles explains how Eastern wisdom is transforming the Western workplace. Smart, hopeful, and inspiring, this is a book with a wide reach and a clear focus."

— Mark Epstein, author of *The Trauma of Everyday Life* and
Thoughts Without a Thinker: Psychotherapy from a Buddhist Perspective

"Gelles deftly show the power of mindfulness to change individuals, business, and our world for the better. Mindfulness is a practice we need to embrace, and we cannot be afraid to follow this path."

— Marc Benioff, chairman and CEO, Salesforce

"This carefully researched, heartfully written, and delightfully readable book tells one of the most interesting true stories of our time: the fascinating and sometimes messy coming together of the wisdom world and the corporate world."

— Chade-Meng Tan, Jolly Good Fellow of Google,
author of *Search Inside Yourself*

"This stunning new book is by far the most insightful, practical guide to mindfulness and meditation. Gelles, who has deep experience with mindfulness, takes us inside leading companies like Google, General Mills, Aetna, and Patagonia to show how meditation is transforming workplaces. *Mindful Work* could change your life."

— Bill George, Harvard Business School, former CEO of
Medtronic, and author of *True North*

MINDFUL WORK

How
MEDITATION
Is
CHANGING BUSINESS
from the
INSIDE OUT

David Gelles

AN EAMON DOLAN BOOK
Mariner Books
Houghton Mifflin Harcourt
Boston   New York

First Mariner Books edition 2016
Copyright © 2015 by David Gelles

For information about permission to reproduce selections from
this book, write to trade.permissions@hmhco.com or to Permissions,
Houghton Mifflin Harcourt Publishing Company, 3 Park Avenue,
19th Floor, New York, New York 10016.

www.hmhco.com

Library of Congress Cataloging-in-Publication Data
Gelles, David (Business journalist)
Mindful work : how meditation is changing
business from the inside out / David Gelles.
pages cm
"An Eamon Dolan book."
Includes bibliographical references and index.
ISBN 978-0-544-22722-4 (hardcover) — ISBN 978-0-544-22632-6
(ebook) — ISBN 978-0-544-70525-8 (pbk.)
1. Leadership—Psychological aspects. 2. Meditation. 3. Mind and body.
4. Social responsibility of business. I. Title.
BF637.L4G447 2015
158.7 — dc23
2014039685

Book design by Greta D. Sibley

Printed in the United States of America
DOC 10 9 8 7 6 5 4 3 2 1

FOR

FRANNY

Contents

Introduction

It is a steamy summer day in Boston. At the Park Plaza, a grand hotel just off the Common, a nerdy crowd packs a high-ceilinged ballroom, stirring under the chandeliers, waiting for a man it reveres as a visionary. The thronging masses — almost all young men — are super-fans of the personal computer, techies at the vanguard of a revolution that would soon upend the way we live and work. Their guest of honor is Steve Jobs.

Just twenty-six years old, Jobs has rocketed to international stardom in recent months. Apple, the company he cofounded and runs, has just gone public. His flagship product, the Apple III, is revolutionizing how people use technology. He is already worth $250 million.

Jobs is in Boston to address Applefest, an event for devotees of his products organized by an eighteen-year-old computer whiz named Jonathan Rotenberg. Applefest was put together without Jobs's knowledge, and he agreed to come only at the last minute, perhaps sensing some kinship with the young, ambitious organizer. Lean and lanky, Jobs sports a full beard and bushy black hair that falls over his ears and past his collar. He could be a folk singer were it not for the dark suit, blue dress shirt, and black tie. Wide-framed eyeglasses cover nearly half his angular face. In the heat, he has removed his jacket, slinging it over his left shoulder.

After lunch, Jobs and Rotenberg walk back to the Park Plaza. All day, hundreds of fans have been tinkering with the newest Apple machines, swapping notes, and dreaming about how computers might change their lives, and the world, in the years to come. Now they're assembled in the ballroom, waiting to hear from the man who has made their futuristic dreams come true.

Despite his youth, Jobs looks cool and collected. A contented grin graces his face, perhaps understandable for a multimillionaire. Yet with nearly one thousand of his most loyal customers in the audience, even Jobs must feel some nerves. These are his early adopters, the hard-core users he's counting on to sustain his company over the coming years. Backstage, ten minutes before the keynote speech is set to begin, the teenage Rotenberg is also a ball of nerves. He and Jobs make some small talk, but both are anxious for the keynote to begin. Then Jobs says, "Jonathan, would you excuse me for a minute?"

Rotenberg turns around, and Jobs is gone. Is it stage fright? Has he just gone to the bathroom? Or is Jobs, already known for his enigmatic behavior, playing one of his mind games? Long minutes drag out. The crowd beyond the stage stirs, restless in the heat. It is now four minutes before the speech is to start and Rotenberg begins to panic. If Jobs gets cold feet and bails, Applefest will be a disaster. Rotenberg will be humiliated. The host paces backstage, searching for his speaker just moments before the main event. A few more minutes tick by. Jobs is nowhere to be found. Then, finally, in a corner of the jumbled backstage area, Rotenberg spots him.

Jobs is sitting on the floor. His legs are crossed. His posture erect, he faces the wall, unmoving. At the precipice of one of the biggest moments of his career, Jobs has paused to meditate.

As Rotenberg looks on, Jobs enjoys another few moments of stillness amid the backstage tumult. Finally, slowly, Jobs gets up, smiles at Rotenberg, and makes his way to the stage. He emerges from behind the curtain and into the spotlight. The crowd roars.

Steve Jobs's ability to be calm and concentrated in the midst of chaos was one of the things that made him such a great leader. Though he was far from perfect, Jobs's focus, insight, and creativity set him — and Apple — apart from the competition. And in that moment backstage, Jobs wasn't praying to any divinity, visualizing any mandala, or reciting some mantra. He was, in all likelihood, doing what he had been trained to do by his meditation instructors — simply paying close attention to the sensations of his own breath, the physicality of his body, and observing the thoughts in his mind nonjudgmentally. He was taking a few moments to be *mindful*.

Jobs was America's first mainstream meditating CEO, a disciple of the Zen Buddhist tradition, and a keen student of Eastern philosophies. But he mostly practiced in isolation, studying intensely with his Japanese teacher, sharing his interest with a few close friends, but rarely bringing his meditation into the office. Today, however, mindfulness is everywhere, almost as ubiquitous and transformative as Apple products themselves.

What was a fringe movement when Jobs addressed Applefest in 1981 is now an increasingly prominent part of the cultural landscape, turning up in businesses, governments, and educational institutions around the world. Senior executives at Ford, Google, and other blue-chip companies are practicing meditation and incorporating contemplative practices into the workplace. Members of Congress are meditating on Capitol Hill. Some corporate campuses have a meditation room in every building, and insurance plans are covering meditation classes. Silicon Valley is swarming with tech-savvy meditators, continuing Jobs's legacy. Even hedge fund managers are using meditation to gain an edge in their trading.

Across industries, there is an elite subculture of accomplished professionals who are discovering the power of mindfulness. They are becoming more effective and more focused and in the process getting better at their jobs. Mindfulness is also allowing workers who practice it to make less-emotional decisions, and to feel happier, too, providing a competitive advantage in the office, and in all realms of life.

Mindfulness, put simply, is the ability to see what's going on in our heads, without getting carried away with it. It is the capacity to feel sensations — even painful ones — without letting them control us. Mindfulness means being aware of our experiences, observing them without judgment, and responding from a place of clarity and compassion, rather than fear, insecurity, or greed.

Scientific research is making the benefits clear. Studies show that mindfulness strengthens our immune systems, bolsters our concentrative powers, and rewires our brains. Just as lifting weights at the gym makes our muscles stronger, so too does practicing mindfulness make our minds stronger. And the most tried-and-true method of cultivating mindfulness is through meditation.

Meditation doesn't require us to wear robes, chant in a foreign language, or sit with our legs folded. Instead, mindfulness meditation simply asks that we take a comfortable position — sitting, lying down, or even standing — and observe our thoughts, emotions, and sensations. Pick a sensation, such as the breath moving in and out of the nostrils, and focus on it. Feel the subtleties of air passing in and out; notice the whole body rising and falling with each inhalation and exhalation. When the mind wanders, as it inevitably will, notice the thought — without getting caught up in it — and return the attention to the breath. When the mind wanders again, sometimes just a few seconds later, bring the attention back to the breath, and begin again.

As a practice, that's it to start with. There are other, more complicated techniques, but basic mindfulness meditation 101 couldn't be simpler. Yet this elementary mental exercise is incredibly transformative. As Steve Jobs knew, and many accomplished workers are discovering these days, mindfulness makes us more focused, more effective, and happier, to name just a few benefits. So it's little wonder why today, in multinational corporations and small businesses alike, more and more people are meditating on the job.

Eager to explore this fascinating intermingling of cultures, I set out on a journey into the contemplative heart of corporate America. For more than a year, I crisscrossed the country, interviewing those who are committed to being more mindful at work. My research took me to small industrial towns in northern Vermont, and into the heart of the world's biggest tech companies in Silicon Valley. I meditated with workers in Minneapolis, Minnesota; Madison, Wisconsin; and Manhattan. I met CEOs who have made mindfulness an integral part of their leadership strategies, spiritual teachers who are grappling with the sudden surge of mainstream interest in the techniques they've been practicing for decades, and everyday workers from various industries who use meditation to become less stressed and more effective at their jobs. Along the way, I also rekindled my own relationship with mindfulness, something that began as an intellectual curiosity when I was a teenager but has profoundly transformed every aspect of my life.

On New Year's Eve, 1998, I was at home in Sausalito, California, after my first semester in college, unsure of which party to attend that night. Buddies from high school were gathering at a big house in Oakland. New friends from college were having a bonfire on the beach. Before I made a decision, however, I picked a slim volume about Buddhism off my mother's bookshelf. I knew that my Intro to Humanities course would be covering the topic in less than a month, so I read the first few pages. Immediately, the elegance of the teachings spoke to me.

I had pored over philosophy and religion books before, trying to find answers to life's big questions after some teenage experiments with mind-altering substances. But the clear messages in that volume were refreshingly practical and even seemed attainable — that we're never satisfied, even when we have it all; that we drive ourselves crazy by wanting things to be other than the way they are, rather than simply observing the world as it is; and that we can get off the hamster wheel of our minds and learn to be at peace. At once simple and profound, the basic tenets of Buddhism resonated with me like nothing else. I kept reading, finishing the book well after midnight. I never made it to any of the parties.

The next morning, I checked in with my friends. One still had her head in the toilet. Another had been punched in the face. A third saw his sister relapse with cocaine. And on the most simplistic level, the equation I had read about the night before — that desire leads to unhappiness — made that much more sense. I went for a walk on the beach, thought about what I had read, and that afternoon opened up the Yellow Pages in search of a meditation center. The next day, I walked into the Green Gulch Farm Zen Center, a utopian compound north of San Francisco, and meditated for the first time.

For the next year and a half, I practiced Zen Buddhism, the same austere tradition that appealed to Steve Jobs. Then, during my junior year of college, I traveled to India as part of a Buddhist studies program. For six months, I lived in monasteries and traveled the subcontinent, learning from meditation masters and sitting for weeks in total silence. It was during this time that I deepened my meditation routine, beginning to understand, through experience, how mindfulness can be so transformative.

Back home for a final two semesters at Boston University, I sought out opportunities to practice. On the morning of September 11, 2001, I was at a secluded cabin in western Massachusetts on a meditation retreat, cutting classes on the first day of my senior year of college. I had been there for four days with Chökyi Nyima Rinpoche, a Tibetan teacher with whom I had studied in India, and a dozen of his students, including the actor Richard Gere, and the meditation luminaries Sharon Salzberg and Joseph Goldstein. There was no TV in the cabin, so when word of the attacks reached us through a few panicked cell phone calls, we huddled around an old Volvo in the driveway, listening to the car radio as the second plane hit. We were shaken and eager to get home, so Chökyi Nyima called the retreat off early — but not before he led us through several hours of compassion meditation, pushing us to feel profound love in conjunction with raging anger, making us mindful of the arising and passing of our complex emotions.

My meditation practice has ebbed and flowed since then. There are stretches when I have a regular sitting routine, starting each morning with an hour on the meditation cushion. From time to time I attend silent retreats, delightful but challenging periods of intensive practice when I refrain from speaking for days at a time. Then there are months when I can't seem to find the time to sit. A demanding job, a busy social life, and a newborn daughter make it all the more challenging. Yet even so, I do my best to practice mindfulness in everyday life.

Despite my time in monasteries, and my devotion to a meditation practice that has its roots in Buddhism, I don't consider myself religious in the slightest. When it comes to questions about the origins of the universe, or the afterlife, I'm a contented agnostic: I have no idea where we came from or where we are going, and I'm OK with that.

What I do know is that many of the techniques I learned from my Buddhist teachers, which are now being taught across the country in purely secular fashion, are effective methods that can help us become happier right now, in this lifetime. What is more, mindfulness meditation as it is being taught today does not require any particular belief system at all. It complements other belief systems, instead of clashing with them. There are Catholics, Jews, and atheists in this book, all of whom find that mindfulness supplements, not rivals, their faith. And meditation, of course, is not uniquely Buddhist.

Every great religious tradition includes elements of meditative practice. St. Teresa of Avila, a sixteenth-century nun, practiced contemplative prayer for an hour at a time, twice a day, and taught meditation as a way to grow closer to God. Many other Christian traditions — from the Trappist monks to the Quakers — have meditative practices at their core. Judaism, too, has a deep contemplative streak, spanning certain Hassidic practices and the meditative branch of Kabbalah. And other Eastern religions, too, from Hinduism, to Jainism, to Sufism, all incorporate forms of meditation. Not all of these practices are the same, of course. Some are intended to bring us closer to a divine spirit, and some are designed to empty our minds. Mindfulness meditation, as practiced today, is designed to make us more aware of our thoughts, emotions, and physical sensations.

I'm far from an expert meditator, and I'm certainly not a meditation teacher. Instead, I've spent most of the past decade as a business reporter for the *Financial Times* and the *New York Times*. Yet over the years I've grown familiar enough with the practice that, when I began to hear about mindfulness being practiced in corporations, I knew it was something I had to investigate. Because mindfulness is not just a simple self-help technique. When practiced diligently, it can help reduce stress, make us more productive, and boost happiness. It can transform not only the way we do our work, but the very work we do. And while it is a practice that can improve our lives, it is also a way of being — attentive, courteous, curious, conscientious, and compassionate.

This is a book about the factory workers, fashion designers, lawyers, and CEOs who have used meditation to change their lives for the better. It's also about how organizations are becoming more mindful — taking better care of their employees, reducing their negative impact on the planet, and finding ways to improve people's lives. And it's about what a more mindful society might look like. As I met workers around the country, I was inspired, humbled, and sometimes skeptical. Accordingly, in these pages I'm sometimes a neutral observer, sometimes a critic, and often an advocate. I try to make the case that mindfulness has become part of the cultural firmament for good reason; that practicing meditation changes our brains, bodies, and dispositions largely for the better; and that when mindfulness imbues individuals and organizations, it can transform the way we work.

In Chapter 1, we'll get familiar with the basic principles of mindfulness and see what meditation practice looks like within one big company. It is inside multinational organizations that many people are discovering mindfulness for the first time, and here, too, where some of the ethical foundations of the practice are being challenged. That makes big companies a veritable laboratory for mainstream mindfulness today, and an ideal place to begin our journey.

But to understand where we're going, it's necessary to know how we got here. In Chapter 2, we'll explore the history of mindfulness. What began as a spiritual practice in ancient India migrated across millennia and continents, eventually arriving on American shores not long after the founding of the country. First embraced by the Transcendentalists, temporarily ignored, and revived by the Beats and hippies, mindfulness in the West has piggybacked on various social movements over the years. And in recent decades, a number of important developments in medicine, science, and technology have allowed the practice to break into the mainstream.

One of the most important such developments has been the emergence of contemplative neuroscience — the study of how meditation affects the brain. In Chapter 3, we'll go inside the laboratory, seeking to understand how mindfulness is impacting not only our behavior, but our very neurological structures as well. We'll meet the scientists who are leading the charge in this emerging discipline and hear from skeptics who believe some of the results are being oversold. And I'll share my own experience of going under the microscope, where I learned what my brain looks like on meditation.

Whether or not every scientific study is bulletproof, however, is not the most pertinent question. What's more important is whether or not mindfulness works. Does it help people become happier? Can it make us less stressed? The answer, as we'll see in Chapter 4, seems to be yes. I experienced as much myself, taking a class in the most popular form of mindfulness training today — Mindfulness Based Stress Reduction — and meeting a swath of workers from various disciplines who have all used meditation to reduce stress, increase their happiness, and improve their health.

Mindfulness engenders a number of benefits beyond stress reduction. One of the most readily attainable is enhanced focus. In Chapter 5, we'll meet workers from disparate fields who have discovered this firsthand. The repeated practice of bringing our attention back to the breath each time the mind wanders, over and over again, cultivates concentration, a useful quality no matter what our vocation.

Being more mindful also cultivates compassion. This may sound surprising at first. How can paying attention to *my* breath make me care about *others* more? And talking about loving-kindness can seem out of place in buttoned-up professional settings. But as we'll see in Chapter 6, compassion spawned by mindfulness is being embraced by politicians, businesspeople, and entrepreneurs alike. They are discovering that compassion, though not normally something associated with corporate life, can be deeply advantageous to all sorts of businesses.

The good news is, many mindful workers are not only practicing compassion with themselves and others, but also extending their efforts to do good in the world well beyond their interpersonal relationships. In Chapter 7, mindful companies that are embracing social responsibility will take center stage. From improving conditions for factory workers, to reducing environmental degradation, to finding ways to bring health care to thousands of new people, the results of mindfulness in action are wonderfully varied.

In Chapter 8, we'll examine what has become one of the most popular applications of meditation in the workplace today: developing mindful leaders. Though perhaps less easily quantifiable than stress reduction, mindful leadership is no less important. Executives hold sway in the workplace, and when they become less reactive, more focused, and kinder, they can create more compassionate workplaces and run more socially responsible businesses.

But not everyone is happy with mindfulness going mainstream. Chapter 9 will take us to the frontlines of the attack on what is being dubbed "McMindfulness." Dissenters say that mindfulness is being subverted and unethically used in the service of big company profits. Purists say it should not be divorced from the traditions from which it came. And some, wary of meditation altogether, just want it to go away.

For better or worse — mostly for the better, I contend — that is unlikely to happen. Mindfulness has been around forever and in this new incarnation is likely to stick around. In Chapter 10, to get a glimpse of what this new, more mindful working world might look like, we go the epicenter of this nascent movement: Silicon Valley. From confabs celebrating mindfulness and technology to a raft of workplace programs teaching meditation in the office, the San Francisco Bay Area is home to the largest concentration of mindful workers in the world. Together, they are hacking corporate cultures to embrace concentration, retooling their algorithms with loving-kindness in mind, and trying to make compassion as commonplace as coding. And since California is, as ever, a cultural bellwether, the mindful workers of Silicon Valley are setting a precedent that is likely to be followed by much of the rest of the world.

As I met this new generation of mindful workers, I was impressed not only with their diligent practice and intuitive wisdom, but also with their bravery in swimming against the tide in today's ultra-competitive workplace culture. As I reported, I learned. And as I learned, I was moved to become more mindful myself. My hope is that by presenting a range of these stories, and a few of my own, this book can inspire still more workers — from those on the factory floor to those in the C-suite — to become more mindful. Whether you are merely curious as to what all the fuss is about, or eager to begin a robust practice, this is an invitation to embark on a personal journey of mindfulness. And whether you are already meditating in the workplace, or are contemplating how it might be scaled within your own organization, you'll find examples here of those who have done it successfully, in a whole range of professions. However it is done, my hope is that with these stories as inspiration, we can all experience the myriad benefits of mindful work.

1

This Mindful Moment

THE MAIN LOBBY of General Mills's headquarters was buzzing with earnest midwestern executives in khakis and pencil skirts, zipping from meeting to meeting as they plotted the future of this $30 billion global food and beverage conglomerate. It was midafternoon on a Tuesday, and I had just arrived at the corporate campus in Minneapolis, Minnesota. Posters on the walls of the spacious, modernist building reminded employees of the brands they were pulling for: Betty Crocker, Hamburger Helper, Pillsbury, Wheaties, and other fixtures of the American cupboard. But in a large conference hall just past reception, an unusual sort of midday meeting was about to begin. Leaders from across the company filed into the room on schedule. Instead of cradling their silver laptops, however, they came bearing purple yoga mats. Instead of rushing in, they entered deliberately, removed their shoes, and left them by the door. Instead of taking seats at a conference table, they settled onto round cushions on the floor, arranged in a large circle. Instead of making small talk, they closed their eyes and took a few deep breaths. And then they began to meditate.

I took my seat among them and surveyed the crowd. The sixty or so employees represented a disparate range of the General Mills corporate hierarchy. One man wore a suit and tie, while a woman to his left had a bright yellow Cheerios T-shirt on. Yet the marketing managers, technology specialists, and financial types were all there at the same weekly gathering and had all shown up for the same reason. They were there to practice *mindfulness,* a deceptively simple practice that has been shown to reduce stress, boost happiness, possibly even make us more productive, and change the way we think about life.

At the most fundamental level, mindfulness is about increasing our awareness of what's happening in our minds, throughout our bodies, and in the world around us. It is about noticing these things, and also accepting them as they are, rather than making ourselves crazy by wishing things were different. And a couple of thousand years of empirical evidence suggests there's one way to cultivate mindfulness that trumps all the rest: meditation.

In the General Mills conference room, a few first-time attendees seemed skittish in the tranquil ambience that had settled. It was an understandable reaction to a vibe that was pleasantly out of step with the hard-driving corporate culture that pervades most American offices. It's unusual that we stop and do nothing during the workday, and that professional velocity kept some participants on edge. But it helped that the woman leading the class was one of the most senior executives at the company.

General Mills's deputy general counsel at the time, Janice Marturano had, over the course of more than a decade, won the trust of her superiors and staff. She had worked on multibillion-dollar mergers and acquisitions and gone head-to-head with regulators at the Federal Trade Commission. So when she proposed teaching a course on mindful leadership, the company let her run with it. Short and quiet with a bob of black hair, wearing plain office garb of black slacks and a blouse, Marturano didn't look anything like the hippie you might expect to be teaching a meditation class. Yet there the top lawyer sat, amid her colleagues in the circle, her legs folded into the half-lotus position.

Once the group was settled, Marturano rang a bell, letting the sound of the chime linger in the room. "Take a posture that for you in this moment embodies dignity and strength," she said in a flat, corporate monotone. "Allow the body to rest, to step out of busyness, bringing your attention to the sensation of each breath."

Marturano's flock exhaled deeply, the stress of the workday falling away. She invited them to focus on their breath, the first step in basic mindfulness meditation. When attention wanders to thoughts, as it inevitably will, simply bring the focus back to the breath, she explained. *Notice how fickle the attention is, how the mind is apt to wander even when we want it to remain stable. Notice how the sensation of the breath arises, only to pass away, and how our thoughts, however vivid, are similarly impermanent.* Marturano soon invited her colleagues to expand their awareness beyond their breath, to the multifaceted sensations rippling through their bodies. *Notice the tingling in the hands, the pulsing in the feet, the warmth of the skin. When the mind starts to wander, as it certainly will, bring the attention back to the present moment and these sensations.*

Seated among the General Mills workers, a reporter in their midst, I followed along as best I could. And though I had meditated on and off for fifteen years, my mind still rambled aimlessly. One moment I felt the gentle current of air passing in and out of my nostrils. The next moment I wondered if I'd find any decent food near the hotel where I was staying. One moment I was engrossed by the oddly pleasant sensation of blood coursing through my veins; then I was thinking about sushi. Thirty minutes later, Marturano chimed the bell to end the meditation session. I had had a few fleeting moments of sustained focus and felt tranquil as I began to stretch my limbs. But mostly, my mind was jumping around like an ill-behaved rhesus monkey, wandering back into the past, and out into the future, but rarely paying heed to the experience I was actually having during those pleasant moments of silence.

Marturano's Mindful Leadership training would continue for another hour and a half, first with a period of gentle yoga, then with a group discussion, a poetry reading, and finally some more meditation. As a business reporter, I've spent a lot of time around big companies, but I had never seen anything like this. At the end of the session, the General Mills employees in the room seemed decidedly more relaxed than they had been when they arrived. No doubt they still had plenty of complaints and lingering stress about their jobs. Practicing mindfulness during the workday is no magic elixir. Yet it also was clear that after the two-hour class, there was a genuine warmth in the room.

There were also some raw emotions present. On the day I was in Minneapolis, General Mills was in the middle of its first round of layoffs in a generation. At least one woman at the Mindful Leadership session had been informed that she was being let go. She cried a bit during the Q&A. Then, as the people in the group went their separate ways, several of her colleagues, including some strangers, approached her to offer hugs and words of support. It was, altogether, a more humane atmosphere than the cutthroat buzz I'd so often encountered at corporate headquarters. People were interacting with each other more like friends than like coworkers.

I had come to General Mills to report on the Mindful Leadership program for the *Financial Times,* the London-based business newspaper where I worked at the time. That reporting would ultimately become a cover story in the *FT Weekend Magazine* titled "The Mind Business," a break from my usual work as U.S. mergers and acquisitions correspondent for the paper. Offbeat though it seemed, the prospect of finding mindfulness in the workplace was a deeply compelling story to me.

As a college student I traveled to India and Nepal, where I sat with some of the most influential meditation teachers of the twentieth century. The techniques I learned along the way had a profound impact on my worldview, affecting almost every aspect of my life. But in recent years, as my personal and professional responsibilities had increased, I was struggling to keep up my practice. My sitting routine waned. Silent meditation retreats, once a regular part of the calendar year, became sporadic. So when I first caught wind of the fact that some companies were encouraging, and even facilitating, meditation in the workplace, I was more than intrigued. I had to report the story.

General Mills was my first stop on this journey. I was curious when I arrived in Minneapolis, but also a bit uncertain of what I might find. Were employees actually sitting in silence, as if the office were a monastery? If so, would it be a form of mindfulness I recognized, or something altogether different? Was it making an impact on individuals, and maybe even the organization? Would anyone even show up?

In Minneapolis, my skepticism quickly abated. Beyond the robust turnout on that Tuesday afternoon, I spent days talking with General Mills employees and could sense that not only was the mindfulness being practiced in Minneapolis authentic and well intentioned, but it was exerting a meaningful influence on employees and the corporate culture. Marturano was certainly the driving force. But the seeds she had planted were already bearing fruit. Two other senior managers had taken up the cause, teaching the large group when Marturano wasn't on campus. Hundreds of employees had taken the Mindful Leadership course. And mindfulness was having an impact beyond the weekly classes. Every building on General Mills's campus now had a meditation room, where workers could slip in for a moment of silence before a tough meeting or presentation. In the teams where managers were practicing mindfulness, workers reported themselves to be happier and more productive. Their managers were better liked. Business, too, was booming. And it all started because one woman was trying to cope with her own stress.

By the early 2000s Janice Marturano had reached the upper echelons of General Mills and was involved in some of the company's highest-priority projects. She led policy work around trade regulation, serving as the company's point person with the Food and Drug Administration. And she worked with the Federal Trade Commission, focusing on antitrust work as General Mills sought to grow through acquisitions.

In 2000, General Mills made a $10.5 billion bid for Pillsbury, the baked-goods company known for its Doughboy mascot. Merging the two would create the fourth-largest food company in the world, a global powerhouse that would dominate supermarket aisles and kitchen cupboards alike. For this very reason, regulators held up the deal, worried it would stifle competition. As an M&A reporter, I was sympathetic to the enormous amount of stress this would have created for Marturano. It's tense enough covering a deal like that, let alone being responsible for getting it through the FTC and Department of Justice. Marturano led the company's dialogue with Washington, working around the clock for eighteen months to prevent the deal from getting blocked on antitrust grounds.

The intensity was not unique to this particular merger, or even to Marturano's field. Many of us know what it's like to work with an all-consuming urgency, when our on-the-job tasks seem like life-or-death challenges. But in the midst of Marturano's negotiations with regulators, an already tough situation became unbearable. In a short span, both of her parents died. That personal blow, on top of her workload, left her emotionally and intellectually drained. She eventually pushed the deal through, allowing General Mills to become an even more dominant force in the packaged-foods industry. But when she returned to daily life at her office in Minneapolis, she had nothing left in her tank. "I thought I'd bounce back. I'd been through deals before," she said. "But I didn't. My mental resilience had become so depleted."

Marturano was still at this low point, exhausted, stressed, and uninspired, when a friend encouraged her to attend a retreat in the Arizona desert led by a man named Jon Kabat-Zinn. She was skeptical at first. A New Age solution didn't seem like the answer to her very real-world problems. But without any other good options, Marturano headed to Miraval, a resort near Tucson that offers an assortment of restorative retreats and luxury spa treatments.

This was no vacation, though. Instead of getting pampered, Marturano got a six-day crash course in an intensive, sometimes challenging technique called Mindfulness Based Stress Reduction, or MBSR. "At the very beginning, Jon said: 'OK, we're going to meditate for about an hour,'" Marturano recalled. "And I thought: '*What*, are you out of your mind? We're going to do *what* for an hour?'"

Soon, it didn't sound so daunting. Over the next few days, Marturano learned to follow her breath, experience the subtle sensations in her body, and notice her thoughts and emotions without reacting to them. In time, her mind began to quiet down. She discovered that beneath the choppy waters of her thoughts, there was a deep reservoir of peace. The all-consuming stressors weren't so paralyzing anymore. Her personal grief from the loss of her parents softened, becoming more manageable. On the last morning of the retreat she woke early and walked into the desert, found a spot near a kiva, and slipped into a deep meditation. Later that day, when it was time to go home, she didn't want to leave.

Back in Minneapolis, Marturano continued to practice, meditating for a little bit each morning before her hectic days began. After a few months of this she noticed something dramatic. All the things that previously made her stressed were still present — work was still intense, she still missed her parents — but she was able to manage them better. She was more emotionally resilient, more focused at work, and more compassionate with herself. She still felt the pain, but it wasn't causing her to suffer as much.

Despite these benefits, she didn't mention her meditation routine to her friends and colleagues at first. Like so many other professionals who taste the benefits of mindfulness, Marturano was concerned that admitting she spent part of each day sitting silently on a cushion would start coworkers' eyes rolling. "I was a closet meditator," she said. But she could keep up the charade for only so long. After a few years, it felt artificial to practice mindfulness at home, then go about her job as if nothing had changed. Even though she had modified her own behavior at work — bringing more presence and attention to meetings and tasks, acting more kindly toward her colleagues — she could take it only so far on her own. Life as a closet meditator was unsustainable.

So Marturano started scouting for allies. After stressful meetings, when colleagues would ask how she managed to keep her cool while everyone else in the room was tense, Marturano would mention mindfulness and ask if they wanted to know more. Some of them did. Before long, Marturano had a list of fellow General Mills executives who said they were interested in mindfulness. With that list in hand, she called up Saki Santorelli, executive director of the Center for Mindfulness in Medicine, Health Care, and Society at the University of Massachusetts and a longtime colleague of Jon Kabat-Zinn, who had taught Marturano in the desert. Together they developed a curriculum, and in early 2006 they took thirteen General Mills executives to a small bed-and-breakfast in Spicer, Minnesota, for a five-day retreat. There, by a lake in the woods, they spent days in silent meditation, learning about mindfulness and beginning a quiet transformation.

Those initial students came back to General Mills changed. "There was quite a buzz when that first group went through," remembered Beth Gunderson, General Mills's director of organizational effectiveness. "Everybody wanted it. It started to take on a life of its own." Soon, Marturano was teaching employees during lunch breaks, and before long, the Mindful Leadership program was born. It helped that Marturano sold the program as training to make executives more competent. But after I watched Marturano teach, there is no mistaking what is at the heart of the program: the very same millennia-old mindfulness and compassion practice I learned from teachers in India. To date, well over one thousand General Mills employees have received the training.

When my article "The Mind Business" was published, I wasn't sure how readers would respond. In previous years, I had interviewed Facebook founder Mark Zuckerberg in Silicon Valley and Ponzi schemer Bernie Madoff in prison. Those articles got passed around plenty, and I was establishing myself as a business reporter. But how would *Financial Times* subscribers respond to a story about meditation?

"The Mind Business" went viral. Readers reached out and asked which other companies were doing similar work. They wanted to know who else was teaching mindfulness to corporations. Mindfulness practitioners and trainers were thrilled to see their burgeoning movement get some mainstream press and wondered when my next story on the topic was coming out. I didn't have all the answers to their questions at the time. But I wanted to find out.

It quickly became apparent that what was happening at General Mills was no anomaly. A little digging revealed that companies including Aetna, Salesforce.com, Green Mountain Coffee, and more were already incorporating mindfulness into their operations in one way or another. And in the past few years, mindfulness has burst into the mainstream, gaining traction within the business world. At the 2013 World Economic Forum in Davos, Switzerland, policymakers from around the globe took time out for a session of mindfulness training; the event was standing room only and covered by BBC Television. A month later *Mindful* magazine launched, giving the burgeoning movement a presence on the newsstand. An article on "mindful leadership" in the *Harvard Business Review* became one of the publication's most-shared stories of the year. From 2004 to 2013, the number of Google searches for "mindful" and "mindfulness" more than doubled. Mindfulness is being practiced at technology start-ups like Etsy and Medium, where young founders and early employees weave it into the corporate culture, doing their part to establish a new norm when it comes to work-life balance. And it is being practiced by big companies like General Mills and even Goldman Sachs, which offers meditation sessions to employees at its $2.1 billion office building in downtown Manhattan.

Viewed one way, the growth of mindfulness in the workplace is the logical next step in the movement toward greater corporate social responsibility. Many companies already strive for profits, aim to help improve society, and are environmentally conscientious. This is the foundation of the "triple bottom line," the modern rubric by which companies assess their holistic impact on the world. Now, some companies are adding a fourth dimension to this framework. In the same way that corporations widely accept that spewing pollutants into the atmosphere is bad for the environment and their reputations, so too are some companies recognizing that it's bad for their employees to be so stressed out that their health falters, or so distractible that they can't concentrate. These companies are beginning to ask how they can also contribute to their employees' — and society's — emotional and spiritual well-being. And they are finding one answer in mindfulness.

So what is mindfulness? Ask a neuroscientist and you'll get one answer. Ask a psychologist and you'll get another. Ask a Buddhist scholar and you'll get a third. The truth is that there is no one universally accepted definition. Yet if you listen closely, you find that each response holds the same essential truth. Mindfulness is about being fully present. It is about attending to the here and now, without being lost in thoughts about the past, or fantasies about the future. It is a quality of being that embodies kindness, curiosity, and acceptance. To be mindful is to actually feel the sensations in your body, even unpleasant ones, without clinging to them or wishing them away. It is to observe your thoughts without letting them become the only version of the truth. It is to attend to your emotions, embracing whatever it is you're feeling in the moment, even if it's not particularly comfortable. It is to be more sensitive and compassionate toward the people and situations around you. And when practiced diligently, it can transform our health, our relationships, and our impact on the world.

The most widely accepted definition of mindfulness today comes from Jon Kabat-Zinn, a PhD who founded the Center for Mindfulness in Medicine, Health Care, and Society at the University of Massachusetts Medical School. Kabat-Zinn has done more than anyone to popularize mindfulness in recent decades. He developed a new clinical framework for training and pioneered MBSR, the course that has introduced so many people to the practice. As if all this were not enough, he has tirelessly taught thousands of people, including Janice Marturano, on countless retreats over the years.

Kabat-Zinn describes mindfulness as "paying attention in a particular way: on purpose, in the present moment, and nonjudgmentally." As a practice, that's it. Mindfulness is just about observing whatever it is we're experiencing, and not allowing our minds to run amok. Yet *mindfulness* is a complex word, with multiple, layered meanings, each building upon the next.

In Sanskrit, the word for mindfulness, *smriti,* means "remembering." And indeed, remembering is a core part of the practice. We must remember to return to the present moment, over and over, even as our thoughts relentlessly try to take us away from it. The word *smriti* also points to a deeper sense of remembering. In practicing mindfulness, we ultimately remember our true nature, a state unclouded with incessant thinking and constant judging. In Pali, the language of early Buddhist texts, mindfulness is translated as *sati,* which means "awareness." This, too, still resonates today. The practice involves keen awareness of the sensations in our bodies, the thoughts in our minds, and the emotions in our hearts. And again, there is a larger meaning to the word — the awareness of the causes and conditions of those very sensations, the awareness of phenomena arising and passing, the awareness of the interconnectedness of all things.

As difficult as it can be to attain, mindfulness is an innate capacity, something that every one of us has experienced. When we take a walk through the woods and are absorbed in the sights, sounds, and smells of nature, instead of our thoughts, that's a form of mindfulness. When a mother looks into her baby's eyes and experiences their visceral bond, that's a form of mindfulness. When we savor a bite of our favorite food, delighting in the tastes rolling across our tongues, that's a form of mindfulness, too. Mindfulness can be quite magical, transporting us from the familiar, often taxing realm of our own distracted minds to a place of pure, focused awareness. But mindfulness is a bit of a rabbit hole. Keep practicing, and the nuances only become subtler, the revelations more profound, the mysteries deeper. Indeed, mindfulness is about much more than simply observing sensations as they occur. It is about what happens to our minds, hearts, and actions when we deliberately continue these practices for weeks, months, and years. Mindfulness is a practice that allows us to achieve more sustainable happiness and to grow more compassionate. And over time, mindfulness requires one to confront thorny concepts like impermanence and compassion.

"The ultimate promise of mindfulness is much larger, much more profound than simply cultivating our attentiveness," said Jon Kabat-Zinn. "It helps us understand that our conventional view of ourselves and even what we mean by 'self' is incomplete in some very important ways. Mindfulness helps us to recognize how and why we mistake the actuality of things for some story we create. It then makes it possible for us to chart a path toward greater sanity, well-being, and purpose."

Practicing mindfulness develops several beneficial qualities: reduced stress, focus, and compassion chief among them. Mindfulness helps us become less stressed by, in part, helping us understand what we can and cannot change. As we observe our breath and bodies, we begin to see that certain things are simply out of our control. We can't always make a pain in our legs go away, but we can control our reaction to it. We can't stop the rain from falling, but we can control to what extent, if any, getting rained on makes us upset. With time, mindfulness reveals just how often our minds are rapidly assessing a situation, passing a judgment, and often causing us stress, making us unhappy. We realize that stress isn't caused by what is happening; it is caused by how we respond to it, which determines our happiness at any given moment.

Practicing mindfulness meditation — the repeated, sometimes frustrating work of bringing our attention back to the present moment — also cultivates focus. When we make an effort to be in the present moment, we quickly see just how rambunctious the mind is, how inclined it is to dwell in the past or race off into the future. Like a puppy, it's simply not well trained yet, apt to chase whatever catches its curious eye. There's nothing wrong with thinking, of course. Our capacity to plan ahead and analyze the past has allowed us to travel to the moon and back. But excessive thinking is not always helpful. And through mindfulness practice we can hone our concentrative powers, training our minds to remain stable and even-tempered for long stretches of time. Just as lifting weights at a gym strengthens our muscles, so too does meditation strengthen our minds, allowing us to develop stable, one-pointed concentration. The mind becomes "as steady as a stone instead of letting it bob about like a pumpkin in water." And stable attention, for many reasons, is an immensely valuable skill to have.

If improved concentration were all mindfulness had to offer, that alone would be a wonderful gift, especially at work. By anchoring us in the present moment, meditation can free us from many of the thoughts and fantasies that so often distract us from the task at hand. Think how much more productive we might be if our minds could operate with clarity and precision on demand. Yet simply becoming laserlike in our ability to focus is not the goal of this practice. For as we become more skilled at mindfulness, watching our thoughts and emotions as they arise and pass, we begin to see the very inner workings of our minds. Each time we notice that we're lost in thought, we put a little distance between the voices in our heads and any notion that what we're experiencing is the only version of the truth. We realize that our thoughts, like our bodily sensations, are impermanent and don't represent the totality of who we really are. With practice, mindfulness makes us less beholden to fleeting desires, and more committed to the pursuit of real, sustainable happiness.

Mindfulness also makes us increasingly attuned to those around us. Through practice we realize that just like us, everyone else in the world is grappling with challenging wants and desires. Just like us, everyone else is grappling with large and small dissatisfactions and anxieties. In this way, practicing mindfulness makes us more empathetic. And as we become more sensitive to our own bodies and minds, we become more sensitive to others, too. We become more skilled at sensing when a colleague, friend, or family member is troubled; we become less reactive, unlikely to snap back at someone at the first sign of conflict or threat. We begin to see that our thoughts, ideas, and judgments are less fixed than we once thought, that there is a different side to our self-centered story. Mindfulness fosters a sense of connection with others and inspires us to be more compassionate, too. It is one of the miraculous side effects of meditation: sitting in silence makes us kinder. "It's clearly a training in concentration, but it's also a training in compassion and kindness," said Sharon Salzberg, a teacher and author who has been practicing mindfulness for forty years. "With mindfulness, we relate to each other and ourselves differently."

But as fundamental as it is to the human experience, it seems we are ill equipped to tap into our innate mindfulness. We need to remember to be mindful because we all, at one point or another, have forgotten how. With few exceptions, we never learned how to turn off our thinking minds, to quiet the voices in our heads. And to reap the rewards of mindfulness, we have to train. We have to unlearn the bad habits that have accrued over a lifetime. Because no matter how sunny our disposition, no matter how generous our spirit, the chattering mind clouds our judgment, moment to moment. And surprising as it may sound, no matter what our age, we can indeed train the wild mind. In the last few decades neuroscience has revealed startling new truths about the nature of our brains. It turns out that they are malleable, and that, with meditation, our neural circuitry can be rewired to make mindfulness and compassion as instinctual as breathing.

This all sounds well and good. But to the human resources manager or the chief executive officer confronted with the choice of whether or not to encourage employees to meditate, it can come off like empty talk without real data to back it up. Fortunately, a growing trove of scientific literature is making plain the benefits of mindfulness practice. Though the research remains nascent, it seems to suggest that sitting still, focusing, and intentionally reducing our reactivity makes us healthier, happier, and kinder, too, as we'll see in Chapter 3. The research tells only part of the story, however. At General Mills, you can sense the difference among those who have trained in mindfulness. Though the company is by no means perfect — still peddling junk food to kids and empty calories to adults — many of its workers are making an effort to be kind to reduce on-the-job stressors, and to be kind to each other and themselves.

Marturano documented the impact of her Mindful Leadership training. After a seven-week course, General Mills employees felt more comfortable being themselves in the office and felt as if they were making better contributions to the team. They were more likely to give their full attention to a conversation, and less likely to let their minds wander. They took more time to prioritize their tasks each day and were more efficient in rooting out unproductive activities. They said they were more focused even on conference calls and in meetings. Furthermore, they were increasingly *self-aware* of these behaviors. They noticed when their minds were wandering and noticed when they were rushing heedlessly from one place to the next. They could tell when they were giving someone only half their attention and knew how to bring their focus back to the present moment.

Throughout this book, we'll hear more stories about the practical impacts mindfulness training has had on companies around the globe. At one Fortune 500 corporation, mindfulness helped reduce health care costs. At another, it helped reduce workplace injuries on the factory floor. Yet the benefits of mindfulness cannot all be measured. In many instances, the effects amount to subtle changes in disposition rather than a wholesale restructuring of some division. And still, if mindfulness can help us be happier with ourselves, kinder to one another, and more considered in our actions in the world, it seems well worth the effort to bring it into the workplace.

• • •

There's good reason that mindfulness is going mainstream right now: it seems as if we're more mindless than ever, especially at work. Just 47 percent of Americans said they were satisfied with their jobs in a recent survey. That was up slightly since the depths of the recession, but still down markedly from the 61 percent job satisfaction level reported two decades ago. Since the global financial crisis, two-thirds of employees said they were spending more hours at work, according to a survey of three hundred big companies by Towers Watson, the consultancy. At the same time, work-life balance has been blurred beyond recognition. With smartphones delivering office e-mails 24/7, many people check in with work before they get out of bed in the morning and check in again right before their heads hit the pillow at night. The nine-to-five job is a quaint relic of a bygone era. Uncertainty in the markets means anxiety in society. Savings are precarious, the real estate market is volatile, and globalization and technology are leaving stalwart industries vulnerable. Corruption without accountability, meanwhile, has left so many jaded.

"In the financial crisis of 2008–2009, we saw the effects of greed played out on a massive scale in the banks and insurance companies," Jon Kabat-Zinn said. "Healing that disease is not just a matter of bailouts, stimulus packages, and magically creating greater confidence in the economy. We need to create a different kind of confidence and a new kind of economics, one that's not about mindless spending but more about marshalling resources for the greater good, for one's own being, for society, and for the planet. Mindfulness can help us open the door to that by helping us go beyond approaches that are based on conceptual thought alone and that are driven by unbounded and legally sanctioned greed."

But imagine if we could change this paradigm and uncover a new way to work. Imagine if work didn't have to be our number-one cause of stress. Mindfulness won't make a bad boss behave better (at least not right away), and it won't make difficult labor any less physically taxing. But by bringing mindfulness to work, we can change the way that boss affects us, and change how we respond to the prospect of tough hours on the job. And in turn, this can change the culture of an organization. Mindfulness can give us a new way to work, and it's already beginning to happen at many companies around the world.

General Mills is just one part of this new generation of organizations. It's not simply that the cereal maker has some modicum of a social conscience. Plenty of other corporations promote fair trade, give away a portion of their profits, and try to take good care of their employees. What sets apart General Mills, along with the other institutions featured in this book, is that it has invited its employees to explore how their minds work and in doing so begun a process to transform the company, and maybe even the world. Marturano and her colleagues understand that the way we're working today just isn't working. And now, finally, these external crises — a stressed-out population, a persistent economic crisis, and climate change run amok — are forcing us to look for internal solutions.

In *The Principles of Psychology,* William James acknowledged that the wandering mind is among our greatest obstacles to self-improvement. "The faculty of voluntarily bringing back a wandering attention, over and over again, is the very root of judgment, character and will," he wrote. "No one is *compos sui* [master of oneself] if he has it not. An education which should improve this faculty would be *the* education *par excellence.* But it is easier to define that ideal than give suggestions for bringing it about."

We now have the tools to bring it about. Mindfulness practice, having made a millennia-long journey from ancient India to the American workplace, teaches us how to control our attention, develop wise judgment, and become more joyous and compassionate.

For solitary craftspeople, manual laborers, call center workers, middle managers, and CEOs alike, it is indeed the education *par excellence.*

Which is not to say mindfulness is a panacea. Meditating for five minutes, or even five hours, a day will not solve all our problems. We will still get sick. Our bodies will still age. Colleagues will frustrate us, and responsibilities will still loom. But meditation practice can soften our responses to them, giving work a lightness, even as colleagues annoy us and responsibilities mount. And in time, it can make us more effective, more resilient, and even give work a new sense of meaning.

Today, with meditation rooms showing up in the halls of big companies like General Mills and politicians sitting in silence on Capitol Hill, many people are hearing about mindfulness for the first time from a corporate well-being program or in a segment on the local news. But in fact, mindfulness has an incredibly rich history, stretching back thousands of years. And to understand all that mindfulness has to offer — even more than benefits like stress reduction and improved concentration — it is first necessary to understand how we got here.

2

How the Swans Came
to the Lake

MORE THAN A DECADE before I sat with Janice Marturano in a conference room in Minneapolis, patiently following my breath, I sat under a Bodhi tree in Bodh Gaya, India, learning how to meditate. It was late 2000, and I was there as part of a study-abroad program organized by Antioch University. While many of my friends at Boston University, where I was a junior, headed to Paris or Milan for the semester, I opted to sweat it out in India.

The subcontinent was a dizzying new experience. I lived in the Burmese Vihar, a guesthouse run by monks where wild peacocks roamed the garden and saffron-robed nuns chanted at sunrise. For decades, it has served as the de facto base camp for Westerners who travel to Bodh Gaya in search of meditation training. Hearing the stories of those who had come before gave me the sense of being part of a rich tradition of exploration and inquiry. And though I had traveled through developing countries before, the onslaught of sensations and the sheer crush of people in India left me with the impression that I had not yet really seen the world until I walked those streets. Simply stepping outside was an overwhelming multisensory adventure. The swirl of colorful saris, dust clouds rising from unpaved roads, and acrid smoke from street-food stands all combined for an intoxicating rush that never got old. Bodh Gaya, due south of the Himalayas, is in Bihar, India's poorest state. Yet poverty does not diminish the region's charm. Bodh Gaya's residents were among the kindest people I've ever met. It's often said that people either love India or hate it. I loved it.

Antioch had brought us to Bodh Gaya because it was the seat of the Buddha's enlightenment. There, living in the Burmese Vihar, we spent months studying with meditation masters from three different traditions: Vipassana, Zen, and Tibetan Buddhism. And as luck — or good karma — would have it, the first of those teachers was regarded as one of the greatest-ever mindfulness instructors of the twentieth century, Anagarika Munindra.

Munindra was a tiny Bengali man who resembled in features, stature, and garb his friend Mahatma Gandhi. A civil servant who began practicing meditation and ultimately came to be caretaker of the complex that marks the site of the Buddha's enlightenment, Munindra-ji also became an accomplished teacher who was particularly skilled at translating Vipassana, or Insight Meditation, for Westerners. Though I was by no means one of his closest students, Munindra and I clicked. In the late afternoons, I would walk with him to the Bodhi tree, often in silence. At nights, I would join him on the roof of the Burmese Vihar under a vast sky filled with billions of stars. In later months, I would visit Munindra at his home in Calcutta and join him in southern India, where he spent each winter. But in those first weeks in Bodh Gaya, I spent most of my time with him in the meditation hall of the Burmese Vihar, sitting in the front row among the other thirty Antioch students, as he taught basic mindfulness practices.

"Moment to moment," he would say in a high-pitched, Yoda-like voice. "Notice the breath from moment to moment." Munindra's teachings emphasized the primacy of the human body. By first instructing us to tune in to the sensations of air passing in and out of our nostrils, he introduced us to techniques meant to bring us back to the present moment, the sensory reality of what was actually happening, rather than letting the mind be lost in our thoughts and judgments. "If you observe your mind, what will you find?" he would say in a typical teaching. "We find that our mind is constantly thinking of something of the past or planning for the future. The past is not real; it has gone. The future also is not real; it has not come. Real reality is the present state. We are living in the present moment only. The present moment is true. So we have to live the life fully, being alive, seeing things as they are in the moment."

Though I had practiced some meditation before I turned up in India, Munindra's words struck a chord. His clear instructions, his focus on the familiar sensations of the body and mind, and his easy, unremarkable demeanor made mindfulness seem extremely accessible. Munindra taught us to use body and mind as a laboratory, observing the impermanence of physical sensations and our own thoughts. He taught us to put some distance between our experience of the world and any universal truth, reminding us that everyone is caught up in his or her own version of reality, none more valid than the next one. He taught us to feel sensations without being overwhelmed by them, allowing us to experience pain without suffering. There was nothing special about his form of meditation. Monks and nuns had practiced it for millennia, and Munindra had given the same instructions to thousands of Westerners before me. But precisely because it was so simple, its results so readily attainable, the impact was profound.

Munindra's teachings changed my life, introducing me to my own body, sharpening my mind, and making me a kinder person. His wisdom has been a touchstone ever since, as I've gone about finding a family and a career. And in a remarkably serendipitous bit of cultural migration, Munindra reappeared, in a way, as I researched this book. Though he died in 2003, some of his closest students went on to lay the groundwork for mainstream mindfulness in America today. As a result, the echoes of his teachings can still be heard in the halls of General Mills, and at other companies around the country.

Mindfulness is a timeless quality that we all possess. Yet it was only about three thousand years ago that holy men in India began to identify it as a powerful tool for spiritual development and behavioral change. The first mentions of qualities akin to mindfulness appear in descriptions of yogic practices in the Upanishads, the scriptural texts of Hinduism that date back as early as 1000 BC. But it was Siddhartha Gautama, the historical Buddha, who zeroed in on the power of mindfulness.

As the Buddha told his disciples, "It is through the establishment of the lovely clarity of mindfulness that you can let go of grasping after past and future, overcome attachment and grief, abandon all clinging and anxiety, and awaken an unshakable freedom of heart, here and now." Indeed, Buddhism revolves around the practice of mindfulness. A fundamental Buddhist teaching is the "four foundations of mindfulness"— mindfulness of body, thoughts, emotions, and consciousness — and the term is sprinkled throughout the tradition's original texts like stars across the sky.

While Buddhism flourished across Asia for millennia, it would take more than two thousand years for it to reach the New World. The first group of Americans to dabble in the practice were the Transcendentalists. In 1840 Ralph Waldo Emerson, a young Unitarian minister in Concord, Massachusetts, started a progressive magazine called *The Dial* with some friends, among them Henry David Thoreau. Though grounded in American virtues and Christian traditions, Emerson and Thoreau were hungry for new ideas and new ways to understand their rapidly changing world. And as original Buddhist and Hindu texts were translated in Europe and sent across the Atlantic, Emerson and Thoreau would publish excerpts in *The Dial* and try to make sense of these foreign traditions.

At times they misinterpreted the esoteric teachings. Emerson sometimes confused Buddhism and Hinduism, and his understanding of
Buddhism's core values was misguided. Their befuddlement was
understandable. There were no Zen priests or Tibetan rinpoches
in Massachusetts in those days, let alone scholars of Eastern religion. What original texts they did receive were translated, sometimes badly. Yet by grappling with these writings, publishing some,
and internalizing bits of the wisdom they contained, Emerson and
Thoreau opened the door for a serious dialogue between American
thinkers and Asia's wisdom traditions. No longer were "Oriental"
teachings merely the curious religions practiced in faraway lands.
In the hands of the Transcendentalists they became new primary
texts, and even words to live by.

It was Thoreau, more than any of his peers, who took the texts
to heart. In an 1841 journal entry, he wrote: "I want to go soon and
live away by the pond, where I shall only hear the wind whisper-
ing among the reeds. It will be a success if I shall have left myself
behind." Though the term *mindfulness* wasn't part of the common
vernacular in pre–Civil War New England, there's no mistaking
Thoreau's intention. He was aiming to observe the world moment
to moment, to let his mind be free from the incessant chattering, to
transcend himself. So one day in 1845, Thoreau marched into the
Massachusetts woods and embarked on what endures even today as
the most famous American experiment in mindfulness.

Thoreau's destination was Walden Pond, an unremarkable body
of water on land recently purchased by Emerson. Thoreau built
himself a small cabin and moved in with the intention to "live deliberately." For just over two years, he remained there in near total
isolation. He spent his days reading, writing, and communing with
nature. The book he wrote about his time there, *Walden,* was an instant classic that helped define the American character. Yet in addition to environmentalism and civil disobedience, themes often

latched on to by many interpreters of the text, Thoreau was also preaching a gospel of mindfulness.

Sometimes, in a summer morning, having taken my accustomed bath, I sat in my sunny doorway from sunrise til noon, rapt in revery, amidst the pines and hickories and sumachs, in undisturbed solitude and stillness, while the birds sang around or flitted noiseless through the house, until by the sun falling in my west window, or the noise of some traveller's wagon on the distant highway, I was reminded of the lapse of time. I grew in those seasons like corn in the night, and they were far better than the work of the hands would have been. They were not time subtracted from my life, but so much over and above my usual allowance. I realized what the Orientals mean by contemplation and the forsaking of works.

As the late Buddhist scholar Rick Fields observed in *How the Swans Came to the Lake,* his excellent history of Buddhism in America, Thoreau "was certainly not the only one of his generation to live a contemplative life, but he was, it seems, one of the few to live it in a Buddhist way. That is to say, he was perhaps the first American to explore the nontheistic mode of contemplation which is the distinguishing mark of Buddhism." Thoreau's friends, too, saw him as a spiritual figure. Moncure Conway, a disaffected Unitarian minister turned atheistic antislavery activist in London, said of Thoreau's time at Walden: "Like the pious Yogi, so long motionless whilst gazing on the sun that knotty plants encircled his neck, and the cast snake-skin his loins, and the birds built their nests on his shoulders, this poet and naturalist, by equal consecration, became a part of the field and forest amid which he dwelt." Fields called Thoreau "pre-Buddhist." He didn't work to cultivate insight, compassion, and an intuitive understanding of interconnectedness. Rather, "he forecast an American Buddhism by the nature of his contemplation, in the same way that a certain quality of transparent predawn forecasts a clear morning."

Thoreau's experience at Walden continues to prove instructive today. Mindfulness Based Stress Reduction founder Jon Kabat-Zinn, writing in his most accessible book, *Wherever You Go, There You Are,* cites Thoreau's adventure in one of his pithy meditation instructions. "Thoreau's two years at Walden Pond were above all a personal experiment in mindfulness," Kabat-Zinn wrote. "He chose to put his life on the line in order to revel in the wonder and simplicity of present moments. But you don't have to go out of your way to find someplace special to practice mindfulness. It is sufficient to make a little time in your life for stillness and what we call non-doing, and then tune into your breathing. All of Walden Pond is within your breath."

For the next hundred years or so, Buddhism — let alone secular mindfulness — had no great boosters in America. Many country-specific movements grew up around immigrant communities, transporting the rituals of Japanese, Chinese, and Korean practitioners to San Francisco, Chicago, Boston, and beyond. But consumed as they were with preserving the traditions from home, these regional movements failed to win many Western adherents. Still, the spread of traditional Buddhism across America nonetheless laid the groundwork for a broader societal acceptance of the relatively exotic religion, a move that would eventually provide fodder for a new group of poets and writers who became engrossed with the philosophies of the East.

The years following World War II saw the next great wave of American engagement with mindfulness. After one hundred years of expanding borders at home and wars abroad, the American zeitgeist was once again poised for self-reflection. It was a time for the country to make sense of its emerging national identity, a task that was enthusiastically taken up in part by the Beat Generation. It began one day in 1953, when Allen Ginsberg was wandering the streets of Manhattan and stumbled upon the First Zen Institute, a collection of original Japanese texts, paintings, and music housed in a luxurious Manhattan apartment. Ginsberg, trim and bespectacled at the time, with slicked-back hair, did not yet resemble the portly, wild-haired sage who would bridge the Beat and hippie generations. This was before "Howl," and the austere vibe of the First Zen Institute intimidated him. Yet Ginsberg was intrigued enough by what he sensed in the place to seek out D. T. Suzuki, who was at the time the most prominent face of Zen in America.

Around the same time, Ginsberg's friend Jack Kerouac, hungry for his own Walden moment, went to a library to read Thoreau. "I said, 'I'm going to cut out from civilization, and go back and live in the woods like Thoreau,' and I started to read Thoreau and he talked about Hindu philosophy," Kerouac once recalled. "So I put Thoreau down and I took out, accidentally, 'The Life of Buddha' by Ashvagosa." As the 1950s wore on, Kerouac nurtured his budding interest in Buddhism, reading whatever original texts he could find. A diligent student, he took copious notes on his readings and compiled them in a volume called *Some of the Dharma*, which he shared with Ginsberg.

In 1957, reveling in the success of *On the Road*, his breakout novel, Kerouac wrote *The Dharma Bums*, a book whose title first introduced the word for Buddhist teachings — *dharma* — to much of the Western world. A semifictional account of his relationship with his friend Gary Snyder, a fellow Buddhist, *The Dharma Bums* was another hit. In one passage, Snyder's character looks into the future and imagines how the next generation will be defined by its spirituality: "I see a vision of a great rucksack revolution, thousands or even millions of young Americans wandering around with rucksacks, going up to mountains to pray, making children laugh, and old men glad, making young girls happy, and old girls happier, all of 'em Zen lunatics who go about writing poems that happen to appear in their heads for no reason, and also by being kind, and also by strange unexpected acts keep giving visions of eternal freedom to everybody and to all living creatures."

With this vision Kerouac foresaw—or perhaps called into being—the hippies of the next decade. For what was that "rucksack revolution" Kerouac spoke of if not the throngs that flocked to Woodstock and on to India? It was the beginning of a new, radical era in American intellectual and spiritual exploration, and it would set in motion the tides of history that, forty years later, would make mindfulness part of the mainstream.

In the 1960s the hippies embraced meditation and the quest for enlightenment part and parcel with bell-bottoms, tie-dyes, free love, and mind-altering drugs. The Beatles went to India to meditate with Maharishi Mahesh Yogi. An American psychologist from Harvard named Richard Alpert went to India and returned as Ram Dass, wrote a seminal book called *Be Here Now,* and began preaching a message of higher consciousness to all who would listen. A supposedly reincarnated Tibetan lama named Chögyam Trungpa Rinpoche studied at Oxford, abandoned his robes, donned a three-piece suit, and opened an accredited college called Naropa University in Boulder, Colorado. It was a busy and bizarre time, with too many characters and movements to comprehensively recount here. Yet a few people bear mentioning, instrumental as they were in laying the foundation for today's mindfulness movement.

In the early 1970s, a new strain of countercultural vagabonds emerged. Less interested in sex, drugs, and rock-and-roll than they were in elevating their consciousness, this set—many of them well educated and well off—traveled to India, Thailand, and Burma to learn from meditation masters. Many were ordained as monks and nuns for spells, spending months and years practicing meditation. And in time, many of them found their way to Bodh Gaya, the same town where I would later meet Munindra. It was there, appropriately, that many of their practices deepened. And while thousands of spiritual pilgrims passed through temples like the Burmese Vihar in those days, three teachers in particular went on to have a lasting impact on mainstream mindfulness.

Joseph Goldstein and Sharon Salzberg met up while practicing in Bodh Gaya in the early 1970s. They later met another seeker, Jack Kornfield. The three studied with Munindra, among other teachers, and became fast friends. Upon returning to the United States, they went about founding a center where they could offer intensive meditation retreats to curious Americans who didn't make the trip to India. On Valentine's Day in 1976 they opened the Insight Meditation Society in an old mansion in Barre, Massachusetts. Later, Kornfield would also establish Spirit Rock, a center with similar aims, in the rolling hills north of San Francisco. At the same time as the IMS and Spirit Rock communities took root, hundreds of other Zen and Tibetan Buddhist centers around the country were also finding large new audiences in what Boston University religion professor Stephen Prothero calls "Boomer Buddhists," middle-aged Americans rediscovering and at times reinventing their own spiritual lives. The flourishing of these groups heralded an important new age in the practice of Buddhism: it democratized meditation. Once largely the preserve of monks and nuns, mindfulness meditation in recent decades has been made accessible to anyone at all. In a recent survey of Americans, 9.4 percent of respondents said they meditated. That's more than 20 million people in the United States alone. Indeed, there are today more meditators on Earth than at any previous moment in human history.

Yet for all their burgeoning popularity, IMS and Spirit Rock were essentially Buddhist retreat centers. If mindfulness was truly going to go mainstream, it needed to be divorced from its cultural roots, stripped of any of the trappings associating the practice with a 2,600-year-old religion. And there is one man more than any other who deserves credit for making secular mindfulness an acceptable everyday pursuit: Jon Kabat-Zinn.

Kabat-Zinn, beginning his work in the late 1970s and continuing today, established the validity of mindfulness as a clinical treatment, developed a rigorous study of the effects of meditation on the human brain, and paved the way for mindfulness training in businesses, organizations, schools, and other professional settings. But try speaking about Kabat-Zinn in even remotely laudatory terms when he's within earshot, and he's liable to shut you down.

"You know how it is with stories," says Kabat-Zinn, a slight, self-deprecating New Yorker. "You can tell the story of yourself in a thousand different ways depending on the effect you want to get across, and whom you're talking to and everything else. So I don't believe any of the stories I tell myself about my past and the arc of my trajectory. But I do sometimes find myself saying that this was something I appreciated very young, maybe five or so."

The son of a scientist father and an artist mother, Kabat-Zinn said his intellectual upbringing suffered from "The Two Cultures" dichotomy, a term C. P. Snow, the British scientist and novelist, used to describe the schism in Western society between the sciences and the humanities. "I just knew there was something missing. I could feel it in the emotional tenor of the family," he says. "And so it became really important to me to understand: what is the unifying factor of different ways of knowing? Now at five, I probably wouldn't have put it that way. But it was kind of like a cellular feeling. There's got to be more to it than this." Kabat-Zinn went on to the Massachusetts Institute of Technology, where he studied molecular biology. But even as he pursued a career in traditional Western science, a deeper curiosity about the nature of reality gnawed at him. "You have to start with physics and chemistry and biology, but what about complexity?" he says. "What about consciousness?"

While at MIT, he was introduced to Buddhist meditation. "I was twenty-two years old, and it was like a wake-up experience," he says. "Holy smoke. This is what I've been looking for my entire life. A way of being that allows us to hold everything without judging it, without putting everything into compartments ... From that point on, even though I did get my PhD in molecular biology, there was always this other element that was very important to me, and that's what I finally figured out how to do as my profession and my love."

The turning point came in 1979. He was working in the gross anatomy lab at the University of Massachusetts in Worcester. In need of a break, he went on a meditation retreat. And while sitting in silence for days on end, he had the kind of epiphany that seems so obvious after the fact. He realized that if mindfulness is a tool to ease our burdens and calm our frayed nerves, he should bring it to the places where people are suffering most — hospitals.

In 1979 Kabat-Zinn set up a stress reduction clinic at the University of Massachusetts. From this perch, he would go on to develop the system known as Mindfulness Based Stress Reduction, or MBSR. An eight-week group course that is led by a trained instructor, MBSR involves a two-hour session once a week, plus one five-hour session. For the duration of MBSR training, participants agree to meditate for at least forty-five minutes a day. Students are taught to observe sensations and emotions, rather than cling to them. They learn to scan their bodies, witnessing the impermanence of both pleasant and unpleasant sensations. They do gentle yoga to develop more acute sensory awareness. They focus on subtle physical experiences — like the feeling of air passing in and out of the nostrils — so that each detail is brought into high definition. They notice how easy it is to let concentration slip from an object of attention — whether it be the breath or the sounds in the room — and become aware of the incessantly chattering mind, leaping around like a monkey. To work through some of these new experiences, students also form a sort of support group with one another, talking through the challenges of their practice with each other and the teacher.

MBSR was slow going at first. Kabat-Zinn taught a few people at a time out of a small room in the basement. Doctors at the hospital in Worcester would send him patients who weren't getting better with traditional treatments, and little by little, word of the cura-tive — if quirky — power of MBSR spread. Patients who were expe-riencing chronic pain would arrive in agony, willing to try anything. After learning MBSR from Kabat-Zinn, they would become fluent at coping with their ailments, more at ease with their pain. Mindful-ness didn't make the hurt disappear, but it allowed them to control their reactions to it. This is one of the key premises of mindfulness as a means of stress and pain reduction: we all experience pain, but that doesn't mean we have to suffer.

In 1993, the television journalist Bill Moyers produced a series for PBS called *Healing and the Mind*. A five-part tour through a range of unconventional medical practices that were just beginning to catch on, *Healing and the Mind* helped pave the way for broad acceptance of alternative medicine in America. In a segment called "Healing From Within," Moyers dedicated almost an hour to Kabat-Zinn and his work, following him and a cohort of MBSR students through the entire eight-week course. Moyers maintained the skeptical tone of a seasoned journalist who has seen it all, but he approached the prac-tice with an open mind, and in the end he acknowledged its effec-tiveness, citing some of the first studies that demonstrated MBSR's clinical efficacy. It was a powerful statement from one of the most trusted men in news: mindfulness was not some New Age hocus-po-cus. It was a legitimate, effective tool to reduce suffering.

The Moyers program was a tipping point, and Kabat-Zinn's renown grew. Two years after the show aired, Kabat-Zinn cofounded the granddaddy of the academic programs focused on mindfulness — the Center for Mindfulness in Medicine, Health Care, and Society. With an institution behind him, Kabat-Zinn and colleagues could now attract grant money, hire staff, train instructors, and scale their efforts. Today more than 720 clinics are teaching MBSR, making it one of the fastest-growing forms of meditation out there, and more than twenty thousand people have been trained at the Massachusetts center alone. Hundreds of thousands more have learned MBSR elsewhere. If stress reduction, improved concentration, general well-being, and a sense of compassion mark the terrain of a more mindful life, MBSR has been proven to be a reliable road map to get there.

Kabat-Zinn, meanwhile, went on to become the face of mindfulness in America and around the world. After handing over the reins of the Stress Reduction Clinic to his friend Saki Santorelli (who helped Janice Marturano develop the Mindful Leadership program at General Mills), Kabat-Zinn transitioned to a full-time circuit of speaking and teaching. He travels incessantly, spreading MBSR around the globe. He teaches retreats for thousands of people each year and leads small gatherings for politicians and business leaders. And besides blazing a trail for the clinical application and study of mindfulness, Kabat-Zinn did another very important thing: he secularized it.

As research into meditation has grown, researchers have struggled with how overt they can be when it comes to acknowledging the religious origins of mindfulness and other contemplative traditions. Lean too heavily on Buddhist terminology, and it's easy for peers in academia to dismiss the whole endeavor as a thinly veiled attempt at conversion. But stray too far from the core teachings of mindfulness, and one risks reducing a rich tradition into a narrow, heartless set of practices and goals. Kabat-Zinn struck a graceful balance early on with his working clinical definition of mindfulness: "paying attention in a particular way: on purpose, in the present moment, and nonjudgmentally."

There's no mention of religion, and yet the instructions capture the essence of the historical practice. It's not that Kabat-Zinn doesn't acknowledge the Buddhist roots of mindfulness. In his books and talks, he freely discloses the origins of mindfulness and uses the occasional story from the Buddhist *suttas* to illustrate his teachings. But he doesn't hit people over the head with it, either, and he's explicit in saying that mindfulness is a secular pursuit. This is one of the secrets of the mindfulness movement: even as it dispenses radical instructions for profoundly changing our way of being, it does so in plain language.

In Buddhist parlance, this could be considered "skillful means," or *upaya,* a term that refers to the importance of adapting a message to an audience. Kabat-Zinn recognized that trying to simply teach Buddhism to Western audiences was sure to fall flat. So he stripped the teachings of any reference to ancient Indian tradition, while still retaining its core tenets. Kabat-Zinn doesn't even think of mindfulness as a spiritual practice. "I tend to stay away from the word *spiritual* as if it had some toxic outpouring," he says. "Because people get very attached to their view of spiritual, and they put that in counterdistinction to everybody else who's not quite as spiritual as I am. So my working definition of spiritual is what it means for us to be truly human. And I leave it at that. Is giving birth spiritual? Is chopping vegetables spiritual? Seeing the look in your daughter's eyes when she comes home from school — is that a spiritual experience? Or is it not good enough? Not really good enough? So from that point of view, what isn't spiritual?"

Today, Kabat-Zinn's influence stretches from the hundreds of hospitals where MBSR is offered as a no-nonsense pain relief technique, to China, where, despite the country's ongoing persecution of Tibetan Buddhism, there is burgeoning interest in mindfulness. Kabat-Zinn has distilled the essential teachings from teachers like Munindra, found a way to communicate them in a relatively efficient eight-week program, and personally taught thousands of people around the world.

But Kabat-Zinn was not going to make mindfulness part of the mainstream all on his own. It would take the efforts of many other academic, business, and cultural leaders to gradually make the practice of meditation an acceptable part of the popular culture. Among Kabat-Zinn's contemporaries working along similar lines was a group of meditating neuroscientists who went to India and studied the brains of Tibetan monks, eventually setting in motion a movement to bring mindfulness into the heart of American academia. We'll hear more about them in the next chapter. At the same time, psychologists like Daniel Goleman, who popularized the concept of Emotional Intelligence, were also deeply influenced by mindfulness. While there was no great groundswell of public enthusiasm for the subject until quite recently, during the seventies, eighties, and early nineties a handful of influential experiments helped pave the way for the mindfulness movement that we know today. One such foray, in particular, forecast today's embrace of mindfulness by major corporations. And the company that embarked on this rather radical endeavor was famously conservative, making its effort all the more remarkable.

In the early 1990s, Monsanto, the world's largest agricultural company, was already controversial. Its "terminator" seeds, which produced plants that could not reproduce on their own, made it public enemy number one for environmentalists. And Monsanto had a famously staid corporate culture, making it an unlikely laboratory for an experiment in mindfulness.

Yet Monsanto also had a new CEO at this time. Bob Shapiro had risen through the ranks to assume one of the most coveted jobs in corporate America. And though he was conventional enough to get the top job at Monsanto, Shapiro also had a long-standing interest in contemplative traditions. So when his friend Charlie Halpern, a lawyer and experienced mindfulness practitioner, suggested Shapiro try out mindfulness practice in the office, the new CEO decided to give it a shot. Halpern had an idea of who might be a good teacher, and in 1996, a mindfulness instructor named Mirabai Bush led Shapiro and fifteen top employees through a three-day workshop on "Deep Thinking Skills" at the Fetzer Institute in Kalamazoo, Michigan. It was the first of what would be a series of meditation retreats that brought mindfulness practice to Monsanto.

Teaching Monsanto executives was a difficult charge for Bush. Before she came to work with Halpern, she had lived in Guatemala for ten years, working on sustainable agriculture projects. "Monsanto was a villain in that world," she said. "I didn't want to do it in the beginning, but I was finally convinced that it was a great opportunity to see if mindfulness would work in a corporate setting." Before the retreat began, Bush went to Monsanto headquarters and interviewed each of the participants, trying to prepare them for what would be a demanding experience — three days and four nights in silence, with instruction on sitting and walking meditation, and loving-kindness practice. She asked them if they had ever spent time in silence and was met with blank stares. "I'm quiet while I read the newspaper in the morning," one man told her. She laughed to herself. A true quieting of the mind was a foreign concept to this crowd.

On the first day of the retreat, the Monsanto employees showed up at the Fetzer Institute wearing suits and carrying briefcases. "People had no idea what they were getting into," Bush said. She led them into the room that would serve as a meditation hall, told them to take off their shoes and lie down, and began a series of relaxation exercises. It was awkward at first, but eventually the students went along with it, proving to be remarkably compliant. "That's the positive side of a traditional corporation," Bush said. "I could tell them what to do, and they did it. They were great. These guys had really great concentration. And when they put their energy toward something, it moved very quickly."

Over the next few days, Bush led the Monsanto employees through rigorous instruction in meditation — long periods of silence punctuated by talks on self-awareness and compassion. It was akin to the monastic retreats practiced at meditation centers like Spirit Rock and Insight Meditation Society. "People were having breakthrough experiences," she recalled. "There was an incredible openness to learning. All the basic awakenings were happening."

Bush had some healing work of her own to do as she sat with executives from the company she loathed. "The stuff I went through was huge," she told me. "I thought I was so compassionate, and I was comfortable no matter who I was with. But when I went to Monsanto, I realized, Oh, my God, I had this whole category of people qualified as the 'other.'"

On the final day of the retreat, the group did loving-kindness practice, wishing for the peace and happiness of all sentient beings. They meditated on the value of all species, including the bugs Monsanto's products were designed to kill. "I opened my eyes toward the end of this practice and saw tears on every face," Bush said. She was surprised to see these Monsanto executives opening up and displaying empathy. "I realized in that moment that I had been holding a lot of judgment too."

After that first retreat, one executive came to Bush and described a minor breakthrough. Part of his job was listening to complaints about the environmental impact of Monsanto products. But he said that when people came into his office to voice their concerns, he couldn't even hear what they were saying, because he was already rehearsing the script he had prepared on behalf of Monsanto. He had to keep those canned responses top of mind, so that whenever someone began airing a grievance he would have the perfect retort to shut them down. But after a few days of practicing mindfulness, he could already feel that facade falling away. He was retraining himself to pay attention, fully, to what was happening around him. And if that included people who were genuinely upset, he was going to have to listen deeply to them, too. It was a small epiphany, but a promising start.

Bush continued to teach Monsanto managers for another few years. In 1997 a retreat for twenty-five executives took place at the Wilderness Lodge in Missouri, and by 1999 Monsanto employees had some momentum of their own, organizing weekly sittings, day-long sessions, and three-day residential retreats. That year Bush gave a talk on "Mindfulness and Business" and expanded her teaching to other Monsanto offices around the country. "We thought we'd plant some seeds and see what would grow," she said. "And it was amazing. Everything we did, people wanted more." Bush saw some signs that mindfulness was making a mark on the company during her work there. Monsanto didn't abandon GMOs. But it was more responsive to its critics for a time, ultimately phasing out the terminator technology. "Monsanto became more open to listening to opposing arguments and different perspectives," she remembers. "I saw a movement toward that while I was working with them."

All things are impermanent, however, including Monsanto's experiment with mindfulness. Shapiro was ousted as CEO of Monsanto in 2000. His replacement sought to eradicate any hint of the former boss's management style and brought a swift end to the most ambitious corporate mindfulness program at the time, at a company that needed it badly. Had Monsanto's mindfulness program taken root today, perhaps it would have survived a changing of the guard. But fifteen years ago, there was hardly any research that demonstrated the power of mindfulness, and virtually no public recognition of, or appetite for, the practice. Nonetheless, the Center for Contemplative Mind in Society continued to work with businesses and other organizations. Bush became its executive director and worked with new clients, including Hoffmann-LaRoche, National Grid, and Hearst. The center also expanded its work to include lawyers and educators and now hosts an annual conference for contemplative practices in higher education. Bush, meanwhile, has had a hand in developing mindfulness training programs at Google and in the halls of Congress.

Arnold Toynbee, the celebrated British historian, is reported to have said that "the coming of Buddhism to the West may well prove to be the most important event of the twentieth century." The statement may be apocryphal, but the sentiment has particular resonance today as secular mindfulness, an outgrowth of Buddhism, begins to exert its influence on Western business. As religious scholar David Loy remarked, "Toynbee may have noticed something the rest of us need to see: that the interaction between Buddhism and the West is crucial today, because each emphasizes something the other is missing. Whether or not Toynbee actually made this observation, the significance of the encounter may be nearly as great as his statement suggests."

Though mindfulness can't be considered Buddhist any more than the law of gravity can be considered English because it was discovered by Newton, the spread of Buddhism is an important part of the history here. For it was only through exposure to the dharma that a new generation of thinkers, tinkerers, and cultural leaders could home in on some of the tradition's essential teachings, strip them of their religious trappings, and offer them up in a purely secular fashion. Kabat-Zinn's work developing MBSR made mindfulness accessible to the medical profession and provided a framework for clinical experiments. Mirabai Bush, working with

Monsanto, provided the first glimpses of how mindfulness and corporate America might mix. But in this empirical world we live in, it would take more than the enthusiasm of these pioneers to make mindfulness a mainstream pursuit, especially in corporate America. It would take evidence, largely in the form of clinical and academic studies, to win over a broader audience. And as we'll see in the next chapter, that has only started to happen in recent years, as hard scientific data has suggested that mindfulness meditation not only changes our behavior. It also changes our bodies and brains.

3

The Science of Sitting

ONE RAINY SPRING DAY I caught the train out of Grand Central Terminal in downtown New York and rode two hours north to the Yale Child Study Center in New Haven, Connecticut. I was headed to visit Judson Brewer, then a neuroscientist doing pioneering work that examines how mindfulness changes the brain. Brewer, a short and energetic man with a well-groomed beard and wire-rimmed spectacles, is a longtime meditator himself. He has spent cumulative months on retreat and has an easy command of the lengthy *suttas* that contain the teachings of Southeast Asian Buddhism. He is also part of a new generation of scientists who are building on the work that Jon Kabat-Zinn began in the 1970s — unpacking the benefits of mindfulness practice with studies that are publishable in peer-reviewed journals. And today, Brewer's primary interest is how secular mindfulness can be used to help everyday Americans.

I had come to interview Brewer about his work and practice. But as we made small talk in a cluttered office and I got my audio recorder out, he asked me how much I had meditated in my life. I told him I had practiced mindfulness on and off for fifteen years, meditating for thousands of hours altogether. His eyes lit up. Before I had a chance to finish my story, Brewer whipped out his phone and called a research assistant. It turned out I was an ideal subject for the study they were conducting, and Brewer was mobilizing his team. The interview would have to wait. Today, he had to investigate my brain.

Twenty minutes later I was seated in the corner of a small laboratory, behind a black curtain, staring at a dark computer screen. Two research assistants were dabbing a cool clear conductive gel in a spiral pattern on my scalp. Behind me an electroencephalograph, or EEG, machine hummed away. On the table next to me was a sort of swimming cap bristling with nodes and wires that would soon envelop my head, measuring the electrical activity in different parts of my brain.

On this day, Brewer and his team were looking at activity in the posterior cingulate cortex, an area in the middle of the brain that forms a central node in the "default network," a circuit that activates when we're daydreaming, dwelling on the past, and generally lost in self-referential thinking. In those moments when we're so absorbed in thinking about our own lives that we don't notice what's going on around us, the default network has taken over. When my posterior cingulate cortex was very active, I was likely to be mind wandering and telling myself stories about my own life. When it was dormant, I was more likely to be mindful. The hypothesis, Brewer told me later, was that when the posterior cingulate cortex goes quiet, people experience what he called "effortless awareness." "It's not just concentration," he said, "but a quality of non-clinging experience."

To begin the experiment, I was asked to practice mindfulness for ten minutes. I just sat still, noticing my breath. While I was meditating, Brewer and his team fiddled with the equipment to make sure they were getting a stable signal. Then the real tests began. On the computer screen in front of me, a series of words flashed, one every few seconds. It was my job to determine whether they could appropriately describe me: WELL-MEANING. ABSENT-MINDED. COURTEOUS. ANGRY. As each word appeared on the screen, I had a few seconds to make a snap judgment. Was I courteous? Was I absent-minded? Was I an angry person? As I later learned, it didn't matter whether the word described me or not. What mattered was that I was judging, telling a story about myself, inhabiting my mind and not my body. As I asked myself each question, deciding what kind of a person I was or wasn't, I reinforced the story of my self. And with each little burst of self-referential thinking, my posterior cingulate cortex lit up.

As soon as a word disappeared from the screen, my job was to immediately slip back into mindful awareness. And at that point, the computer screen switched from showing words to displaying a progressing bar graph representing activity in my posterior cingulate cortex. I could tell that when the bar graph was moving up, I was being more mindful. When I began mind wandering, it dipped down, falling below the x axis. One way I knew was that when the graph came on the screen, I could also see the graph from the previous minute, when I had been doing word associations. That graph had a stable baseline punctuated by sharp peaks downward, like stalactites hanging from a cave ceiling. These were the moments when I was telling myself stories about my own identity. When I stopped and just became mindful of my breath, the graph moved the other way, swelling upward like a mountain.

We did dozens of these runs over the course of two hours, as I meditated, then watched the words flash before me on the computer screen. Each time, I had bursts of self-referential processing as I did the word associations, activating my posterior cingulate cortex. And each time, I would then slip into meditation, sending the bar graph up — an indication that my default network wasn't active, that I wasn't thinking about myself. Thoughts would arise, of course. And I could watch in real time as the bar graph wavered and dipped, showing the activation of the posterior cingulate cortex. When that happened, I renewed my effort, focused on the breath, and the bar graph moved back up.

Once, late into the experiment, I decided to begin meditating, then intentionally let my mind wander. I wanted to see if I could really manipulate the EEG graph on command. After the word association I began focusing on my breath. Then after about thirty seconds, I thought of the most stressful thing I could think of: a job interview. Two days later, I was scheduled to have my final interview with the executive editor of the *New York Times*. I was instantly lost in an anxious train of thought about my job application, interviewing with my potential future boss, and the drama of having to quit my current role at the *Financial Times*. And sure enough, on screen, the bar graph plummeted. Any modicum of mindfulness had evaporated instantaneously.

The next run, I tried to repeat the experience. First I did the word associations, then I began meditating, and then I thought of my interview with the boss again. But this time, the bar graph didn't plummet. I wasn't having as severe a stress reaction to that thought, wasn't getting caught up in my own personal narrative. I just noticed that I was thinking about my job interview and returned to awareness of my breath. It was as if my mind had already seen that part of the movie, didn't particularly enjoy the experience, and didn't need to watch it again. Instead, thoughts of my job interview flickered away in the background, without taking over my attention.

This was the moment Brewer and his team were looking for. They wanted to see if longtime mindfulness practitioners could have stressful thoughts without reacting to them. "The hypothesis is that there's a common element to thinking and anxiety and judgment, as opposed to just noticing," Brewer told me later. "It's about one's relationships to one's thoughts. If you're caught up in your thoughts, you may have a physiological fear reaction, and that's different from consciously noticing your thoughts and being with them, which is not 'clenchy.' It's about getting caught up versus not getting caught up with your thoughts. It's what I describe as getting out of your own way. It's not about *not* thinking; it's about how we're relating to the thinking."

Before I left Brewer's lab we did one more run. I wanted to see what loving-kindness meditation looked like on the EEG graph. Loving-kindness, or *metta,* is a type of meditation that's often taught in concert with basic mindful awareness. The practice is deceptively simple, but very powerful. All *metta* asks is that you wish well for yourself, for those around you, and for all beings. To practice, simply recite a few phrases silently: "May I be happy, may I be healthy and safe, may I be free from suffering." After a little while, we expand it to those around us: "May everyone in this room be happy, may everyone in this room be healthy and safe, may everyone in this room be free from suffering." Finally, we wish well for everyone. "May all sentient beings be happy, may all sentient beings be healthy and safe, may all sentient beings be free from suffering." With *metta,* there's no expectation that our wishes will actually impact the outcome of any given event. Nor is it about praying to a deity who might deign to lend a helping hand. Instead, *metta* hones our ability to conjure up feelings of compassion, goodwill, and caring on demand. It's also an effective practice that makes us less concerned with the self, and more concerned with others.

During this final run, the word associations — RUDE, HELPFUL, CURIOUS — elicited the now-predictable stalactite graph, as activity in my posterior cingulate cortex spiked each time I thought of myself. Then I shifted into *metta,* and the graph immediately shot upward. Though I was wishing well for myself, it wasn't eliciting the same kind of self-referential response that I'd seen with the word associations. After twenty seconds I began wishing well to everyone in the room — Brewer and his assistants. The graph moved up even higher. Whatever activity there had been in the posterior cingulate cortex was diminished further. My default network was shutting down as I directed my attention to the world outside me. Finally

I began wishing well to all sentient beings. The bar graph spiked higher. The further out I extended my loving-kindness, the less I dwelled on my own unhappiness.

It was a wonderful demonstration of the power of science, and the power of mindfulness. With these simple practices, I was able to rein in one of the most stubborn parts of consciousness — the self. Brewer, meanwhile, was able to glean new insights into the inner workings of the human brain.

Brewer and his team at Yale are at the vanguard of a scientific revolution of sorts. At the best research universities around the globe, some of the brightest minds are exploring mindfulness. Whole centers have sprung up at Stanford, UCLA, and the University of Massachusetts, among others, where scientists and psychologists are studying longtime meditators. In very short order, the study of meditation — not long ago dismissed as a pseudoscientific self-help technique at best — has become part of everyday academia. And if there is one vein of research that has gained traction above the others, it is how mindfulness affects our brains. The devotees of this emerging field even have a wonderful name for themselves: "contemplative neuroscientists."

The paradigm shift hasn't happened overnight. Broad acceptance of mindfulness as a practice worthy of serious scientific inquiry, a practice with viable clinical applications, has been a long time coming. In 1983, R. Adam Engle, an American businessman who had been practicing Buddhist meditation for a decade, heard that the Dalai Lama, the spiritual leader of Tibet, was both interested in Western science and eager to share his understanding of contemplative practice with the Western scientific community. Engle was intrigued and wondered if he might have a hand in facilitating the conversation. The next year, Engle met with the Dalai

Lama's youngest brother in Los Angeles and laid out a plan for a weeklong dialogue between the Dalai Lama and a group of Western scientists. A few days later word came back — the Dalai Lama was in, and Engle was authorized to set up the event. Around the same time, Francisco Varela, a Chilean neuroscientist living in Paris, met the Dalai Lama at the Alpbach Symposia on Consciousness, in Austria, and the two struck up a conversation about the intersection of Buddhist practice and science. Though Varela didn't know Engle, he too was interested in creating a formal setting where Eastern wisdom and Western science could have a meaningful dialogue. In 1985 Varela's friend Joan Halifax, a Zen nun who at the time was running the Ojai Foundation, heard about Engle's effort and suggested the two join forces. The teams met at the Ojai Foundation in 1985 and formed the Mind and Life Institute. Two years later, Engle, Varela, and colleagues were on their way to Dharamsala, the remote mountain town in northern India that is the seat of the Tibetan government in exile, and home to the Dalai Lama.

The cognitive scientists who made the trek to present to the Dalai Lama weren't sure what kind of response they would get. Would the spiritual leader of Tibet really care about their work in the labs? But instead of an off-putting religious leader, they found a curious monk brimming with smart questions, who chimed in with his Buddhist perspective when asked. "He didn't have an agenda," said B. Alan Wallace, a translator for the Dalai Lama. "It was a meeting of minds."

That first Mind and Life event was an intimate gathering in the Himalayan foothills. Since then, Mind and Life has hosted dozens of dialogues and gone on to publish a growing body of books and papers, roping in dozens of esteemed scientists from various fields. Daniel Goleman, the psychologist who popularized Emotional Intelligence, participated in the second Mind and Life gathering, in

Newport Beach, California, in 1989. Like his friend Jon Kabat-Zinn, Goleman was trained in Western medicine and science but developed a deep affinity for the meditative practices of the East. "Buddhists have been developing ways to encourage positive emotion through meditation for thousands of years," he said.

The next year, he was moderating the third Mind and Life dialogue and invited Kabat-Zinn to attend. With the Dalai Lama in attendance, Kabat-Zinn and others described their research, recounting how the cultivation of pro-social behavior — often through meditation — improved physical, emotional, and mental health. Though Kabat-Zinn and others had been teaching secular meditation in the form of Mindfulness Based Stress Reduction for years, the Dalai Lama had not yet endorsed the practice. After hearing from this group, however, he began to come around. Meditation, the Dalai Lama began to believe, didn't necessarily have to be the preserve of monks and nuns. It could make an impact on ordinary people, too.

Before science went all in on mindfulness, technology had to catch up. And it was one new piece of scientific equipment in particular — functional magnetic resonance imaging, or fMRI — that helped the scientific community make a big leap forward. When fMRI results began to come in, the Mind and Life meeting participants began discussing more than theoretical connections between brain science and meditation; they began examining actionable studies that produced meaningful results.

The beauty of fMRI technology is that it shows, in real time, what areas of the brain are active. In an angry brain, certain areas light up. In a pleasured brain, other areas become active. After examining the brains of the same individuals, scientists quickly began to see that the neural pathways of the brain seemed to change over time. The brain wasn't fixed, as had previously been the belief. It changed, it could be trained, and it was as malleable as plastic.

Contemplative traditions had believed this to be the case for millennia. A basic tenet of Buddhism is the belief that we can up-root unvirtuous habits and replace them with virtuous ones. Now scientists could see this happening on their computer monitors. When the Dalai Lama learned about fMRI technology at the 2000 Mind and Life meeting, he was intrigued. Soon, he began encouraging neuroscientists to study the brains of Buddhist monks. "His Holiness wanted proof the techniques were useful and, if it was shown they were, to distribute the results widely so that others could benefit," said Goleman. Before long, a new generation had taken his words to heart.

Since then, the Mind and Life Institute has organized dozens of dialogues between senior scientists and meditators, drawing thousands of people to events at MIT, Harvard, and other universities around the world. Grants from the institute have funded the work of a new generation of contemplative neuroscientists, its summer programs have provided mentorship opportunities for this new cohort, and its publications have helped bring the science of meditation out of the monastery to the university.

One of the scientists who described fMRI to the Dalai Lama at early Mind and Life meetings was Richard Davidson of the University of Wisconsin at Madison. With big boyish eyes and a wild tangle of salt-and-pepper hair, Davidson oversees a small empire that conducts research into mindfulness and is today the de facto face of contemplative neuroscience. But he almost never went down this path.

As a graduate student at Harvard in the 1970s he hung around with counterculture heroes like Timothy Leary and Ram Dass and began meditating. Davidson went to Sri Lanka to study with Buddhist monks for three months and experienced firsthand the way meditation and mindfulness changed everything from his brain to his body, making him calmer, less emotionally reactive, and healthier. When he returned to Cambridge, he was convinced he could make a career studying mindfulness and the brain. If only. When he told his advisers he wanted to study meditation, they steered him away. It was a career ender, they said. So Davidson went on to become a successful conventional neuroscientist, even as he kept up his own meditation practice.

Had Davidson ignored his mentors and plowed ahead with mindfulness research early in his career, he may not have gotten very far. In the early seventies, what little research on meditation there was tended to be poorly executed and prone to wildly overstating the benefits. One study suggested that crime dropped in neighborhoods where people were doing Transcendental Meditation, a different type of practice. What is more, Davidson acknowledged that "the science and the methods of the time were not suited to the task of studying subtle internal experience." That is, technology had not yet caught up. Without fMRI technology, which wasn't widely available at the time, scientists couldn't witness real-time changes in brain activity. Nor did scientists fully appreciate epigenetics, the way gene composition can change over the course of a life. Most importantly, Davidson said, "we lacked an understanding of neuroplasticity. It is now widely accepted that the brain is an organ designed to change in response to experience and, importantly for our work, in response to training." But that wasn't the case in the seventies.

Then, in 1992, Davidson met the Dalai Lama and confessed his longtime dream of merging his personal practice with his professional research. Much had changed over the past twenty years. The Mind and Life group had helped legitimize the scientific study of meditation, more academics were coming out of the closet — announcing themselves as unabashed meditators — and the technology had improved. Soon Davidson, already a successful professor with a bright future ahead of him, took a gamble that would have previously cost him his career. He made the science of meditation his primary research area. And before long he was conducting some of the first neurological research on meditators, using new technology to see how brains changed in response to meditation. The studies confirmed his hypothesis that the mind — what we think — can change the brain — that mass of gray tissue inside our skulls. Eventually, he was invited to present to the Dalai Lama at a Mind and Life gathering. And now, despite his humble midwestern roots, Davidson is a sort of celebrity neuroscientist.

In 2009 Davidson founded the Center for Investigating Healthy Minds at the University of Wisconsin at Madison. It is now one of the leading research centers that focus on the effectiveness of meditation training on the brain, and the center itself is a testament to the power of mindfulness in the workplace. "It's had a radical impact," Davidson told me. "We have a meditation space in the middle of our lab that's used for research as well as our own personal practices. We have regular sittings there. It's a regular feature of what we do." Of the more than sixty people who work at the center, most meditate. "The whole environment has been radically affected. There is a kind of underlying dharma connection that makes everyday operating very different. As the nominal leader of this, my leadership skills have been deeply affected by this. And to have this plunked down in the middle of a competitive academic environment is amazing."

Mainstream credibility hasn't come easily for Davidson and his colleagues. Until recently, positing that hours of sitting meditation over the years could alter the structure of the brain would have been heresy. Right up into the 1990s, scientific convention held that after a critical period of "plasticity" early in life, the brain's basic architecture is set in stone, essentially fixing our neural wiring in place for life. If anything, the brain would degrade over time. But there was little belief that we could control how it aged, let alone make it stronger, or more inclined to focus on positive emotions like compassion. Yet at the same time Kabat-Zinn was pioneering MBSR in clinical settings, neuroscientists like Davidson were beginning to reveal new truths about our most complex organ. And today, dogged research by scientists around the globe, along with advances in fMRI and other neuroimaging technologies, has led to a revolution in how we think about our own brains. Thanks to their work, we now understand that our neural pathways continue to develop throughout our lifetime. This is a key finding of modern neuroscience — the architecture of our brains is not static; it can change. This notion of "neuroplasticity" has upended the study of the brain at academic institutions around the world, and now it is changing the way researchers assess mindfulness.

One of the earliest and best-known indications of neuroplasticity came from studies of London's taxi drivers. To earn the right to drive a black cab through that city, applicants must memorize a complete map of London's labyrinthine streets. To master "the Knowledge," as it is known, aspiring cabbies need to know hundreds of street names, dozens of popular routes, and myriad shortcuts. Learning the Knowledge can take years, and many who study diligently still don't pass the final exam. Yet there is a discernible difference in the brains of those who have mastered London's serpentine streets. Several studies have shown that the gray matter of the hippocampus — an area associated with memory and spatial awareness — in accomplished London cabbies is substantially thicker than that of non-cabbies. The same is true for other highly technical vocations. A study of violinists revealed that the parts of their brains associated with the motor mechanics of their left hands, used to hold the strings against the violin's neck, were far more developed than in non-violinists. It works the same when it comes to our intellectual and emotional muscles. The more we use the parts of the brain associated with concentration, and even compassion, the easier it is to focus, or feel love and kindness toward others. Scientists call this "use-dependent cortical reorganization." In plain English that means the way we use our minds affects how our brains work. But a simple way to think of it is this: what you practice becomes stronger.

In a way, research on neuroplasticity just confirms age-old truths. "Whatever one frequently thinks and ponders upon, that will become the inclination of his mind," said the Buddha. The modern variant, oft quoted by neuroscientists, is: "Neurons that fire together, wire together." It is a simple but profound truth: with training, the neural pathways that regulate our emotions, thoughts, and reactions can be rewired. "The mind can change the brain, and a changed brain can then change the mind," Davidson told me. "And some of those changes can be beneficial."

Indeed, mindfulness seems to change the brain in some specific ways. Broadly speaking, mindfulness increases activity in parts of the prefrontal cortex, an evolutionarily recent region of the brain that is important for many of the things that make us human. This region is the seat of much of our higher-order thinking — our judgment, decision making, planning, and discernment. The prefrontal cortex is also an area that seems to be more active when we are engaged in pro-social behavior — things like compassion, empathy, and kindness.

One way to measure this phenomenon is by looking at cortical thickness, so-called gray matter, in the brain. In a 2005 study, Harvard researcher Sarah Lazar and colleagues investigated whether meditation changed the brain's physical structure. To test the hypothesis, Lazar used fMRI scans to measure variations in the thickness of the cerebral cortex in experienced American practitioners of Insight Meditation, which emphasizes mindfulness in all aspects of life, then compared them to the cerebral cortexes of non-meditators. Lazar and her colleagues showed that in long-time mindfulness meditators, the cortical regions associated with processing sensory input were thicker. The results provided some of the first evidence that meditation could change the structure of the brain. They also suggested that regular meditation might slow the inevitable age-related thinning of the frontal cortex.

In another study, researchers showed that meditation increased gray matter in "brain regions involved in learning and memory processes, emotion regulation, self-referential processing, and perspective taking." That's quite a list, suggesting that mindfulness can help our minds in more ways than one. The results demonstrated measurable changes in the brain regions linked to memory, self-awareness, stress, and empathy. In the study, sixteen participants had their brains scanned at regular intervals before, during, and after an eight-week MBSR course. Practicing mindfulness exercises for an average of twenty-seven minutes per day, the participants reported feeling less stressed after learning MBSR. But their brains spoke louder than their responses to a questionnaire. The before and after images showed that over the course of just two months, gray matter density had increased in the hippocampus, a center of learning, memory, and self-awareness.

"It is fascinating to see the brain's plasticity and that, by practicing meditation, we can play an active role in changing the brain and can increase our well-being and quality of life," said Britta Hölzel, a research fellow at Massachusetts General Hospital and Giessen University in Germany who worked on the study. "Other studies in different patient populations have shown that meditation can make significant improvements in a variety of symptoms, and we are now investigating the underlying mechanisms in the brain that facilitate this change."

Studies like these are just beginning, and our understanding of the brain is far from complete. But already the work of Davidson,

Lazar, and others is demonstrating a direct connection between the practice of mindfulness and the architecture of our brains.

Our plastic brains can also work against us. If we indulge our basest inclinations, reacting to each negative emotion by stewing in ruminations about past wrongs or planning efforts to get even, these patterns will only become more ingrained over time, trapping us in a mental prison of our own making. Neuroscientists can see this on the readouts from fMRI; in consistently agitated subjects, the parts of the brain associated with fear, clinging, and reactivity come on-line at the slightest disturbance and are slow to settle down. But through the same biological mechanisms, the practice of mindfulness changes our brains, and our behavior, over time.

One area of particular interest to contemplative neuroscientists is the amygdala, an almond-shaped region in the middle of the brain. The amygdala, it seems, plays a central role in our stress reactions. When we experience a stressful situation, two main regions of the brain are activated — the hippocampus and the amygdala. The hippocampus, a seahorse-shaped region near the base of the brain, receives the information taken in from our senses. If it determines the situation at hand to be threatening, it activates the amygdala. And when the amygdala is activated, our fight-or-flight response kicks in, pumping cortisol and other hormones through our system, raising our blood pressure, and clouding our judgment. We get angry. We react aggressively. We're apt to make the situation worse, not better. Neuroscientists affectionately call this an "amygdala hijack."

Needless to say, this kind of all-or-nothing, fight-or-flight reaction isn't suited to the modern world, especially not in the office. A minor setback can seem like a career ender. Fleeting disagreements can fester into deep-seated grudges. And when the amygdala is constantly ramped up, it is more easily excited, more sensitive to the next disturbance. Agitation becomes a vicious cycle.

The good news is, a little bit of mindfulness has been proven to be an effective defense against an amygdala hijack. In one study run out of Massachusetts General Hospital, researchers showed that meditation reduced the size of the amygdala after just eight weeks of practice. That is, mindfulness made practitioners less likely to overreact, less likely to let their anger get the best of them.

It seems these sorts of changes are lasting, too. Mindfulness doesn't just change the brain during meditation. The effects continue long after we get off the cushion. The same study that showed that meditation reduced the size of the amygdala also demonstrated that the emotional regulation cultivated by meditation endured long beyond the time spent in sitting practice.

Davidson and the Center for Investigating Healthy Minds remain at the center of the contemplative neuroscience universe, taking advantage of the increasing sophistication of fMRI scans, and the growing acceptance of the study of meditation as a tool to rewire the brain. Like the EEG that Jud Brewer used on me at Yale, fMRI gives researchers a window into how different activities affect the workings of the brain. "Functional images show the dynamic activity within the brain over time," said Davidson's colleague Antoine Lutz. "We can try to observe, for example, how the brain regions associated with attention or empathy function differently for an expert practitioner compared with a novice practitioner when they focus their attention or cultivate compassion during meditation."

Some of Davidson's other colleagues, Lisa Flook and Laura Pinger, conducted another research program that studied the effects of mindfulness on pre-kindergarten students as well as teachers. The practice centered on cultivating kindness, as well as mindful awareness. Over eight weeks, the children in the study practiced breathing and movement exercises, listened to readings about kindness and caring, and engaged in exercises designed to demonstrate caring activities to their peers. Compared to a control group that didn't get the training at the same time (but received it later on), the students who received the kindness training were more attentive and had better control of their emotions. "We examined the effects of the training on students' attention and emotion regulation, relationships with classmates, and pro-social behaviors," said Flook. "Children completed computer tasks measuring their attentional ability. Teachers completed reports of the children's behavior in the classroom, while parents reported on children's behavior at home. Our research suggested that there were improvements in attention and increases in pro-social behaviors among children who received instruction." It worked for the teachers, too. "Mindfulness training can enhance teachers' sense of well-being," said Flook. "It can also provide a buffer against the stress that arises from the demands and challenges of the classroom environment."

Another of Davidson's colleagues, Melissa Rosenkranz, has worked to understand how positive and negative emotions affect the immune system — in other words, the mind-body connection. She worked with Davidson and Kabat-Zinn on a seminal study, which demonstrated that mindfulness training activated the left prefrontal cortex of the brains of workers at a biotech company and also boosted their immune systems. Since then she has continued to study "just how much power the brain can have over the health of the body." One recent study examined whether or not mindfulness could help treat asthma. The hypothesis is that if patients train their minds to become less reactive, the stress reactions that can often exacerbate asthma attacks might be mitigated. Though the study wasn't completed, initial results suggested that Rosenkranz was headed in the right direction.

During the few days I visited Madison, Davidson was hosting a confab that brought together the Dalai Lama, the pundit and entrepreneur Arianna Huffington, and a handful of Nobel laureates. At the hotel newsstand, *Madison Magazine* featured a cover story about Davidson and the Center for Investigating Healthy Minds. After the Dalai Lama spoke, Davidson signed copies of his new book for a throng of fans. Later in the week, VIPs were invited to attend a screening of a movie that featured his work and sumptuous visuals of his sparkling new research center. For someone who almost didn't go down this path, Davidson seems remarkably at ease on the frontlines of contemplative neuroscience.

Davidson initially didn't study meditation's effects on the brain, for fear it would ruin his career. Young neuroscientists face no such stigma today, and a cohort including Brewer, Lazar, and others is pushing the research in new directions each year. How mindfulness practice changes the brain and how it can be beneficially applied in a clinical setting are being studied by leading researchers at Harvard, Yale, Stanford, and dozens of other research universities.

One measure of the burgeoning academic interest in meditation is the volume of peer-reviewed papers addressing mindfulness. Studies on mindfulness funded by the National Institutes of Health jumped from two in the year 2000 to 128 in 2010. The National Institutes of Health's National Center for Complementary and Alternative Medicine (NCCAM) spent less than $2 million on research into meditation in 2002. By 2012, that number had jumped to $14 million. Now articles with titles like "A Quest for Compassion" and "Why Is It So Hard to Pay Attention, or Is It?" are showing up regularly in *Science, Frontiers in Human Neuroscience,* and other preeminent scientific journals. There is even a peer-reviewed journal called *Mindfulness,* published by academic powerhouse Springer.

Josephine Briggs is director of the NCCAM, the largest funder of research into meditation and mindfulness. A Harvard-trained physician, Briggs spent most of her career working at the pinnacle of conventional medicine and has watched the study of mindfulness slowly gain traction in recent decades. She says the field is now at a tipping point, where the rigorous study and clinical applications of meditation are becoming thoroughly mainstream. "There are two reasons for that," she told me. "One is scientific. The development of neuroscience tools to study the human brain, particularly neuro-imaging methods, has improved dramatically. Now there is real excitement that we can understand, anatomically, what happens when you move your finger." Meditation, Briggs said, is just another physical function that the scientists can study. "It's clear that by focusing your attention you do change your mental state."

The other reason research into mindfulness has hit a tipping point is more practical, Briggs said. "It has to do with the fact that a body of work has been coming together that suggests that these approaches are helpful to people," she said. "They may help with the acknowledged limitations of pharmacology in managing bothersome systems." That is, mindfulness might assist where drugs fall short. A whole field is emerging that joins pharmacological treatment with brain-training exercises that improve the effectiveness of the medicines. "These practices are no longer in any ways peripheral," Briggs said. "This is a sea change."

Indeed, open discussion about self-awareness, meditation, and compassion is no longer inherently taboo, something only for New Age weirdoes or patchouli-scented dropouts. Sure, there will be naysayers. But the stigma is falling away, and the change started in the halls of academia and the labs of Ivy League researchers. In the same way that science has led the way in making other once-outrageous subjects dinner conversation — like the ills of smoking, the importance of exercise, and the threat of global warming — so too is it helping make mindfulness part of mainstream medical research and treatment. In the same way that mindfulness has been proven to change our brains, it is also changing our bodies. Practicing it activates the regions of the brain associated with pro-social behavior and positive emotions and may even lead to weight loss and the amelioration of long-term illnesses. These findings point toward a new way of thinking about health and wellness. Instead of a purely remedial approach that often calls for copious amounts of pharmacological treats, today some of the most prominent voices in the American medical establishment are espousing the healing powers of mindfulness, meditation, and self-awareness.

Despite this flurry of research activity, mindfulness as medicine remains a nascent field. Though it's clear that the practice can be enormously beneficial in a wide range of settings, we're only just beginning to understand exactly how it works. Determining precisely why simply paying attention can have such transformative effects on an organism as complex as the human body is at this point still more art than science. Clinical research into the field is only getting started, and we're still at the early stages of understanding how the mind affects the body, and vice versa.

And really, what are all these studies actually telling us? The truth is that all the science, fascinating as it is, has limited practical utility. It may tell us what is happening in the brain when we practice, and this in turn may provide some measure of validity to skeptics. But fMRI and EEG do not tell us how to live or point the way toward some ultimate achievement. The goal is not a less reactive amygdala. The goal is true, sustainable happiness.

Furthermore, there is some skepticism, even among meditation researchers, about just how much the research is really revealing. Willoughby Britton, a professor of psychiatry and human behavior at Brown University Medical School, has emerged as one of the field's de facto ombudsmen. A devoted meditator herself, Britton nonetheless has some sharp words for many contemplative neuroscientists. She reserves particularly harsh judgment for those who seem to use research to advance a Buddhist agenda. "That is not the purpose of science — to confirm the dharma," she said. "And if that is what people are doing as scientists, they need to seriously step back and look at the ethics of that. To use science to prove your religion or worldview — there is something really wrong with that." It's a particularly fraught issue when it comes to research into mindfulness because, as is the case with Kabat-Zinn, Davidson, and others, many of those conducting the studies are also longtime meditators. "Our natural bias to confirm our own worldview is very much at work," Britton said.

More broadly, Britton believes that there is undue excitement about just what studies of mindfulness are actually proving. "Public enthusiasm is outpacing scientific evidence," she said. "The public perception of where the research is is way higher than the actual level." Mindfulness is no panacea, she reiterates. And the scientific community has a responsibility not to oversell the benefits of meditation. "People are finding support for what they believe rather than what the data is actually saying," she said. "Ironically, we need a lot of mindfulness to 'see clearly' the science of mindfulness."

Britton is right. It's important not to place too much faith in the power of science to explain the power of mindfulness. Real understanding can come only through practice. Nor should studies be used as marketing tools for emergent worldviews. And still, the volume of research being done on mindfulness and its initial findings is compelling. Moving the discussion of the benefits of mindfulness from the realm of theory into the laboratory was a big and important step in its own right. But science moves slowly, and contemplative neuroscience is at the very early stages of development. It will take many more years, decades even, before a substantial body of research exists. And even then, we may only be scratching the surface.

Two days after my visit to the Yale lab, I had my job interview at the *New York Times*. I was a few minutes early, and Jill Abramson, then the paper's editor, had someone else in her office. When her assistant asked me to wait in a nearby chair, I figured that instead of surfing the Web on my iPhone, I'd do a little *metta*. I began wishing well for myself, then for all the people in the building. Then I did some *metta* for my potential future boss. At this point, something unexpected happened. I stopped thinking of Abramson as the formidable executive editor of the *New York Times,* who in just moments would decide whether or not I was qualified to work at the paper. Instead, she was just another person like me. Abramson, I could see, had all the same motivations, frustrations, joys, and confusions as the rest of us. I was wishing well for all sentient beings when I was called into her office.

The interview went well enough, and I was invited to join the *Times.* But before I left Abramson's office, we began talking about my interest in meditation. It turned out she was getting into yoga and had been reading up on mindfulness, too. As I opened up, I mentioned the experiment at Yale, and how when I needed a stressful experience to think about, this very meeting was what came to mind. Abramson laughed a little and said, "Well, this wasn't so bad, was it?"

It wasn't, and that's the point. Despite all the energy I had spent stressing about my interview, it went fine. How often do we play out this very same routine, worrying about something for no reason at all? How often do we get worked up about something before it happens, only to discover the source of our fears to be a nonevent? Too often, to be sure. But mindfulness can help us break this cycle. In the next chapter we'll see how the practice can be an effective antidote to this most common tormentor: stress.

4

Less Stressed

RIGHT AROUND THE TIME I began hearing about mindfulness at work, and plotting my trip to visit Janice Marturano at General Mills, I got a promotion. This was back when I worked at the *Financial Times;* after I had been covering media for a few years, my editor asked me to become the paper's sole mergers and acquisitions reporter in the United States. It was a big offer, but I was reluctant to accept it at first. I enjoyed covering media and felt as if I was just hitting my stride. There was also the reality that covering M&A is notoriously competitive. Reporters on that beat are expected to be on call 24/7 and often work Sundays, chasing the deals that might break on so-called Merger Mondays. And in the United States, the *FT* was outmatched, competing against large teams of reporters at the *Wall Street Journal* and Bloomberg. Nonetheless, it was a great opportunity to take on a prominent beat, and I accepted the job, even as I expected that the stress would be immense.

I was right. The job, instantly, was overwhelming. For the first three months I had breakfast meetings, lunches, and after-work drinks on top of long days at the office. Anytime a deal broke, or was even rumored, I was expected to match the story or take it forward. It was exhausting, and I noticed my stress levels ratcheting up. Luckily, I knew what to do. Though mindfulness works best as a preventive medicine, it can also prove an effective remedy. And after a few intense weeks of M&A reporting, I sensed it was time to recommit to meditation.

Though I had practiced mindfulness on and off for almost fifteen years, I had gone all that time without ever trying out what is probably the most popular form of meditation training today: Mindfulness Based Stress Reduction. MBSR, more than any other class, curriculum, or teacher in the last thirty years, has helped mindfulness go mainstream. As a reporter, I had to figure out what it was all about. And at a personal level, reducing my stress level sounded pretty good, too. My job was more intense than ever, and I was trying to write a book on the side. With this kind of a schedule, I figured I could use all the mindfulness I could get. So with stresses at work mounting, I signed up for my inaugural training in MBSR. I even managed to convince my wife, Alison (never much of a meditator herself but often the most considerate person in the family), to join as well.

It was a difficult time for us. In addition to our busy work lives, we had just suffered a personal blow: Alison had had a miscarriage, and we were reeling, trying to process a complex flood of emotions. Like Marturano when she went off to the desert and learned from Jon Kabat-Zinn, we were personally and professionally depleted. And yet I knew I needed to renew my practice, and Alison intuited that mindfulness would help her heal. Which is how it came to be that at 8:30 p.m. on a Thursday evening, after a long day at work, while our friends were dining out or going to a show, we were at our first MBSR class, staring at a raisin.

We were at the Open Center, a New Age mecca in the shadow of the Empire State Building. We had entered through the gift shop, an incense-scented store hawking biodynamic brown rice wraps and crystals. We hustled through and made our way upstairs to a large classroom, where we took our seats in a big circle, along with twenty-eight other professionals from across Manhattan.

My butt was planted on an uncomfortable metal folding chair. The room we were in, a large space with double-high ceilings and big windows facing north onto the bustling streets, had seen better days. The mauve carpet was stained, and a fluorescent ceiling light flickered. It wasn't the most soothing environment, but then, mindfulness asks that we be at peace even in uncomfortable situations. From down the hall, squawks from a Native American flute class pierced the air. And while my classmates were all there of their own volition, there was definitely some trepidation in the air. An introduction to mindfulness, it turned out, can be a cause for stress.

Our teacher for the eight-week course was Amy Gross, the former editor of *O* magazine, the print arm of Oprah Winfrey's media empire. A compact woman with smooth features, a bushel of dark hair, and warm eyes, Amy did her best to make the group feel welcome in an admittedly awkward environment. Everyone seemed to know things were going to get intense, but no one knew quite what to expect. But I figured we were in good hands. Because she had worked with Oprah for years, I suspected Amy knew a thing or two about stress at work. And after dispensing with some formalities and doing a round of introductions, she got down to business.

Eager as I was to learn MBSR, it was a challenge to be fully present. I'd just had an intense day at the office, full of rolling deadlines, screaming editors, anxious colleagues, and evasive sources. I was still thinking about the story I'd just filed, which would be posted online any minute. The turmoil from the miscarriage continued to demand my emotional attention. Even though I was sitting down, I could feel the momentum of the day still trying to carry me along, as if I had just stepped onto solid ground after hours on a train. And now, a half-hour into the first class, we were staring at a raisin, which was supposed to be the object of our attention for the next ten minutes or so.

Amy told us to examine the raisin in our palm as if we'd never seen such a thing before, as if it were an alien object that magically appeared from another planet. Consider it anew, she said, with all five senses. We began with sight. What did it resemble? A rock? A piece of bark from a tree? The skin of an elephant? I examined the small pebble of dried fruit, noting the contradictions in its form. It had sharp ridges covering its globular body. Between its creases were flecks of a dried white substance, the sugar from its evaporated juices, clinging to its shriveled flesh.

Next: sound. What noise does a raisin make? None, I figured. Bringing it close to my ear, I squeezed gently. In fact, I could hear a small crackling. Turns out raisins have a voice, after all. It was a delightful little surprise that brought a smile to my face.

Now touch. It was tough yet supple, sticky yet dry. Its nib, once connected to a small stem, was almost sharp, capable of leaving a small scratch on my skin. It weighed almost nothing, yet had a distinct volume between my index finger and thumb.

Smell. These weren't the freshest raisins, and there wasn't much fragrance coming from their small bodies. Nonetheless, when I brought it very close to my nose, nearly shoving it up my nostril, I caught a faint whiff of sweetness. And that little smell was enough to set my mouth salivating.

Finally: taste. I bit off a third of the raisin. Immediately my taste buds lit up, more saliva flooding around my gums. Though small, the little piece released enough flavor to dominate all my other senses.

All the while, Amy asked us to also monitor what thoughts or feelings, likes and dislikes, the raisin elicited. Was I disappointed by its lack of freshness? Annoyed by the stickiness? Left salivating after smelling food? Did I notice the impulse to eat the raisin? Could I be aware of the intention to place it in my mouth before I actually made the motion to do so? Finally, when it was time to swallow the piece I'd chewed, could I feel the muscles in my throat impulsively moving before I followed through with the action?

The purpose of the exercise was twofold. Bringing our full attention to the raisin made it clear how much richer even mundane experiences can be when we are fully present. This is true of everything, from brushing our teeth to walking down the street. Every moment of our lives, there is a lot going on that we fail to notice.

The second intention was subtler. By encouraging us to examine our impulses, emotions, and desires, Amy was, with a few baby steps, helping us cultivate self-awareness. Instead of simply eating the raisin on autopilot, we were putting just a little space between our preconceptions about eating the raisin and the act itself. We were not just noticing the sensations of the experience, but also becoming aware that we were having an experience in the first place.

Though I ate that raisin a long time ago, I still remember each detail of it vividly. That's the power of mindfulness. For those few minutes I was so engrossed in the totality of the raisin, no other thoughts were distracting me from the present moment. As a result, the shriveled grape remains among the most memorable meals of my life. And the lesson from MBSR is simple: we can bring that same clarity, purpose, and self-awareness to all our experiences.

Learning to appreciate the depths of a raisin was just the first step in MBSR. After the raisin, it got much harder. For the next two months, in class and during exercises at home, we practiced a variety of mindfulness techniques. Certain routine activities — riding the elevator, for me — became prompts to pay attention to the sensations in our bodies. Mornings took on new contours as Alison and I practiced breathing meditation and the body scan — feeling the sensations throughout all our extremities and organs — in bed before starting the day. In class, we discussed our experiences throughout the week and practiced further. We built up the duration of our meditation sessions, from five to ten minutes, then to thirty and forty-five minutes.

And in time, as the class went on, Amy introduced concepts including impermanence, self-compassion, and the importance of practicing acceptance. Understanding impermanence, she explained, is a useful way to reduce stress. When we know that whatever is agitating us will not last forever, it is harder to get hung up on unpleasant sensations, be they aches and pains or emotional sorrows. Self-compassion, meanwhile, is a practical tool that cultivates forgiveness for oneself and others. Because stress arises from a mismatch between what we want to be happening and what is actually happening, simply accepting things as they are — and having the wherewithal to let go of any strong emotional reactions — is an extraordinarily useful skill. We can't always change what's happening, but we can change our responses.

At some level, Amy's MBSR instructions were familiar territory to me, reminiscent of the teachings I had heard in Bodh Gaya some fifteen years prior. Now, in Manhattan, it was refreshing to hear these ideas presented anew, free from any of the cultural baggage associated with India. It wasn't quite the same as walking around the Mahabodhi Temple with Munindra, but the MBSR course offered by the Open Center was a comprehensive curriculum, and Amy was a skilled teacher.

Alison and I took the teachings to heart, sitting together in the morning, practicing mindful awareness throughout the day, and doing body scans and loving-kindness meditation together before we went to sleep each night. Most of the other students also seemed to benefit, too. One was an emergency room nurse who worked thirty-hour shifts, making life-and-death decisions about patients without taking care of her own emotional and physical needs. Another worked in a fast-paced financial firm and was always on call. By the end of the session, most in the group professed to being better able to manage their stress.

We went to a total of nine MBSR classes over a two-month period, amounting to about twenty hours of instruction time. At home, our diligence varied from day to day and week to week, but we made time for formal mindfulness practice most days, doing either breath meditation or body scans. Say that amounted to another thirty hours of practice. That's less than an hour a day for about eight weeks of our lives — a good chunk of time, to be sure, especially given the schedules young professionals keep in New York City, but not insurmountable. After all, the average American watches thirty-four hours of television per week. Just imagine if people spent even a fraction of that time practicing mindfulness.

By my lights, MBSR isn't perfect. It's a bit too focused on individual outcomes and doesn't do enough to encourage students to be kind or address issues like their environmental impact on the world. But as an introduction to mindfulness, MBSR shares the qualities of the best consumer products on the market: high quality, deeply reliable, and well worth the investment.

Ten weeks after beginning MBSR, my own practice was renewed, and Alison had a new foundation for her own emerging mindfulness routine. But the most surprising outcome of the course was that Alison and I had a new vocabulary we could use to discuss our experiences and our relationship. Our reactions became less absolute. Little conflicts became easier to defuse. When I was upset about those spousal habits that drive the other person nuts — if she'd left all the kitchen cabinets open, for example — I would watch my reaction flare up, then explain to her that I was noticing some anger around my dashed expectations that cabinets would actually get closed. When I put some distance between me, my reaction, and her actions, the whole situation felt less charged. Alison heard me out and pledged to be more mindful about closing cabinets. I, in turn, was gently called out on my own bad habits, and I pledged to try and replace the garbage bags after I took the trash out. Mundane, perhaps, but these were small victories that made a big difference. If mindfulness can make marriages a bit easier, we all ought to be practicing.

At work, the same thing was happening. Though my deadlines didn't go away, they didn't elicit the same paralytic effect they had

had on me just months earlier. Certain colleagues still bugged me, but I found myself wishing them well and sympathizing with them, instead of trying to strike back in a spat. And though I still took my job seriously, my time at the office had a new lightness to it as I found ways to be mindful even in the midtown newsroom of the *Financial Times*.

Kabat-Zinn wisely decided to make stress the focus of his effort to bring mindfulness to the masses. Stress is something we all experience, a universal form of suffering. "Most people are first drawn to the practice of mindfulness because of stress or pain of one kind or another and their dissatisfaction with elements of their lives that they somehow sense might be set right through the gentle ministrations of direct observation, inquiry and self-compassion," Kabat-Zinn wrote in his book of reflections and teachings, *Coming to Our Senses*. "Stress and pain thus become potentially valuable portals and motivators through which to enter the practice."

Sure enough, just about all of us are stressed for one reason or another. It seems to be an integral part of the human condition. We get stressed about little things — whether we have enough milk in the fridge, whether the cats were fed, or whether our favorite team is going to win. And we get stressed about big things — the well-being of our friends and family, our jobs and finances, wars and the environment. None of this worrying makes us any more effective, of course. Nor does stressing about these things help us find effective solutions to them. It's just the way our minds work.

Work, in particular, seems to keep us up at night. The top three causes of stress are money, work, and the economy, according to the American Psychological Association. Sixty-nine percent of employees report that work is a significant source of stress, 41 percent of people say they typically feel tense or stressed out during the workday, and more than half of employees say stress reduces their productivity. Over the past thirty years, stress levels have increased 18 percent for women and 25 percent for men, according to Carnegie Mellon research.

Stress is also a killer. One hot spring day I attended a conference on the mind-body connection in a posh SoHo loft owned by Arianna Huffington. Huffington is a big booster of mindfulness, capitalizing on its burgeoning popularity with her own unique blend of conferences, books, and online promotion. During a panel discussion on the benefits of mindfulness, the celebrity doctor Mark Hyman explained to Katie Couric just how bad stress is for the body. "If you really knew what was happening to you when you are stressed, you would freak out. It's not pretty," he said to a room full of highly stressed New Yorkers. "A stress response is an automatic, reptilian, lizard-brain, dinosaur response to some stressful thing. Stress is a perception of a real or imagined threat to your body or your ego. So it could be a rhinoceros chasing you, which I had happen in Africa. Or it could be you think your boss is mad at you or your spouse did something that they never did, and it's totally all in your head. You have the same physiological response, which is that cortisol increases, which is your stress hormone. Adrenaline increases, and it shifts a cascade of events in your body that leads to increasing belly fat, it raises the bad cholesterol, it lowers the good cholesterol, increases inflammation, lowers testosterone, increases infertility. For women it makes hair grow on their mustaches and lose hair on their heads. It causes muscle loss, insomnia, palpitations, dizziness . . ."

"Stop!" Couric finally screamed.

But Hyman went on. "The thing about stress is that it's automatic," he said. "It finds you. You don't have to go find it. The problem with relaxation, or mindfulness, is that it's a lot of frickin' work. It's an active process, it's not something that happens to you. Stress finds you. You have to go looking for relaxation."

As Hyman said, our biology doesn't discriminate between the

big things and the little things. In our brains, the same regions fire up no matter if we're worrying about groceries or global warming. In our bodies, the same hormones are released whether we're beating ourselves up about a missed appointment or a lost job. Reacting to a mundane concern can be just as agonizing as worrying about the state of the world. In cases of acute stress, those triggered by a particular event, our heart rates elevate, we sweat, our chests tense up, and our brains race. As one corporate mindfulness trainer said, "We're basically the descendants of nervous monkeys."

Evolutionarily, stress was, at times, a big help. It was the impulse that led us to run from that rhinoceros. That's why even today, when something unpleasant comes up, we have a "fight-or-flight" response. Our adrenal glands release a surge of substances including epinephrine and cortisol, increasing the heart rate, pumping oxygen into the brain, slowing nonessential functions like digestion, activating our energy stores, and heightening our reactivity. In cases of chronic stress, the ongoing activation of the fight-or-flight response can lead to a variety of long-term ailments. Blood sugar levels can rise precipitously, leading to diabetes. Blood pressure rises, too, increasing the risk of heart disease. Constant stress can result in diminished concentration, irritability, and depression. And excess cortisol can depress the immune system and even lead to weight gain. Highly stressed people are at greater risk for a panoply of illnesses, including heart disease, cancer, diabetes, depression and anxiety, fatigue and muscular pain. This all takes a toll on organizations because highly stressed workers are less productive and incur more health care costs than their less-stressed colleagues.

According to the World Health Organization, stress costs American businesses as much as $300 billion per year, much of that in the form of higher health care costs. Writing in a Harvard Business School paper, professors Michael Porter, Elizabeth Teisberg, and Scott Wallace said that U.S. employers often spend two to three

times more for the indirect costs of health care — reduced productivity, sick days, and absenteeism — than they do on actual health
care payments. Their recommendation: that companies "mount an
aggressive approach to wellness, prevention, screening and active
management of chronic conditions."

But for all this talk of stress, we rarely examine its root causes. If
stress results from out-of-control thinking, the solution, it stands to
reason, is learning how to, if not control our thoughts, at least not let
them control us. William James knew as much when he said, "The
greatest weapon against stress is our ability to choose one thought
over another."

That's where mindfulness comes in. Stress isn't something im-
posed on us. It's something we impose on ourselves. As a popular
saying in mindfulness circles goes, "Stress isn't what's happening.
It's your reaction to it." We're either worried about what's about to
happen, or we're ruminating on what just occurred. Acute stress,
the most common form, comes from "demands and pressures of the
recent past and anticipated demands and pressures of the near future," according to the American Psychological Association. That is,
stress emanates from a mismatch between our expectation of how
things should be and the way things are. It is the result of us not
being able to control our own thoughts. It manifests when our mind
hijacks itself, taking us on a rollicking tour of places we don't exactly
want to go. And stress is contagious. When we're stressed, we are
prone to be harsher on ourselves, sharper with our friends and family, and less sensitive to the needs of strangers. By bringing us back
to the present moment, mindfulness can break the cycle of constant
amygdala responses.

Mindfulness frees us from stress by giving us the mental flexibility to choose one experience over another, to direct our attention away from negative experiences and instead focus on neutral
or positive ones. Even more powerful than choosing one thought

over another, as William James suggested, is choosing how we respond to the thoughts and situations that arise. Mindfulness allows us to fully experience negative events and emotions without letting them become all-consuming. This is why mindfulness is such a powerful antidote to stress. By learning to attend to what is happening right now, without thinking about the past or future, we can free ourselves from stress — for a few moments at a time to start, but ultimately for much longer. Indeed, research is already proving as much.

Because MBSR is a highly structured course that has endured for three decades now, it is often used as the framework for clinical studies. As a result, there's a tremendous volume of literature documenting its efficacy. In one of the first evaluations of mindfulness's impact on a corporate setting, a team of scientists including Richard Davidson and Jon Kabat-Zinn administered MBSR to the employees of Promega, a fast-paced biotech company in Madison, Wisconsin. Over the course of eight weeks, Kabat-Zinn himself led forty-eight employees through a full MBSR course. Before the course began, the researchers tested how stressed the employees were, what their brains looked like using EEG technology, and how strong their immune systems were. Then the Promega employees, along with a control group who had applied for the course but didn't get in, went about business as usual.

Before learning MBSR, the participants reported feeling highly stressed. No surprise, given their jobs. But after the course, the meditators reported that they were less stressed, felt less anxiety, and had more energy at work. And indeed, their brains seemed to have changed. EEG recorded the electrical activity in their brains through sensors placed on their scalps, and the researchers observed consistent changes in the neural activity of the mindfulness group. Compared to their colleagues, those who had taken the MBSR course showed greater activation in the left prefrontal cortex, an area associated with, among other things, stronger immune systems.

But to really test whether the immune systems of the mindfulness practitioners had gotten stronger, the researchers came up with a novel approach. They gave both the meditators and the control group flu shots, then measured the antibody levels in their blood. The group that practiced mindfulness had significantly more flu antibodies circulating in their blood. That is, mindfulness appeared to actually make the body stronger, to give it more weapons with which to fight off illness.

Just as important, Promega employees sensed the benefits in their own lives. "I really am an empiricist in every aspect of my life," Michael Slater, a molecular biologist at the company, later recounted. "I doubt dogma, and I test it. I do it at the laboratory bench, but also in my personal life. So this appealed to me, because I could feel the reduction in stress. I could tell I was less irritable. My wife felt I was easier to be around. So there were tangible impacts. For an empiricist, that was enough."

Since that study at Promega, the results have continued to pile up. In a meta-analysis of studies examining the effect of mindfulness on stress and other ailments, a team of German professors found that the practice helped treat a wide range of conditions including depression, anxiety, eating disorders, and pain. A UC Davis study put a spotlight on the stress hormones, showing that mindfulness reduced cortisol levels in a study of intensive meditators. Another study from the University of Exeter found that mindfulness increased happiness and easefulness among secondary school students. In the survey of 522 students from the UK, ages twelve to sixteen, those who went through a nine-week introductory mindfulness course reported fewer symptoms of depression and stress compared to those who didn't learn mindfulness. It works for teachers, too. In a study of educators in the Madison, Wisconsin, area, those who practiced were less stressed and had fewer symptoms of burnout than those who didn't.

Mindfulness has also been shown to reduce stress even in the most trying circumstances. In 2007 a group of employees from the University of Texas Medical Branch in Galveston began an MBSR course as part of a research project by staff from the pediatric and psychiatry departments. When the study was done, there were predictable variations between the mindfulness students and a control group. Those with MBSR training came out on the other end of two months reporting less perceived stress than they had before, and less than the control group. Then Hurricane Ike hit. A Category 4 hurricane with sustained winds of 145 miles per hour, Ike turned out to be the third-costliest tropical cyclone in history. On the morning of September 13, 2008, it leveled Galveston. The storm surge crested a seventeen-foot-high seawall and destroyed some neighborhoods. When the clouds cleared, 3,500 families were homeless. The UT Medical Branch became a community center of sorts, drawing everyone in the community into the recovery effort. And yet when the researchers came back a year after the MBSR classes were delivered, the results had held. Despite enduring such devastation, the meditators were still less stressed than peers who hadn't practiced mindfulness. A year later, changes wrought by mindfulness practice had withstood even a Category 4 hurricane.

Other research continues to prove how our immune systems benefit from mindfulness. In another study of how mindfulness can improve health, UCLA researchers worked with HIV-positive adults in the Los Angeles area. Over the course of an eight-week MBSR training, just like the one given to the Promega employees and the one I took in New York, the Los Angeles group did not change their HIV treatment in any way except for meditation. And yet something dramatic happened. The CD4+ T cells, which are the so-called brains of the immune system, and the ones targeted by HIV, stopped deteriorating in the group that practiced mindfulness. Meanwhile, a control group exhibited steady declines in their CD4+ T cells, the classic sign of the disease's progression. A person's dedication to the practice seemed to matter as well. Those who attended more classes had higher CD4 counts than those who missed sessions.

And in one of the most famous studies conducted by Kabat-Zinn and his colleagues, a large group of patients with psoriasis, the skin disease, were given a conventional treatment that involves spending time in an ultraviolet light box. While receiving the treatment, half the group listened to mindfulness trainings, and the other half did not. In results that seem almost too good to be true, the group that listened to mindfulness instruction saw their psoriasis heal three times faster than the group that underwent light box treatment without mindfulness. The only difference was the quality of their awareness.

This simple truth — that the quality of our attentiveness can change the way our bodies and minds work — means that old habits can be uprooted if we're more mindful. And it means that we have the power to change behavioral patterns that might seem deeply ingrained, becoming more resilient along the way.

Take the case of Cesar Quebral, who manages technology infrastructure for financial groups. It's a demanding job for Quebral, as he's responsible for keeping servers up and running, 24/7. He began practicing mindfulness after learning about it from Jeremy Hunter, who incorporates it into his classes at Claremont Graduate University in Southern California. Quebral's practice developed over time and eventually proved useful in the workplace. In a recent job, Quebral's boss wasn't necessarily a mean man, but he wasn't the most empathetic one either. Often when Quebral came into his boss's office to talk about an important issue, the boss would continue looking at his phone, or working on his computer, as Quebral made his points. Quebral could feel himself tensing up whenever this happened. His chest tightened, his blood pressure rose — he was having a stress reaction just from being ignored. His amygdala was flaring up, and a cascade of negative emotions flowed through his body.

Previously, Quebral would simply go back to his desk and let the resentment simmer. He loathed his boss for being so insensitive, and he silently berated himself for not doing anything about it. But after practicing mindfulness for several months, he developed the confidence to address the root cause of his unhappiness. Through meditation, he had grown to understand that the dynamic with his boss was causing him a tremendous amount of stress. He also realized he could change it.

Quebral started by working on his own reaction to being ignored. When his boss ignored or interrupted him, he just noticed the experience, then noticed his brewing unhappiness, then returned to his breath. It wasn't always easy, but in time, he was able to let it go, little by little. His amygdala response was no longer so intense. He had some room to maneuver, the space to communicate clearly without being overwhelmed by his anger. Finally, he confronted his boss in a reasoned, calm manner. He told him that he felt disrespected when he was ignored, that he didn't feel he was being listened to, and he asked for his boss's full attention.

His boss was caught off-guard. Quebral was prepared for him to react with anger. But instead, his boss truly heard him for the first time. It was a turning point, Quebral said. "As soon as that happened, the walls were down," he said. His boss apologized and didn't treat him with the same disrespect as he had before. Quebral is under no illusion that his boss has changed for good. "You're also dealing with someone who has their habits," he said. "But at least there's that mutual understanding that things he does bother me and we're able to work with it."

Applying this same equanimity throughout the workday has also allowed Quebral to be more effective in meetings. He is clearer and more focused on finding solutions that are in the interest of the entire team, not just himself. "Prior to this I always thought that decisions revolved around me," he said. "I thought outcomes that were best for me were most important. But now I see that what's best for the team, and what's best for my boss, will move us all forward."

Quebral has even brought his mindful communication practice home with him. Though he's happily married, he acknowledges there are times when his wife says something that hurts his feelings. "It's rare, but sometimes she does it," he said. He used to let it slide, but he stewed on it privately, just sweeping the painful comment under the rug and moving on, suppressing his own feelings about the incident, even as his internal alarm bells were ringing, his amygdala going off. But recently, as Quebral was washing the dishes, she tossed a barb his way and it stung. Instead of ignoring it, he turned the faucet off and, with the same equanimity he used to address his boss, told her she had hurt his feelings. His wife was receptive, and the two had a warm, sincere conversation about the issue. "I always thought that if I said something it could escalate," he said. "Through mindfulness, and being calm and not overreacting, it allows me to frame it constructively, and have a different mindset."

Moments of anger are ripe opportunities for practice. Had Quebral simply lashed out at his boss, relations would have undoubtedly deteriorated. But by bringing a compassionate tone to a confrontation — or even practicing loving-kindness meditation in the heat of anger — we can transform a moment of conflict into one of practice, challenging ourselves to see our own reactions at the same time we look for the good aspects in whomever we're mad at. "There's that onerous practice of looking for the good in someone," meditation teacher Sharon Salzberg told me. "Or just reminding yourself that indeed, that really sucked, and indeed, that's not the entirety of the reality. The truth of a person is usually more complex. Just like the truth of ourselves is more complex."

Stress reduction isn't just an individual pursuit. In some offices, it is part of the corporate culture. And at Green Mountain Coffee, based in Waterbury, Vermont, mindfulness has become a part of the fabric of the company.

What began with Green Mountain's founder offering meditation classes to some of his top executives has evolved into a company-wide stress reduction program. Today, one of the overseers of the program is Laura Fried, who joined Green Mountain in 2008 as a sales development manager, training the company's growing army of marketers. She had taken a few years off to raise her children and was struck by the frenetic pace at the company she returned to as it went through a growth spurt. "The multitasking and concentration were overwhelming," she told me. Fried's father was a physicist, and she still remembers when he taught her about the big bang when she was five years old. That moment laid the foundation for a life-time of inquiry, which was finally engaged when she began practic-ing mindfulness with Green Mountain's in-house instructor.

Over time, she grew to be particularly adept in mindfulness, and its instruction, and Fried now teaches meditation to her colleagues at Green Mountain. "We're focused on building concentration, mak-ing it easier for things to arise and pass," said Fried. Her students are taking a closer look at their thoughts and sensations, how they ap-pear then fall away. Noticing that once-intense experiences disap-pear as easily as they arise leads to ruminations on impermanence, and an understanding that even our most extreme experiences are fleeting. It's not always easy. Training the restless mind is one of the hardest things we can do, and progress doesn't always come quickly.

"I don't want to see folks who are just doing poorly and think that mindfulness is going to work miracles," said Fried. "Some people get upset when the first thing we teach them doesn't work. They say, 'This was supposed to help, and I don't feel good.' But it's hard work."

At Green Mountain, mindfulness training started with the top executives and soon spread to midlevel employees. But Fried and her colleagues realized that much of the workforce was still not being served. The frontline workers who put in twelve-hour shifts roasting coffee beans, packing boxes, and shipping them off to supermarkets around the country also needed a bit of on-the-job stress relief. In fact, they were perhaps the ones who needed it most.

So the company turned to Prudence Sullivan, Green Mountain's director of continuous learning and organizational effectiveness, looking to scale the program. Sullivan had been involved with the company's mindfulness training from the start. Now, in a bid to reduce injuries, and perhaps increase mental well-being as well, she made it mandatory that all frontline workers do a series of mindful stretching exercises before beginning their shifts.

It is early morning in Waterbury, and at a massive complex of buildings, dozens of line workers are preparing to start their shifts. American flags hang on the wall, and a banner strung from the ceiling reads USE YOUR BEAN. For the next twelve hours their sweat and effort will help Green Mountain continue to churn out packaged coffee. Some of the workers will operate the heavy machinery that roasts coffee beans by the ton; some will pack and ship the boxes that deliver that coffee to restaurants, gas stations, and grocery stores. Yet before any of them begin, they have assembled in a co-ed preparation room lined with bright red lockers, where together they will do yoga. Led by one of their colleagues, the workers do a series of stretches, including gentle lunges, lifting a leg and rotating their ankles, and rolling their necks. All the while, a colleague is coaching them as if it were Lamaze. "Breathe in . . . breathe out."

The stretches are designed to hit all the areas in the body where people hold tension.

This is a scene repeated around the country, at all of Green Mountain's roasting, packaging, and distribution facilities, recalling the calisthenics for laborers that are popular in Japan. And it's had an impact — workplace injuries are down across the company. Some of that change is likely attributable to more limber muscles, which can better handle the strains of factory work. But some of it, workers and Green Mountain managers say, also is attributable to the fact that the Mindful Stretching program has made workers more attuned to their surroundings, more aware of their own behavior, and therefore more disciplined in the execution of their tasks on the factory floor. "When I first started stretching, I actually didn't enjoy it at all," said an employee named Eric, who operates one of the K-cup machines. That's not so surprising; at first glance Eric is not the type you'd expect to start the day with yoga — a Boston Red Sox cap is pulled down low above leery, no-nonsense eyes, and he sports a goatee around a set of small lips. Yet asked about the Mindful Stretching program, he opens up. "As you do your job throughout the day, you realize how important it is. It keeps you limber and more flexible. I was hurting a lot less after the end of the day. You realize how important it really is to do. That's when I started focusing on the stretches more appropriately."

Tom, another K-cup machine operator, had a similar story. "I feel less tense at the end of a workweek; my feet don't hurt as bad," he said, standing in the locker room after a stretching session, wearing a camouflage bandanna and a hooded sweatshirt. "Lifting things is easier. I don't ever get knots in my back when I move in funny ways."

Mark Plamner, Green Mountain's safety and health specialist, said a few key features distinguish the program. "The relaxation is an important form of mindfulness," he said. "It helps us maintain positivity, positive thoughts throughout the workday. It helps us stay centered and see the things we need to see to be productive and to work safely. The mindfulness is beginning to be part of the routine now. You're going home feeling a little less pressure, hopefully a little less stressed out, your muscles a little less impacted from the day's work, and we are seeing our accident rate go down because people are more flexible."

Green Mountain offers Mindful Stretching in every factory the company owns, and more than five thousand employees are mindful stretchers. It took buy-in from the founder and CEO, the head of human resources, and most critically the workers themselves, but today Green Mountain has become one of the biggest advocates of mindfulness in the workplace. In doing so, the company found ways that mindfulness could help employees at every level. Executives became better communicators, midlevel employees became more focused, and critically, thousands of manual laborers became less stressed. And while it may be hard to draw a direct line from the mindfulness program to the bottom line, Green Mountain is thriving. Though meditation is no guarantee of a rising stock price, Green Mountain's market capitalization increased fifteen-fold in the five years after it introduced mindfulness, before coming back down a bit. And managers like Laura Fried view the company in a new light. "Look at this as a whole spectrum of offerings," she said. "Basic services that we provide to people who are dealing with their morning commute, and people like me who are facing existential issues . . . We are providing them with opportunities to enhance their own experiences at work and at home."

A particularly nefarious kind of stress is known as burnout. A potent mix of feeling exhausted, overwhelmed, and spread too thin, burnout often afflicts workers in high-intensity roles, such as first responders and doctors. Yet mindfulness seems to be an effective remedy here, too. Michael Krasner, a professor of clinical medicine at the University of Rochester, has put himself on the frontlines of such efforts. "Mindfulness allows us to be in a whole host of situations with a sense of equanimity," he said. "We don't get sucked into how charged an experience is but are simply having that experience."

In one study led by Krasner, seventy physicians from Rochester began practicing mindfulness in an experiment designed to ease burnout. Like so many other doctors, they were running on autopilot for most of the day, hurtling from one crisis to the next without ever truly being present with their patients or themselves. "They barely recognized certain experiences as either powerful or challenging before they moved to the next experience," Krasner said. They "kept their nose to the grindstone." They almost never reflected on the life-and-death work that they did each day. "It becomes easy to look at our patients as objects," Krasner said, "rather than appreciating the meaning and joy of an experience, even if that experience is difficult. But lack of meaning goes hand-in-hand with ineffectiveness and a lack of well-being as a physician."

One day a week over the course of two months, the doctors took a few hours out of their busy days and learned to meditate, practiced mindful conversation, and participated in writing exercises designed to cultivate self-awareness. After just eight weeks, the physicians reported feeling less burned out, less emotionally drained. They also reported feeling more empathetic and more sensitive to patients' mental states—both attributes that are correlated with better patient care. "Patients know when their doctors are or are not present," Krasner said. "As a practitioner, I know when I'm really there for my patients and when other things are pulling me away and I'm not."

The training not only allows doctors to be more present with those in their care, it also improves their technical skills. "If something goes wrong and you fail to notice," said Krasner, "you end up going down one path in your care. But if you fully accept these challenges — not resign yourself to them but fully accept them — you can see more clearly and proceed down a path where you have a better chance of success."

In a related study of employees at a bank in Johannesburg, researchers from several South African universities found an inverse correlation between trait mindfulness and job burnout. The more mindful the employees were, the less likely they were to feel overwhelmed, used up, and spit out by their jobs. "Mindfulness can be a source of employer value proposition and may in the long run provide organizations with a valuable tool to manage high burnout levels of employees within the workplace," the researchers wrote.

And just as mindfulness is ameliorating burnout, it's also relieving depression. Mindfulness Based Cognitive Therapy, an offshoot of MBSR, has emerged as an effective alternative to pharmacological treatments of anxiety and depression. Developed by a group including a British psychologist named John Teasdale, MBCT marries elements of a standard MBSR course with cognitive behavioral therapy, an approach that seeks to address specific problems in a patient to relieve depression. By pairing the two approaches, MBCT has become an effective technique to get people out of their own heads. Studies have demonstrated that the technique is more effective than antidepressant medications in preventing relapses in depressives. In one led by Teasdale that examined 145 people with chronic depression, a sixty-day mindfulness program significantly decreased the chances of relapse. Yet even before MBCT caught on, therapists with their own mindfulness practices were incorporating mindfulness techniques into their sessions with clients and using them as a tool to deal with their own on-the-job issues. Mindfulness, therapists report, complements traditional analytic methods in several important ways. Because mindfulness makes patients less reactive, mental health professionals have been able, in some cases, to break the cycle of dwelling on negative emotions. Little setbacks don't turn into paralyzing catastrophes. Patients see that depressing thoughts are just that: thoughts. And they pass.

"Depression is often kept going, from one moment to the next, by streams of negative thoughts going through the mind, such as 'My life is a mess,' 'What's wrong with me?' 'I don't think I can go on,'" said Teasdale. "Redirecting attention away from these ruminative thought streams by becoming really aware of what we're doing while we're doing it can 'starve' the thought streams of the attention they need to keep going. That way, we 'pull the plug' on what is keeping us depressed, and our mood can begin to improve."

Mindfulness is a powerful way to weaken the vise grip of those negative thoughts, "particularly if we bring awareness to the sensations and feelings in our bodies," Teasdale continued. "By doing this over and over again, we end up living more in the actuality of the present moment and less 'in our heads,' going over and over things that happened in the past, or worrying about the future."

At work and at home, stress comes in all shapes and sizes. There is the nagging anxiety over a job poorly done, the heavy burden of ambitions unfulfilled, and the simmering concern that others will let you down. Some jobs — like my own — are calm at times but punctuated by moments of stress, such as when a story is breaking. Other jobs may lack drama but induce a constant, low-grade stress reaction. And in some jobs, there are constant, intense, life-and-death stressors. In such professions — medicine, the military, psychoanalysis, to name a few — being able to manage stress is an essential skill. Who wants to be treated by a frazzled doctor? Or defended by an emotionally depleted soldier? Yet as is all too often the case in professions of all stripes, stress management is rarely — if ever — taught to people who fill these essential roles. Doctors learn how to operate on a dying patient. But when do they learn to take care of their own minds? Soldiers can hit a target a hundred yards away. But can they zero in on their own emotional states and prevent blowups before they arise? Though mindfulness training is not mandatory for doctors, soldiers, and therapists, it has, over the past couple of decades, proven to be an effective tool in combating some of the most intense work-related stressors there are. By grounding us in the present moment instead of letting our minds wander to the past or future, and by encouraging us to accept things as they are, instead of wishing for them to be otherwise, mindfulness can make us more resilient, capable of skillfully managing previously torturous situations. It can reduce our stress, improve our health, and ameliorate depression.

Ratcheting down stress is an important first step in developing a more mindful relationship to work and life, and one that nearly everyone who begins to practice enjoys. It allows us to manage our emotions more effectively, to take better care of ourselves and others, and to be healthier and happier. It's also an essential hurdle to clear if we want to experience some of the other benefits mindfulness has to offer — focus, a renewed sense of meaning, and enhanced leadership skills.

5

More Focused

IT WASN'T LONG AFTER beginning MBSR that I began to reap the dividends of my renewed mindfulness practice. As my meditation routine grew more stable, with a session of sitting in the morning followed by a body scan in the evening, coupled with a commitment to bringing some self-awareness to my reactions, my already laid-back demeanor grew positively chill. But I knew that reining in my perennial, low-grade attention deficit disorder would be the real test.

In my job, I'm always expected to be on call. If a story breaks before dawn, the *Times* is on it. If another breaks just before my head hits the pillow, the *Times* is on it. I'm almost never offline. I wake up early to check my e-mail in bed, my eyes half open. If there are no urgent queries from the editors, I might roll over and get a few more winks. Before long I'm up, confronting dozens of messages that have filled my four inboxes overnight. As I make an espresso at home, I check Twitter, Facebook, and the websites of four or five news organizations — the *New York Times,* the *FT,* the *Wall Street Journal,* Bloomberg, and Reuters. Then it's on to the blogs — Quartz, Dealbreaker, Business Insider, and more — scanned as I gobble down a bowl of cereal with fruit, not always eating so mindfully. Deals are often announced in the morning, so as I commute across midtown Manhattan from our apartment to my office, I check my iPhone every couple of minutes along the way, making sure I haven't missed any breaking news. If an e-mail comes in, I'll respond as I walk, firing off edits, story suggestions, and questions as I plow toward my desk. This can make my pedestrian commutes rather hazardous. I've barreled into children, nearly been run over by bicycle deliverymen, and wandered into traffic more than once. Having reached my desk, I turn on twin computer monitors that nearly fill my entire field of vision. Both are dominated by full-screen Web browsers, each sporting at least a dozen tabs. My e-mail accounts are always open. TweetDeck emits an endless stream of quips. Websites constantly refresh. If the day is particularly busy, I'll break out my laptop or iPad as well, propping it atop a pile of newspapers on my desk. Like so many other contemporary professionals, I spend a lot of time in front of screens. While I may be overly reliant on technology as I go about my day job, I do try to be more judicious about managing my attention outside office hours. And one long weekend when I was still with the *FT*, I had an opportunity to use mindfulness to this effect.

On a Friday morning not long after I began the MBSR course, I got a tip that two large pharmaceutical companies were in talks about a deal, but the details were sketchy. All day I chased that lead, calling sources around the world in hopes that I might be able to land a scoop. By the afternoon, I heard that a competing news organization was chasing the same story. But I still didn't have it confirmed. Eventually I had to leave the office to start a three-hour drive to Pennsylvania, where my wife and I were visiting family for the Easter weekend. As we drove out of Manhattan and down the New Jersey Turnpike, I took a few more calls through my Bluetooth. My colleagues in London had made some progress, and we were close. But the details were still too flaky for us to publish the story. Then, just as we pulled into the driveway, an e-mail came in. The competition had published a story saying the two companies were in advanced merger talks, and a deal was to be announced on Monday.

I felt as if I had been punched in the stomach. For a reporter, there's almost nothing worse than getting scooped, especially when you know you almost had it. I beat myself up for not going with what we had. I wondered how we could have landed the scoop for the *FT,* but I also wasn't quite sure the other newspaper had it right. The details were also spotty in its story, and we had been steered away from this being a done deal.

After my wife and I said our hellos and exchanged hugs with family, I made another round of calls and sent another batch of e-mails chasing the story. It was getting late on a Friday night of a holiday weekend, and my sources, understandably, were moving on with their evenings. So after a few minutes of calls and e-mails, I decided to focus on my family. I had done everything I could up to that point. Worrying about the deal wasn't going to get me anywhere as I sat down for dinner. In fact, all it could do was keep me distant and distracted from the people I love most in this world. I turned my attention fully to my family and didn't think about the deal again for hours.

This was a small moment of mindfulness in action. I made a conscious choice to stop dwelling on the deal, to refrain from mulling over whom else I could have called, what my editors might be thinking about my reporting skills, and what the competition would be writing next. Instead, I focused on being aware of and attentive to the people around me. After a few hours, I checked to see if any new e-mails had come in. But that took all of a minute, and then I returned to the present moment, to enjoy a wonderful meal and conversation.

It wasn't always the case that I could direct my attention with this kind of discipline. Before I began practicing mindfulness, I would cling to negative events, mulling over my failings and what I could have done differently, wasting hours and getting nowhere. If I haven't been practicing mindfulness regularly, or am in a particularly agitated state, it's still easy to get lost in negative thoughts that lead nowhere. If my practice hadn't been strong, dinner would have been ruined. But on this weekend, thanks in part to the fact that I was in the middle of my MBSR course and had been practicing regularly, I was able to diligently focus my attention on my work as was appropriate and otherwise relax into the present moment.

The next morning I woke up with the deal on my mind. But after checking my e-mail and seeing no updates, I put my phone down and went on to enjoy breakfast with my family. I knew that information would come in when it came in, and that we'd write the most accurate story we could as soon as we were ready. Then, early on Saturday afternoon, an important source that I couldn't reach on Friday rang me back. I decided to take his call. It was a calculated choice — slipping out of a lovely conversation with my family to pick up the phone. It was the right move. He had seen the competitor's story, of course, but he had good information for me: that story was wrong. He explained that the two companies had been in talks, but that the talks had fallen apart the previous Wednesday. "It's been pencils-down for days," he said. The deal was dead, and I was delighted. I called yet another source, whom I hadn't reached the previous day, and he confirmed that the deal had been dead even before our competitor ran its story. Soon we published our story, explaining that the deal had gotten close but had fallen apart. It was the last word on the subject.

It wasn't the most dramatic professional feat, just another mergers and acquisitions story coming together over a weekend. But had I let it, that deal could have ruined my weekend. I could have worried through the night about getting scooped, woken up in a foul mood, spent the morning rereading the competition's piece, and altogether missed an opportunity to be present with the people I love. Instead, the story was simply a task I had to attend to — intermittently — over the course of a few days. I was still taking my job seriously. I worked the phones as hard as I could and chased every lead

I had. The difference was that when I was working, I was working, and when I wasn't, I wasn't. I was focused.

While distraction can seem like the norm today, we shouldn't simply accept that it's OK to do our jobs inattentively. Without sustained attention, it's unlikely that we're being effective at work. We owe it to ourselves, and our employers, to fully attend to the task at hand. If we're thinking about what we're going to cook for dinner or remembering what we did last night—let alone playing solitaire or idly surfing the Web—we are robbing ourselves of potentially rich moments pursuing our craft, and our employers of valuable hours they are paying for. "A person should be able to carry out his or her job without interruption, and meditation supports this approach," wrote Chögyam Trungpa, a Tibetan teacher and the founder of Naropa University. Trungpa advocates a holistic approach to mindfulness, encouraging us to treat every experience, however mundane, as an exercise in awareness. "With this approach, if you are making a cup of tea, you are in complete contact with the process: with what kind of tea you are going to brew and what kind of kettle and teapot you are going to use. It is a matter of relating with those little things, which is not a big deal particularly."

But it's not just about being focused while doing our jobs. We should be fully present no matter what the activity. When we're at work, we should work, not get lost in daydreams about our personal lives. And if we are spending time with our children, we should spend time with our children, not think about work. It's not about excluding certain activities, or eliminating the use of technology altogether. It's about doing whatever it is we're doing *fully*, one thing at a time. It just happens that by doing so, we can become more efficient workers.

At General Mills, the employees who took Janice Marturano's Mindful Leadership course reported dramatic spikes in their ability to "focus on a project from beginning to end," to be "fully attentive in meetings, conference calls, and presentations," and "to notice when my attention has been pulled away and redirect it to the present." At Green Mountain Coffee, learning how to meditate has helped keep employees on task. Ryan Dremiller, a graphic artist who works for the company in Vermont, said practicing mindfulness has given him a leg up as he spends hours staring at his screen, trying to perfect the company's graphic identity. All those hours spent focusing on his own breathing, returning attention to the rising and falling of the breath, have allowed him to zero in on the task at hand as he sits in his cubicle. "The concentration piece has been the biggest boost," he said. "Doing design work, it's critical to be able to be absorbed in a task. It also allows me to be more intuitive as well, and to discover things in the process I might not otherwise have. On a subtle level, doing practice improves your baseline happiness. Having positivity brought to the workplace is important. I'm a better person to work with and deal with than I was eight years ago." So important was Dremiller's renewed ability to focus, he said mindfulness training was among the best things Green Mountain has going for it. "The meditation is the biggest benefit this company offers," he said. "Even if only one or two students show up, you can effect some serious change. Even in a company of six thousand people, if ten people are doing it, that's a huge thing. They can go bring it to other people and maybe effect some change in the world."

Meditation practice strengthens our mental muscles, giving us the ability to sustain our focus and deepen our concentration. In mindfulness meditation, we bring our attention back to a particular object — like the breath — time and time again. When the mind wanders and we begin thinking about what we're going to do after this tiresome meditation session, we bring our attention back to the breath. When we catch ourselves daydreaming about a particularly nice meal we just had, we bring our attention back to the breath. In time, the attention grows more stable and the mind wanders less frequently. We are able to stay with the sensation of the breath for minutes, and sometimes even hours, simply experiencing the gentle inhalations and exhalations that sway the body. And through these countless moments, one breath at a time, we are strengthening our concentrative muscles. Though incredibly simple, this basic practice is one of the most powerful tools to rewire our minds and make them more stable. And indeed, our monkey minds can be tamed. Though there are many ways to achieve this, mindfulness meditation is among the most effective.

In one study, researchers at Liverpool John Moores University, in the UK, compared how meditators and non-meditators performed on various attention tests. All twenty-five meditators in the study had practiced mindfulness for some time and came from various professions. The twenty-five non-meditators, mostly recruited from a local credit management company, included telephone operators, team leaders, IT technicians, financial workers, account managers, marketers, and senior executives. To assess each group's attentional powers, the Liverpool researchers employed what is known as the Stroop Test. Named after John Ridley Stroop, an American psychologist who worked in the 1930s, the Stroop Test uses a wry trick of cognitive dissonance to evaluate how quickly and accurately someone can focus on the task at hand. In the test, subjects are presented with a list of various colors: BLUE, ORANGE, PURPLE, BROWN, and so on. But in each case, the color of the ink for each word is different from the color the word describes. The word BLUE might be printed in pink ink. The word BROWN might be printed in green ink. In the popular variation on the test used in Liverpool, the subjects' task was to name the color of the ink, not the word itself.

The meditators and non-meditators got the same test and were given two minutes to identify the color, as opposed to the word, in as many of the 120 mismatched word-color combinations as they could. The meditators completed the test in a room at their local meditation center, while the non-meditators took the test in a quiet room at their office. And while most all of the conditions were the same — the groups even got the same amount of sleep the night before taking the test — the results were unequivocal. "Meditators performed significantly better than non-meditators on all measures of attention," the researchers wrote. Not only did the meditators answer more questions during each two-minute test, but they also committed significantly fewer errors. "High levels of mindfulness are correlated with high processing speed, good attentional and inhibitory control, and a good coordination of speed with concurrent accurate performance," the authors wrote. The researchers concluded that "cognitive processes that became automatised can be brought back under cognitive control and previously automatic responses can be interrupted or inhibited." In other words, mindfulness training can undo our conditioning, reforming the bad habits of incessant mind wandering and instead cultivating sustained focus. "These results support the hypothesis that mindfulness would correlate positively with task performance," they wrote.

In another study, this one involving a group of human resources professionals in San Francisco and Seattle, a group of researchers from the University of Washington wanted to see how practicing mindfulness might change the ability of office workers to stay on task. Thirty-eight participants were separated into three groups — one control group, one that learned relaxation techniques, and a third that learned mindfulness. The mindfulness training was based on the work of Darlene Cohen, a Zen priest who died in 2011; instead of emphasizing the importance of acceptance, she placed primacy on the practice of focused attention. Students were trained in how to narrow or widen the focus of their attention, and how to relax in awareness of the present moment. They learned how to voluntarily shift one-pointed focus from one thing to another, and how to cultivate intense focus on their breath, body, and other objects.

After eight weeks of training, the UW researchers wanted to see if anything had changed with their HR workers. So they designed a test that would measure just how well they could multitask. Researchers rigged up a one-person office with a laptop computer and a telephone, then installed sophisticated monitoring technology that allowed them to observe and record the subjects, as well as track the content on their computer screens, their keystrokes, and the movements of their mouse. The participants were asked to imagine that it was their first day at a new company and that they had to complete a series of tasks, including scheduling a meeting by coordinating when a group of people were all available, finding a free conference room once they had a meeting time, writing a draft announcement of the meeting, eating and drinking throughout the day, and writing a memo that proposed a creative agenda item for the meeting. The information they needed to complete all this came at them rapid fire in a series of e-mails, instant messages, phone calls, and knocks on the door. As if all that weren't enough, they had to complete everything in twenty minutes and were occasionally interrupted by unrelated calls. In other words, it was a lot like real life. When you realize these are the conditions in which most of us work, it's amazing we get anything done at all.

So how did the meditators fare at multitasking versus their peers who simply learned to relax? On the face of it, perhaps not so much better. The mindfulness group didn't perform their entire set of tasks any faster than the control groups. But when the researchers looked at *how* the workers spent their time, significant variations emerged. Over the course of the twenty-minute experiment, HR professionals who hadn't done mindfulness training did an average of fifty-four activities per session. That is, they jumped between reading a document, answering the phone, and sending an e-mail about every twenty seconds. The group that had learned mindfulness, when tested, did an average of forty activities per session. After just eight weeks of focused attention training, they were 20 percent more concentrated on the tasks at hand, 20 percent less likely to bounce around from one thing to the next. They kept their attention focused on a task for more than half a minute, as opposed to less than half a minute for the participants without mindfulness training. "Meditation therefore seems to *reduce* task-switching," the researchers wrote. "Meditation seems to *increase* time spent per activity." The mindful workers were more focused.

Being fully present is important in any job. But it's essential in the world of sports, a profession that has for decades served as an unlikely laboratory for a string of experiments in mindfulness.

Phil Jackson, the most successful professional basketball coach ever and a longtime Zen practitioner, has used mindfulness to get the most out of his players for twenty years in the NBA. In his memoir, *Eleven Rings,* Jackson described how he used meditation to help coach the Chicago Bulls and Los Angeles Lakers to a combined eleven NBA championships. Jackson turned to mindfulness because it is what he described as "an easily accessible technique for quieting the restless mind and focusing the mind on whatever is happening in the present moment." For basketball players, "who often have to make split-second decisions under enormous pressure," it's a powerful tool.

Jackson used a variety of techniques to train the likes of Michael Jordan, Scottie Pippen, Kobe Bryant, and Shaquille O'Neal in mindfulness. To begin with, he taught them basic breath meditation, body awareness, and exercises that promote awareness of thoughts and emotions. But Jackson also used less conventional teaching methods. In one drill he would lead the team in breathing exercises, getting all the players to synchronize their respiratory rhythm. "It helped align them on a nonverbal level far more effectively than words," Jackson wrote. "One breath equals one mind." At other times, he used techniques that got his teams out of their comfort zones. He made the Bulls practice in silence one day. Another day, he made them scrimmage with the lights out in a darkened arena. These exercises might not seem like mindfulness at first glance. But they are in fact the same kinds of techniques, ones that force us to stop relying on habits and instead bring us back into the present moment. "I like to shake things up and keep the players guessing," he wrote. "Not because I want to make their lives miserable but because I want to prepare them for the inevitable chaos that occurs the minute they step onto a basketball court." The same principle can be a valuable lesson for workers no matter what their profession. Challenging situations may seem like unfair setbacks when they're happening. But inasmuch as these occasions open up our senses and get us to drop our expectations, they are good opportunities to practice mindful awareness.

As Jackson brought meditation into the locker room, he helped some elite players develop greater self-awareness. Michael Jordan, already a fierce competitor, took to the practice with particular zeal. Beyond simply honing his on-the-court focus, Jordan also attained some measure of insight through mindfulness. He developed a greater awareness of his role as a leader and his effect on group dynamics, and he grew eager to connect with his teammates. Though the greatest basketball player of all time understandably had an ego on the court, he softened a bit off the court, at least among his fellow Bulls. Practicing mindfulness got him to become more attentive to the feelings of his teammates, at least nominally, allowing the team to jell. After he came back from his year and a half playing minor-league baseball, Jordan didn't know many of his new teammates and felt alienated from the group. But with mindfulness, he made the extra effort to listen to what his new teammates were saying, take stock of his own strengths and weaknesses at that point in time, and ultimately reconnect with his team. He eventually led them to another three rings. Jordan wasn't always a model citizen, of course. But thanks to the mindfulness training Phil Jackson brought to the locker room, he was able to be a better teammate, and a more successful player.

When Jackson arrived in Los Angeles to coach the Lakers, he was struck by their short attention spans. Unlike the Bulls, who were preternaturally calm and composed, the Lakers team he took over was fidgety and distractible. So he began again, introducing mindfulness, starting with just one minute of meditation before practice. He built the duration up over time, eventually getting the Lakers to calm down, open up their senses, and play intuitively, as a team. With Jackson at the helm, that Lakers team would go on to win five championships.

Jackson cites mindfulness training as a critical component of his extraordinary success, and he wasn't alone in bringing mindfulness to the world of sports. A testosterone-fueled, capitalistic spectacle that often rewards violence, the sports world depicted on ESPN isn't always the most serene environment. Yet there's good reason athletes have an affinity for mindfulness. When playing any sport at its highest level, competitors must become deeply attuned to the sensory worlds around them. They must slip out of a conceptual mode and into an experiential one.

Many other coaches have been espousing the virtues of mindfulness for years now. By talking about being in the present moment, focusing on processes rather than goals, Hall of Fame coaches including Dean Smith and Mike Krzyzewski have been teaching players to be mindful — if only by a different name. Bob Rotella, a sports psychologist who works with golfers, talks about the importance of "letting go of memories of shots, staying in the present, accepting whatever happens without judgment, and looking for rhythm in the game." And in perhaps the first direct application of mindfulness to sports, Jon Kabat-Zinn and colleagues trained the 1984 U.S. Olympic men's rowing team in mindfulness. Not much data from the training is available, but many rowers who medaled said the training improved their mental preparation and performance on the water.

Getting into the body, or "coming to our senses" as Jon Kabat-Zinn calls it, is an important part of being mindful. All the better if we can allow our bodies to act spontaneously, without preconceived actions gumming up the works. This is particularly true when playing sports, and one reason why teams like the Bulls and Lakers were receptive to mindfulness training. "Athletes in general can only be successful if they are mindful," Mason Fries, a professor at National University, wrote in the *Journal of Academic and Business Ethics*. "They cannot dwell on past missed baskets, strike outs, interceptions, etc. Champions must stay in the present moment and 'let go' of the past immediately."

Fries, a former college wrestler and mindfulness researcher, described a situation when the lack of mindfulness caused him to slip out of a flow state, with disastrous consequences. At a national wrestling tournament, competing with his teammates at Oregon State University, Fries was on the mat, winning a match against a past national champion. Fries had his opponent pinned with both shoulders on the floor. Victory was just a few moments away. But instead of keeping focused on the match, Fries's mind began to wander. "I can't be winning, he is a national champion," he thought. "If I do win, I will be so excited. What an accomplishment!" As Fries was daydreaming, his opponent took advantage. Fries's absent-mindedness caused him to loosen his grip, and before he knew it he had lost his edge. He went on to lose the match by one point. "Not being mindful cost me the match," Fries said.

While coaches and athletes have been practicing mindfulness in the locker room and on the court for years, only recently have they publicly embraced meditation. "For a long time I believed I had to keep my personal beliefs separate from my professional life," Jackson wrote. But over time, as he grew comfortable with the principles of mindfulness and how they could be effectively applied to the realm of professional basketball, Jackson decided he had nothing to lose by going public. "Though at first I worried that my players might find my unorthodox views a little wacky, as time went by I discovered that the more I spoke from the heart, the more the players could hear me and benefit from what I'd gleaned."

Today, mindfulness is appearing more often in professional sports. Pete Carroll, the coach of the Seattle Seahawks football team, is using mindfulness and other meditative techniques to give his young team an edge on the gridiron. Carroll employed Mike Gervais, a sports psychologist with a penchant for meditation, to teach mindfulness to the players before practice. It's not required of them, but about twenty players show up to sit quietly before strapping on pads and hurtling themselves at each other. Carroll and Gervais aren't pitching the players on mindfulness as a means to simply promote happiness—that wouldn't go over too well in the NFL, where the opposing team's crushing defeat is a weekly goal. And mindfulness alone doesn't account for the Seahawks' success. Instead, quieting the mind and eliminating distractions is one component of a sophisticated regimen of performance enhancement techniques designed to help a group of elite athletes tap their full potential. But it's an important part, and it seems to be having an impact. The Seahawks won the Super Bowl in 2014.

"Meditation is as important as lifting weights and being out here on the field for practice," said Russell Okung, a six-foot-five offensive tackle with a $48 million contract. "It's about quieting your mind and getting into certain states where everything outside of you doesn't matter in that moment. There are so many things telling you that you can't do something, but you take those thoughts captive, take power over them, and change them."

Even student athletes are studying up on mindfulness. Tim Frazier, who was a point guard on Penn State's men's basketball team, has a regular meditation practice that he says enhances his performance on the court. Frazier, the school's all-time leader in assists, learned mindfulness from a yoga instructor who was brought in to help the team focus. And he says that learning to be aware of his thoughts, nonjudgmentally, has made a difference in his game. "The game moves so fast, it's hard to focus on the here and now," he said. "Meditation slows me down, keeps me more relaxed and more focused." One key way it has helped is by keeping Frazier immersed in the current play, rather than letting himself dwell on a missed opportunity from a few possessions ago, or worrying about the next defensive set he might face. "Sometimes during the game, you focus on whether past plays were good or bad, but meditation brings you back to the play at hand," he said.

Michael Baime, a director of the University of Pennsylvania Program for Mindfulness, said that besides cultivating sharper focus, the physiological benefits of mindfulness practice are of enormous value to athletes in particular. "What impairs performance more than anything during competition is the effect of negative emotions on biology and on the ability to maintain perspective and continue to perform at the level at which you're capable," he said. "Mindfulness practice really isn't that different from athletic training.

"If you want to get neuroscientific about it, mindfulness practice changes the structure of the brain through which awareness operates," he said. "Just as running increases the strength of the quadriceps muscle, mindfulness practice strengthens the executive control function of the brain. Elite athletic performance is mostly a mental game. Mindfulness improves working memory and what you're able to do in the moment of a challenging situation. It helps you to focus on the information you need to perform."

Getting athletes to focus in the age of social media is especially challenging today, said Pat Chambers, the Penn State men's basketball coach. "There are so many distractions with Facebook, Twitter, Instagram, etc., that I think you need a solution on how you can rid yourself of all that for a few minutes to refocus," he said. "My hope is that before practice, our guys can find a technique they like to clear their heads. That for a few hours they can stop worrying about their test the next day or the argument they had with a friend, so that once they step on the court, all they are worried about is getting better today."

The mindfulness found in locker rooms doesn't emphasize decreasing emotional reactivity, let alone cultivating compassion. Athletes need to be quick, decisive, and aggressive. But by helping football and basketball players and other athletes to enhance their concentration, mindfulness is giving them a taste of what meditation has to offer. It may not be the whole hog, but it's better than nothing at all. And for a few players who are inclined to go deeper, a practice in concentration might just be the first step of a longer journey.

As Chambers saw in his players, we need to beef up our concentrative muscles now more than ever. While humans have always had wandering minds, technology now allows us to indulge our distractive tendencies like never before. What began as channel surfing a few decades ago led to Web browsing, which gave us social media such as Facebook and Twitter, with their ever-refreshing feeds of easily digestible nuggets of news and gossip. Smartphones, never far away and always on, give us the ability to check our e-mail, feeds, and updates with ease and impunity. Research abounds demonstrating the perilous impact of our newfound addiction to technology. Our attention spans are getting shorter, our long-term memory is degraded, and as a result, we are feeling less connected to one another. But all too often what is left out of discussions about the negative impact of excessive texting and Tweeting is any mention of an antidote.

Enter mindfulness. Though mindfulness and technology are not mutually exclusive — we can be mindful of the fact that we are distracted by our devices — regular meditation can cultivate more sustained focus and make us more sensitive to the detrimental effects of our low-grade ADD. "Concentration bolsters mindfulness . . . and in turn is strengthened by mindfulness, because we can let go of distractions more and more easily as we grow more mindful," wrote meditation teacher Sharon Salzberg in her book *Real Happiness at Work*. "Turbulent thoughts, futile regrets, anxious wanderings may arise, but they arise accompanied by less and less 'glue.' Then they don't take hold of our attention and spin us away from the home base of the present moment."

Just like athletes who can become absorbed in the present moment thanks to mindfulness training, we can become more regularly immersed in whatever is happening to us at any given moment and less caught up in whatever might be happening on social media. And as people become more aware of their thoughts and emotions, many realize that perpetual distractedness is not a productivity enhancer or a pleasant diversion. More often, it is a cause of profound dissatisfaction for themselves and others.

Until he began meditating a few years ago, Joe Ens was typical in how he consumed information throughout the day. A fortysomething Canadian with action-hero good looks who works at General Mills in Minneapolis as a vice president of marketing, he would wake up in the morning and immediately check his BlackBerry to see if any crises had erupted overnight. As he worked out in his home gym, then got the kids ready for school, he would monitor incoming e-mails to get a sense of what the day would hold, barely attending to his exercise or his family. Was there a problem with one of the new ad campaigns he managed? Did one of his employees have an issue that needed immediate attention? As he drove to work, he would think through the day's meetings and presentations. Would his bosses be satisfied with his work? Would his leadership impress others? By the time he showed up at his desk, he was already exhausted. He was in a state of what scientists call "continual partial attention," only slightly aware of what was happening around him, and very much lost in thought. It's a state familiar to us all.

Then Ens began practicing mindfulness with Janice Marturano. He wasn't the most obvious candidate. An avid sports fan and huge heavy-metal listener, Ens was more interested in hanging out with his friends and family than hanging out with his own thoughts and emotions. But, at Marturano's urging, he gave it a try. At first, simply practicing was a breath of fresh air for Ens, a few moments during the day when his attention was focused on the present moment, not racing ahead to deal with the next problem, or dwelling on the past. But before long, he began to see how his habits throughout the day were sapping him of energy and focus. That incessant checking of e-mail, that voice in his head that never stopped planning his next step and judging his last move — it was all counterproductive. Gradually, Ens began to redesign his life in small ways.

Now when he wakes up, he goes downstairs to his home gym and walks right by his phone, which he leaves on the kitchen counter, not on the nightstand next to his bed. When he's finished exercising, he ignores his phone again and fixes breakfast for his two daughters. Only once they're out the door and on the bus does he check his e-mail. "My habit is not to jump into someone else's agenda by opening all the e-mails they've sent me overnight," he said. "My habit is to start the day on my terms."

Ens's discipline continues throughout the day. As he drives to work, he uses his time in the car to practice mindfulness, rather than letting his mind wander. He focuses on the road ahead of him, experiencing the sensations of seeing, moving through space, and controlling the car with his hands and feet. Because the mind is prone to wander, especially in the car, he sometimes listens to a guided meditation by Saki Santorelli, Jon Kabat-Zinn's colleague from the Center for Mindfulness. Once at the office, Ens arrives at his relatively simple workstation. Instead of having two computer monitors, as he once did and as most of his colleagues still do, Ens has just one. Whenever the IT department installs an instant messenger service on his computer, he uninstalls it. He also takes his mindfulness practice with him throughout the day. As he moves around the General Mills campus, he is careful not to check his phone too often, not allowing new e-mails to divert his attention from the task at hand. "Mindfulness has profoundly changed my perspective on technology," he said.

Mindfulness has impacted the way he works in many other ways, too. Each Monday he has a nonnegotiable block of time during which he reflects on the previous week and sets his priorities for the week to come. On his office wall is a poster with a quote from Lao Tzu, the Taoist Chinese philosopher and author of the *Tao Te Ching*:

> Do you have the patience to wait
> Till your mud settles and the water is clear?

Ens said this small verse encapsulates how mindfulness has transformed his work life. Instead of reacting impulsively, he now lets the appropriate response emerge from a place of quietude. He responds based on what he and those around him need of him in that moment, rather than reacting from a place of fear or judgment. He is also more deliberate in his communications. "One of the things that has changed in my leadership style is that I'm very comfortable with silence," he said. "I used to just jump into an answer without knowing what I was going to say. Now I'm very comfortable letting myself sort through the clutter of my thoughts before I respond."

Once, while I was talking on the phone with Ens, the line went silent. Long seconds passed without a sound. "Hello?" I said, expecting no response. "Hello?" But Ens was still there. He laughed and explained he was just waiting for the right reply to come to him. He does this often now, letting the silence linger in ways some might find uncomfortable. It drives his team crazy. Those pauses punctuate conversations with so many mindfulness practitioners I've met over the years. They have the confidence to hold silence for a moment, the knowledge that saying something just to fill the space could have unintended consequences.

As Ens found out, our deepening reliance on technology is a profound source of distraction. We are beholden to our devices, reliant on them for navigation, communication, entertainment, and so much more. "Even before smartphones and the Internet, we had many ways to distract our selves," Jon Kabat-Zinn once posted on his Facebook page, of all places. "Now that's compounded by a factor of trillions."

Thoreau saw this coming. In *Walden* he forecast our affinity for technology for technology's sake, our lust for speedy information, and even our obsession with celebrity gossip. "Our inventions are wont to be pretty toys, which distract our attention from serious things. They are but improved means to an unimproved end," he wrote. "We are in great haste to construct a magnetic telegraph from Maine to Texas; but Maine and Texas, it may be, have nothing important to communicate . . . We are eager to tunnel under the Atlantic and bring the Old World some weeks nearer to the New; but perchance the first news that will leak through into the broad, flapping American ear will be that the Princess Adelaide has the whooping cough. After all, the man whose horse trots a mile in a minute does not carry the most important messages."

Yet even Thoreau couldn't have foreseen the wired world in which we now live. There are more cell phones on the planet than there are people. We wake up and look at screens, digesting whatever messages and news we may have missed overnight. On the way to work, we may spend more time surfing the Web from our mobile devices. Once at work, we likely stare at screens for seven, ten, twelve hours a day, doing whatever it is that we do. Coming home, we're surfing again, until we finally arrive at our televisions. There are screens pumping out information in elevators, on gas pumps, and affixed to bus stands. It's only getting worse. Wearable computing like Google Glass is embedding screens into our very apparel.

As we grow more distractible as a society, the dark side of multitasking is becoming increasingly clear. Not only is it unproductive, it can often be deadly. In 2013, the driver of a high-speed train in Spain that crashed outside of Santiago de Compostela, killing more than eighty people, was on his phone at the time of the accident. In New Jersey around the same time, a bus driver lost control of his vehicle while texting and killed an eight-month-old girl in her stroller. This isn't a situation that is unique to train conductors, bus drivers, and airline pilots. Many of us drive to work, or even drive as part of our job. By 2009, distracted driving was a factor in 5,474 deaths in the United States alone, or 16 percent of total auto fatalities. Nearly half a million more people were injured as a result of people paying attention to their devices instead of the road.

And yet, we persist in believing we can be immersed in technology and attend to the present moment at the same time. We can't. Multitasking is a myth. It's impossible to do two things at once. Instead, what we think of as multitasking is actually switching between two or more activities very rapidly. "Most people get overwhelmed because they can't stay in the present, and they convince themselves with the belief that multitasking will make them faster," said Stephen Josephs, a coach who uses mindfulness to help his clients, including many Silicon Valley entrepreneurs, to become more effective at their jobs. "But they're deluding themselves. They're just being less efficient. The cure to multitasking is to understand what the right sequence of tasks is and do them one at a time."

Of course, our minds were wandering long before Apple began selling the iPhone. Distractibility, the compulsion to follow our thoughts wherever they lead in a never-ending train of free association, is as much a part of our humanness as our capacity for work, and our capacity for mindfulness. Some call it "monkey mind"—our thoughts jumping around, untamed as a wild ape. It's been true for millennia, and it affects everyone the same: by and large, we're not in control of our own thoughts. Just think of the last time you were on a conference call and decided to clear some e-mails out of your inbox during a stretch of conversation that didn't involve you. Return your attention to the call, and in all likelihood you have no idea what was just said for the several minutes prior. Often all that wandering can be helpful, allowing us to plan, process, and make sense of our lives. But our monkey minds can also get us in trouble and leave us seriously unhappy.

The title of a 2010 paper published in *Science* by Harvard doctoral student Matthew Killingsworth and his professor, Daniel Gilbert, gave away the punch line even before they delivered the joke: "A Wandering Mind Is an Unhappy Mind." "Unlike other animals," they wrote, "human beings spend a lot of time thinking about what is not going on around them, contemplating events that happened in the past, might happen in the future, or will never happen at all." In other words, they're pointing out what we have already learned so far—that most of the time, we're not very mindful. Killingsworth and Gilbert posit that the default mode of the brain seems to be mind wandering, and that while our ability to contemplate the future and consider the past is a "remarkable evolutionary achievement," it comes at an "emotional cost." Given that "many philosophical and religious traditions teach that happiness is to be found by living in the moment, and practitioners are trained to resist mind wandering and 'to be here now,'" it seems right to assume that these traditions suggest that a wandering mind is an unhappy mind. To find out whether the traditions are right, the authors did what any enterprising scientists would do in this day and age: they designed a mobile Web application optimized for the iPhone.

The app, found at www.trackyourhappiness.org, prompts users throughout the day and asks them how they are feeling and what they're thinking about. A question like "How are you feeling right now?" is followed by "What are you doing right now?" which is subsequently followed by "Are you thinking about something other than what you're currently doing?" By the time they published their paper, more than five thousand people from eighty-three countries had submitted a quarter million data points.

The data revealed three key findings. First, "people's minds wandered frequently, regardless of what they were doing." That's no surprise. What was more interesting is that "people were less happy when their minds were wandering than when they were not, and this was true during all activities, including the least enjoyable." That is, the very thing we're hard-wired for — mind wandering — is the very thing that seems to make us unhappy. Even when people were daydreaming about a delightful fantasy, they were unhappier than when they were focused on the present moment.

The final finding in the paper is perhaps the most telling. "What people were thinking was a better predictor of their happiness than was what they were doing," the authors wrote. In other words, it didn't matter if someone was at work, goofing around on the computer, doing chores, or enjoying a meal with friends. What mattered was whether they were paying attention to what they were doing, and not dreaming about the future or ruminating about the past. "A human mind is a wandering mind, and a wandering mind is an unhappy mind," Killingsworth and Gilbert conclude. "The ability to think about what is not happening is a cognitive achievement that comes at an emotional cost."

It might seem a fool's errand to try to wean people off their smartphones, especially today's youth, the first generation of true digital natives. But early research is suggesting that in fact, mindfulness can make an impact even on restless teens and aloof college students. If that is indeed the case, mindfulness training — which is already appearing everywhere from kindergarten to grad schools — could have an impact on the way we learn.

A group of Canadian professors ran an experiment to assess how mindfulness impacted the energy levels and emotional states of a group of undergraduate students who were studying to be teachers. The researchers had previously done similar work with nurses, who experienced all the expected benefits of a mindfulness-based stress reduction program. The nurses became less "emotionally exhausted," a tremendously beneficial change for frontline health care workers who deal with death and dying on a regular basis. And this was only with a brief MBSR program, not the standard eight-week course.

The researchers, from the universities of Toronto and Manitoba, figured the students would respond similarly to their brief program. So they offered an elective course focusing on stress and burnout. As part of the course, they taught a brief Mindfulness-Based Wellness Education program. In addition to the traditional components of an MBSR course, this program emphasized health and wellness promotion. Lectures during class time were a part of the training, and students were given homework — in addition to studying from a

CD and wellness workbook, they were asked to meditate five days a week for fifteen to twenty minutes.

Though some students complained that the meditation homework was too demanding ("Five times a week exercises," one said; "if you reduced that a bit then the students could actually do the exercises more willingly"), the MBWE course delivered results at the end of eight weeks. Compared to the control group, students who participated in the course exhibited more mindfulness and greater satisfaction with life, and they said that they felt healthier. And though there were variations in some other measures of the efficacy of the training, there was one area that simply did not square with the hypothesized results. When it came to how the training impacted students' psychological distress, practicing mindfulness didn't move the needle in this group. "The Mindfulness Based Wellness Intervention did not have the hypothesized influence on psychological distress," the researchers wrote glumly in their conclusion. In other words, not even mindfulness can prevent school from being a truly nerve-racking experience.

But in another study of mindful students, psychology researchers at the University of California at Santa Barbara studied the relationship between mind wandering and academic achievement, wondering if a little dose of mindfulness might improve test scores. The team had a hunch. They had already discovered that there was an underlying connection between mind wandering and things like working memory capacity and intelligence. Not surprisingly, mind wandering didn't help. More attentive subjects had better working memories, which in turn led to better scores on reading comprehension tests. To test their hypothesis, the Santa Barbara team studied a group of undergraduates who went through a two-week intensive mindfulness program. The result: their mind wandering decreased, and their working memory got stronger. Then, when given the Graduate Record Examination, the standardized test students take when applying to graduate school, they performed better than peers who hadn't trained in mindfulness.

In this study, mindfulness was proven to be more effective than other seemingly beneficial lifestyle changes like diet and exercise. The researchers signed up forty-eight UCSB undergrads and split them into two groups, telling each that the study was about improving cognitive performance. Half were given a new, healthy diet regimen and asked to keep a daily diary of what they ate. The other half embarked on a compressed version of MBSR, learning to focus on their breathing and stay in the present moment. Two weeks later the groups were reassessed for mind wandering, working memory, and reading comprehension. The nutrition group's results hadn't changed. But the mindfulness group was more focused and had better memories, and their GRE reading scores jumped from an average of 460 to 520. Mindfulness practice, it appears, can improve test scores.

There is a growing body of research that offers us clues as to what's happening on the neurological level here. A team led by Harvard researchers at Massachusetts General Hospital in 2011 showed that practicing mindfulness led to marked changes in the part of the brain associated with memory. The study, which used fMRI scans of a group of participants before and after they took an MBSR course, showed increases in gray matter density in the hippocampus, the region of the brain known to be critical to our learning and memory skills. In 2007 a study by researchers in Dalian and Beijing showed that when given just five days of integrative mind-body education that included mindfulness meditation training, Chinese students exhibited better concentration; lower anxiety, depression, anger, and fatigue; a decrease in the stress hormone cortisol; and better immunoreactivity.

The Dalian study is a reminder that mindfulness is never doing just one thing at once. Even when done with the aim of improving concentration, mindfulness is at work elsewhere in our hearts and minds — making us more sensitive to the needs of others, and even improving our health. Even when Michael Jordan's meditation was aimed at making him more focused on the court, it also made him a nicer person for his teammates to be around. In addition to building up our concentrative muscles, mindfulness makes us more perceptive about a whole range of things, from thoughts, to emotions, to physical sensations. All that noticing adds up. We become more attuned to what is bugging us, what makes us feel good, and what delivers lasting happiness. In time, we also begin to notice what makes us dissatisfied, and what makes other people unhappy. Mindfulness doesn't only develop concentration. It changes the way we understand the world around us, giving us a subtler sense of cause and effect. In the next chapter, we'll see what happens when a practice evolves, becoming less about attending to our own fleeting desires, and more about serving the needs of others. And our first stop, of all places, is the U.S. Congress.

6

Compassionate

THE DAY AFTER President Barack Obama was sworn into office for his second term, I made my way to Capitol Hill for a visit with Congressman Tim Ryan, one of the most unlikely mindfulness advocates in America. Ryan represents Ohio's Thirteenth District, which includes impoverished swaths of the Rust Belt and down-and-out cities like Akron. Yet with his boyish good looks, bright eyes, and wide smile, Ryan is his district's ambassador of happiness. Broad-shouldered and towering, he still has the build and the swagger that made him a star high school quarterback. He is also about as clean-cut a midwesterner as you can find.

On the day I dropped by, a handful of constituents lingered in the waiting room outside his personal office, and staffers buzzed about, finalizing arrangements for the last events of the inauguration celebrations. Alone in Ryan's inner sanctum for a few minutes before he arrived, I surveyed the souvenirs from his ten years in office. A seal of the Buckeye State and pictures of Ryan and the president adorned the wall. But other trinkets were more surprising. A singing bowl, used to open and close meditation sessions, sat on his desk. Also there: a stone engraved with the words "WHAT WE THINK, WE BECOME."— BUDDHA. A do-not-disturb door sign pilfered from a hotel read SHHH, I'M MEDITATING. On his shelves were colored binders full of research on mindfulness as it applies to education, sports, the military, and health. Ryan finally burst in and gave me a vigorous handshake. He apologized for being late, but his schedule

was off that day, partly the result of getting a slow start after celebrating at inauguration parties into the early-morning hours.

Ryan began practicing mindfulness in 2008, after he was re-
elected for his fourth term. Despite presiding over a very safe district, Ryan could feel himself getting mired ever more deeply in the
political gridlock that pervades Washington. He is a centrist Democrat, and his views were becoming more resolute as his colleagues
on the other side of the aisle became more extreme. So before being
sworn in, Ryan went on a five-day silent retreat with Jon Kabat-
Zinn at the Menla Mountain Retreat Center in the Catskills. He had
dabbled with meditation before that, but Ryan, a Catholic to this
day, had never given it much of a chance. While on the retreat with
Kabat-Zinn, however, he began settling into the practice. "I just kept
getting more and more quiet," he told me. "I was in the zone. My
mind and body were synchronized, in the same place at the same
time. And I thought, 'My God, why didn't someone teach me this
when I was a kid?' It would have been so different. I went to Catholic school all these years and it was supposed to be a good education,
but no one taught me this."

This, for Ryan, was a whole new way of going through his pres-
sure-filled days, a whole new way of interacting with regulators, fellow members of Congress, and lobbyists. It was an opportunity to
reframe the way he paced himself and took care of his mind and
body. During his first three terms, he had worked around the clock,
with the intensity of a quarterback trying to win the game with one
final drive. He was motivated by the desire to serve his constituents, sure, but he was also ambitious and eager to get ahead in the
cutthroat world of politics. And though he was only in his late thirties, that drive was already taking its toll. Ryan was perpetually exhausted and had gained weight. The usually jovial man voters had
elected was becoming sharper with his colleagues and friends. But
as his practice deepened in 2009 and he began a regular medita-

tion routine, Ryan mellowed in some important ways. It's not that he worked any less hard. In fact, he was clearer about his goals on the Hill. But within months, he was being much more deliberate in his actions, even with his own staffers. Whereas previously he would make offhand remarks that could set his staffers off on a series of tasks they hoped would fulfill a vague request, he began managing more effectively, being very clear about what he needed done. "I can do and say things that waste their time because I didn't think before I spoke," he said. He was trying to ease their burden, even if only by a little bit. Mindfulness, though he didn't entirely realize it right away, was making him more compassionate.

Soon he could sense it when meeting with constituents, too. Ryan was more conscientious, giving them his entire attention instead of letting his mind wander to other issues while they spoke. And their stories—everything from tales of unemployment to instances of domestic violence—touched him like never before. "It just gets more enjoyable to be with them, rather than letting myself be distracted," he said. "Even the sad stories, I'm there for them."

Before long, mindfulness began changing Ryan's legislative agenda. Previously content to simply hew to party lines, he began researching the effects of mindfulness and saw the powerful impact that it could have in educational environments and as a remedy for high-stress jobs. So in recent years, Ryan has become a champion of broader investments not just in education, but in social and emotional learning as well, including the teaching of mindfulness in schools. In his district back in Ohio, he has gotten funding for pilot programs for teaching mindfulness in classrooms, helping children in poor school districts learn social and emotional skills that can help them navigate treacherous dynamics at home and in school. And he also advocates for using mindfulness in the military, working to bring stress reduction practices to active-duty troops and veterans alike.

Ryan's mindfulness practice has even changed his relations with his colleagues on the other side of the aisle. He is an ardent liberal, but meditation allowed him to have empathy for his ideologically opposite colleagues, even when he didn't agree with them. "I'm a lot more patient than I used to be, a lot more tolerant of other people's views," he told me. "I'm still not persuaded by my Tea Party colleagues. But I do try to listen to them more than I did previously and try to find that kernel of something we can work on together, find some common ground." And when he does find himself in a spat, he is more judicious with his tone and language. "I'm more thoughtful with my actions," he said. "Even if I'm saying the same thing, I'm not as aggressive about it. I don't want to add to the aggression of the political system and the anger."

After a few years of practice, Ryan was moved to write a book about his findings, *A Mindful Nation*. A breezy tour of his own journey and his ideas for making mindfulness an acceptable alternative to Ritalin for hyperactive kids, or Prozac for vets with post-traumatic stress disorder, *A Mindful Nation* was also Ryan's coming-out party. No longer just a clean-cut politician from the Midwest, he was now the congressman who meditated. He sent a copy to every representative on the Hill and spoke about it to anyone who would listen.

At first, it was fodder for some snickering in the halls of the Capitol. Staffers wondered what had become of their representative, constituents wondered what his priorities were, and colleagues thought he had opened himself up to attacks. "I'm not blind to the fact that this could be used against me and bastardized," Ryan told me. "But that's a risk that I'll take."

For all its polarization, however, Washington can be a remarkably tolerant city. And after the initial shock wore off, most people now just accept Ryan as the mindful congressman. Even some Republican colleagues, who would rather not be named, read the book and dabbled in mindfulness. Ryan started a "Quiet Time Caucus" that meets before votes are cast on Monday or Tuesday. The gathering attracts a few people each week, who come together and share a few minutes of silence before entering the chaos in the House chamber. "I just want to create some space on the Hill, before the week starts, where we can have some quiet time," Ryan said. "Just to put some value on it. Just to say: this is important. In today's society, you've got to do it."

Ryan is now a tireless advocate of incorporating mindfulness training into schools and the military, leading workshops around the country and still talking about his practice to anyone who will listen. Since meeting him in his office, I've seen him at local Buddhist centers like the Interdependence Project in New York, at mindful techie events in Silicon Valley, and once at a reception sponsored by Dom Pérignon in Jon Bon Jovi's $40 million New York apartment. At times, it seems he is as much a representative of mainstream mindfulness as he is a voice for his district.

And Ryan has a vision for mobilizing the mindful into a voting bloc. Using the on-the-ground network of yoga studios, he believes it might just be possible to get practitioners engaged around issues like funding for education, environmental preservation, and health care for veterans. "When you think about the yoga-mindfulness platform, in the sense of being a part of a political movement, I think it could be really beneficial," Ryan told me. "There are yoga studios in every community, and you could get into suburban America that isn't really hard-core Democratic. When you talk about personal responsibility, taking care of yourself, being a conservationist, it cuts through the political divide. Who's not in favor of taking care of themselves?"

Ryan said that by giving him a bit more space — space to observe his own reactions, space to think before he spoke — his mindfulness practice has made him less self-centered, and more concerned with

others. "You actually slow down enough to pay attention to someone other than yourself," he said. "When your stress levels are up,
you're short with somebody on the phone: 'Yeah, yeah, yeah. OK,
bye.'" But with mindfulness in his life, "you slow down, you really
start to appreciate that there is another human being across from
you," Ryan said. "And if you practice enough, and you slow down
enough, you know some of the pain that you have, and you see that
obviously someone else is going to have that too. So you're a little
more sympathetic, empathetic, or compassionate."

With time, the practice of mindfulness often generates a feeling
of compassion for ourselves, and for others. As we observe our
thoughts and experiences, we begin to understand that our own
frustrations are not so unique. Like the pain felt by everyone else
in the world, it arises from a mismatch of our expectations and the
way things are. Though it can sound a bit heavy, this understanding actually becomes a liberating force in our lives. No longer are
we beholden to the tyranny of our fleeting desires. We develop self-
compassion, knowing that our minds are programmed to dwell in
the past and leap to the future, are naturally inclined to cling to de-
sirable sensations and reject unpleasant ones, and also knowing we
have the power to reduce how much all these reactions upset us.
Like a loving parent comforting a restless child, we comfort our dis-
tressed minds, knowing that whatever is bothering us will pass soon.

With that little bit of breathing room — understanding that our
own problems are fleeting, and that we control how much they drive
us crazy — we can, with time and practice, begin to direct our attention to the needs of others. We begin to understand that literally
everyone around us is fighting the exact same battles. We all endure
minor annoyances that grate on us, and we all face big challenges at
work and at home. Through meditation, we can give ourselves the
space to maneuver around these obstacles. And, recognizing how

universal they are, we can also develop some care for others who are fighting the same battles. In time, mindfulness both creates the room for compassion and inspires us to help other people, too.

Compassion arises spontaneously as we become more mindful. It's a natural outgrowth of a diligent meditative routine. Yet there are also specific practices, often taught alongside basic mindful awareness, that are designed to cultivate sustained feelings of love and kindness. Just as mindfulness meditation makes us more aware of our own thoughts, emotions, and sensations, so too does compassion meditation open up our hearts to new depths of empathy and joy.

One of the most common techniques is *metta,* or loving-kindness. It's the practice I did in Jud Brewer's lab at Yale, and it is often done for five or ten minutes at the beginning or end of a regular mindfulness meditation session, though it is sometimes an intensive practice in its own right. *Metta* simply involves wishing well for yourself and others. By repeating phrases like "May I be happy; may I be safe and protected; may I be free from suffering," we can generate feelings of goodwill for ourselves. Then, extending those thoughts to include people we care about, our benefactors, and even people we dislike, we can cultivate empathy for others. Finally, by wishing well for all sentient beings, *metta* generates compassion that extends well beyond ourselves.

Much in the same way that mindfulness has sparked a scientific revolution of sorts, so too, in recent years, has compassion. Stanford's Center for Compassion and Altruism Research and Education, or CCARE, is a growing hub of research into positive emotions in the workplace that recently collaborated with Thupten Jinpa, the longtime translator for the Dalai Lama, to create a new working definition of compassion. Compassion, Jinpa and his team said, is "a mental state endowed with a sense of concern for the suffering of others and aspiration to see that suffering relieved."

On its own terms, compassion is proving to be a robust field of inquiry. Well beyond the confines of CCARE, scientists and professors are making it the focus of their studies, and organizations and businesses are working on ways to incorporate it into their everyday operations. Meanwhile, researchers are finding that there is a strong connection between mindfulness and compassion, and that the former can cultivate the latter.

An experiment conducted by researchers at Northeastern University added heft to the notion that mindfulness leads to more compassionate behavior. In a variation on a classic experiment, thirty-nine people from the Boston area took part in their first ever meditation course, learning mindfulness. Twenty of the participants took the course first, and the other nineteen were put on a waiting list. After the first group completed the eight-week course, all participants were brought back to the lab for an experiment that they were told would test their memory and attention. When they arrived at the lab, however, they were placed in a waiting room. In the room were three chairs, two of which were already occupied when the participant walked in. After the participant sat down in the third chair, a person using crutches and wearing a boot around one foot entered the room and "audibly sighed in pain as she leaned uncomfortably against the wall." The other two seated people, also in on the experiment, didn't stand to offer their seats to the woman on crutches. The question was whether the participant in the experiment would. "Would he act compassionately, giving up his chair for her, or selfishly ignore her plight?" the researchers wanted to know. The answer depended on whether or not the participant had completed mindfulness training. Among the group that hadn't yet had the eight-week course, only 16 percent of participants offered their seat to the woman on crutches. Among those trained in basic mindfulness, that number increased to 50 percent. "This increase is impressive not solely because it occurred after only eight weeks of meditation, but also because it did so within the context of a situation known to inhibit considerate behavior: witnessing others ignoring a person in distress — what psychologists call the bystander effect — reduces the odds that any single individual will help," the authors wrote in the *New York Times*. "Nonetheless, the meditation increased the compassionate response threefold."

The compassion generated by mindfulness practice is not just externally directed. Mindfulness practice appears to generate compassion for oneself, as well. The phenomenon was recently studied by Kristin Neff of the University of Texas at Austin and Christopher Germer of the Harvard Medical School. "Self-compassion involves being touched by one's own suffering, generating the desire to alleviate one's suffering and treat oneself with understanding and concern," they wrote in the *Journal of Clinical Psychology*. "Self-compassion is relevant to all personal experiences of suffering, including perceived inadequacies, failures, and painful life situations more generally." The authors said that self-compassion is characterized by self-kindness, instead of self-judgment, a sense of common humanity instead of isolation, and "mindfulness versus over-identification when confronting painful self-relevant thoughts and emotions."

In their research, Neff and Germer pointed out that mindfulness and self-compassion are not the same thing but are closely intertwined. "One important difference between self-compassion and mindfulness is that self-compassion includes feelings of kindness and common humanity," they said. "An increased perception of shared humanity is likely to be related to increased feelings of social connectedness, while the soothing qualities of self-kindness are likely to reduce depression and anxiety."

To study how effective mindfulness was in generating self-compassion, Neff and Germer developed a version of MBSR with extra exercises designed to encourage participants to be kind to themselves. A few dozen professionals were fielded in the Boston area and introduced to mindfulness meditation for the first time. In addition to formal sitting practice — where they learned to follow their breath and observe their thoughts, emotions, and sensations — they were given extra instruction in loving-kindness, or *metta* practice. After eight weeks of training, "participants reported significantly increased self-compassion, mindfulness, life satisfaction, and happiness, as well as decreased depression, anxiety, and stress," the researchers reported. The results were no fluke, either. The more participants practiced formal meditation, the more self-compassionate they were. "This implies that self-compassion is a teachable skill that is 'dose dependent,'" they said. "The more you practice it the more you learn it."

The same dynamic is at play in sports, too. When negative thoughts do arise, especially self-critical ones, mindfulness can help athletes overcome sometimes paralyzing harsh judgments of their own performance. Diane Reibel, director of the Mindfulness Institute at Jefferson University Hospitals in Philadelphia, said that self-compassion has proven to be a useful tool for athletes who are trying to overcome mistakes in the heat of competition. "Picture an athlete who missed the field goal," Reibel said. "What does he do now? He could spend time beating himself up over it or say, 'I'm human, I make mistakes, and I'll do better next time.'" Frazier, the former Penn State point guard, concurs. "Sometimes during the game, you focus on whether past plays were good or bad," he said, "but meditation brings you back to the play at hand."

Being compassionate, however, doesn't mean we have to be soft. Compassion can inform our disposition in all types of work, even jobs that require constant conflict. Sometimes, in fact, compassion calls for conflict.

Cheri Maples came to mindfulness the way so many of us do: she was in pain. A police officer in Madison, Wisconsin, Maples tweaked her back while pulling a stolen moped out of the trunk of her squad car and landed in the chiropractor's office. There, on the waiting room table, was a book about mindfulness by Thich Nhat Hanh. A year before this moment, in 1991, she wouldn't have bothered to read the first page. But she had recently gotten sober and in the process had become a little more receptive to spirituality. Now, with three weeks of leave mandated so her back could heal, Maples went all in, signing up for a nearby retreat with some of Thich Nhat Hanh's monks and nuns.

Maples arrived at the retreat skeptical that other participants would understand her, given that she was a cop. When she was asked to take the five mindfulness trainings, the first of which is Reverence for Life, Maples said she couldn't do it. Her job, she explained to one of the nuns, could require her to kill. "Who else would we want to carry a gun except someone who is mindful?" the nun responded. That moment served as a small opening for Maples. No longer did her identity as an officer of the law preclude her having a much more expansive, compassionate side to her being as well. Since that retreat, she has been a committed practitioner.

The first way Maples began bringing mindfulness to work was by checking her intentions each time she responded to a call. Instead of letting each call over the radio trigger an amygdala hijack, pumping her up with adrenaline as she prepared to confront a potentially dangerous situation, she took a mindful pause. She cultivated a sense of service and remembered that her role was to create a situation that minimized harm. With that wholesome intention in place, she would be on her way to the crime scene, committed not only to defusing a potentially dangerous situation, but also to helping those in need. Over the years, this saved lives. Maples was more prudent in her reactions. "I never did have to shoot anybody even in situations where, by policy, I could have," she said. "Carrying a gun can be an act of love when armed with mindfulness."

The next step came as she became more mindful of how she was doing in the wake of intense calls. Instead of simply rushing back onto the street, succumbing to the peer pressure that drives cops to handle as many calls as possible, she would take her time. She would reflect on what had just transpired and with self-awareness evaluate her own performance on the job. Had she responded skillfully? How could she have improved her behavior? If she was rattled or exhausted, she gave herself room to recover. Maples was practicing self-compassion, too.

Back at the station, Maples worked to curb gossip, which was rampant among the officers. She understood that negative speech was corrosive, weakening the ties that bound the police force together and ultimately leading to officers who were less unified in their mission to protect the public. The popularity contest at the station was also among the biggest of the job stressors, and Maples knew that removing some of that anxiety from the workplace could only help. She even began speaking up against injustice, though it was at times at her own peril. When peers made a wisecrack laced with sexism or racism, Maples found a way to gently push back.

Later in her career, as she began to train new recruits, she added some mindfulness practices to their regimen. In one exercise, she would have them write value reflections, prodding them to explore their own compassion, even if it was latent. "I wanted them to get in touch with the values in their lives that were most important," she said.

Bringing compassion to work gave Maples a new career of sorts. It turned policing from something Maples did, a job that defined her, into a process she participated in where she could effect some positive change in the world. It turned her role as a cop from a hard-edged vocation fraught with peril into an opportunity to help, practice compassion, and heal the people in her community. "It's not like I didn't make an arrest, or didn't have to use force," she said. "I always was going to protect myself and the person I'm arresting from unconscious habit energy. But I went about it with a different intention, and it made a difference."

When the prospect of practicing compassion on the job is raised, many people balk. Being loving and kind doesn't square with workplaces that are often competitive and aggressive. "We do not always view compassion and loving-kindness as the strengths they are," Sharon Salzberg wrote in *Real Happiness at Work*. "They are often viewed as secondary virtues — at best — in our competitive culture: If you can't be brave or brilliant or wonderful, then you might as well be kind. But kindness is not an insignificant virtue; in fact, it is a potent tool for transformation since it prompts us to step outside our own conditioned response patterns." As Maples demonstrated, embracing compassion doesn't mean we have to roll over and be soft. It's true in the police station, and it's true in a newsroom, too.

Dan Harris, the ABC anchor of *Good Morning America Weekend* and *Nightline,* discovered that being compassionate in the midst of a tough job is not only possible, but deeply rewarding. Harris, who initially approached meditation with skepticism, if not outright disdain, began practicing mindfulness after experiencing a drug-induced nervous breakdown on live national television. In *10% Happier,* his lively account of his conversion from cynic to advocate, Harris recounts his efforts to incorporate compassion into what was already a difficult meditation routine. At first, he worried it might just not work. Though he knew that compassion was good for the mind, and the body, he was concerned it might make him lose the edge that got him to the anchor's chair so early in his career. "I worried that in competitive career fields like TV news, compassion was not adaptive," Harris said. "Also, I still wasn't a huge fan of doing *metta,* which felt forced and artificial to me. But I wanted the aforementioned benefits. So, with some trepidation, I added a parallel track to the ongoing science experiment I'd been conducting on myself."

For Harris, the results were readily apparent. "In the months after I started adding compassion into my meditation practice, things started to change," he said. "It's not that I was suddenly a saint or that I began to exhibit extra-virgin extroversion, just that being nice — always important to me in the abstract, at least — now became a conscious, daily priority."

Harris, previously tightly wound and competitive, began willing himself to make eye contact with colleagues and smile. Weirdly, he enjoyed it. "It was like I was running for mayor," he said. "The fact that my days now included long strings of positive interactions made me feel good (not to mention popular). Acknowledging other people's basic humanity is a remarkably effective way of shooing away the swarm of self-referential thoughts that buzz like gnats around our heads."

Harris also began to see more clearly just how destructive it is when other people lose their tempers. When he witnessed travelers becoming apoplectic at Transportation Security Administration workers in the airport, he empathized with them. He could relate to their pain, and he knew the unpleasant feeling of anger, the chest tight and "toxins running through their veins." This only reinforced his motivation to be kind to himself, and to others.

But Harris's newfound compassion practice was challenged when he sat down to interview Paris Hilton. He knew Hilton's star was fading and rightly asked her a provocative question about what it was like to lose her luster. Hilton, miffed, walked out of the interview, creating a made-for-TV moment. When it aired a few days later, it went viral, and Hilton was pilloried in the press. Harris, however, was conflicted. "While ridiculous on a thousand levels, this incident did raise some serious questions about my compassion policy," he said. "Had I just committed an egregious violation?"

Harris had known Hilton might react this way, and he even admitted that he sort of hoped she would, knowing the ratings would be great. But had he set Hilton up? Was he rude to her? "There was a larger issue at play here," Harris said. "Was journalism—or any high-stakes, competitive profession, really—incompatible with *metta*? My job required me to ask provocative questions, to 'go in for the kill,' as we say—and, often, that wasn't so nice."

As a journalist myself, I've often pondered that question. I routinely publish stories that upset the people I write about. Newspaper reporters have their own version of going in for the kill. "If you're not pissing someone off, you're probably not doing your job," the saying goes. And while I don't go out of my way to hurt people's feelings, I don't shy away from an important story just because it might ruffle some feathers. Instead, I try to be clear about my intentions. So long as I'm not causing anyone to suffer just for the sake of it, but am instead pursuing a story with legs, I'll keep doing my job. And meanwhile, I'll continue to do my best to cultivate compassion for myself, and others, too.

Individual actors like Dan Harris and Cheri Maples are the seeds that will allow a more mindful society to take root. If each of us practiced a little more compassion for ourselves and others, life at work, and at home, would undoubtedly be much more harmonious. But on our own, or even in small groups, efforts to bring compassion into the workplace can go only so far. To scale compassion, it will have to be woven into the very fabric of businesses' products, not just their cultures. And fortunately, there are some software engineers in Silicon Valley who are trying to do just that.

• • •

My first job at the *Financial Times* was writing about Silicon Valley from the San Francisco bureau. It was a plum assignment, and I got to cover Facebook and Twitter as they grew from dorm room curiosities to world-changing technology juggernauts. I hung around Facebook quite a bit during those days, but I never heard its engineers talk much about mindfulness, let alone meditation. Whenever I interviewed Facebook founder Mark Zuckerberg, he would talk about making the world "more open and connected." It seemed like a noble enough goal (even if persistent privacy gaffes stoked concerns of a real-life Big Brother). But when I went back to visit my friends at Facebook a few years later, I was surprised to find that the principles of mindfulness were showing up in the very architecture of the world's largest social network, and that some of Zuckerberg's closest allies are deep mindfulness practitioners. Even more surprising, at Facebook, compassionate engineers are retooling the site, one feature at a time, in a bid to facilitate more empathetic communication among Facebook's one billion users.

It began when Arturo Bejar, a director of engineering, was tasked with reviewing the process through which users flag photos as inappropriate. As Bejar and his team scanned the endless digital archive of photos that had been reported, three things struck them as unusual: most of the flagged photos didn't violate Facebook's terms of service and weren't offensive, in most cases the person reporting the photo was featured in it, and most often that photo had been uploaded by a friend of the person doing the reporting. Some were pictures of friends at a party, and the user doing the reporting felt embarrassed or uncomfortable. Some showed a user who was trying to cultivate a professional image drinking a beer, or in a bathing suit. Others showed the reporting user with his or her ex. These photos didn't violate Facebook's terms of service. They violated its users' sense of personal comfort.

When Bejar began looking into this problem, users had just a few drastic options if they didn't like a photo. They could report it as inappropriate, an action that could get the offending user's account suspended. Or they could unfriend the person, or even block the user from ever contacting them again. The one way to request that an awkward picture be taken down without going nuclear was to ask the person who posted it to take it down, through either a message or a comment. "It's hard to tell your friends that they have done something that is hurtful or embarrassing to you, especially in a public comment," Bejar told me.

Around this time, Bejar attended a gathering of mindful techies called Wisdom 2.0, at the Computer History Museum, a charming little institution that chronicles the rise of Silicon Valley and makes a few decades ago seem like the distant past. While there, Bejar had his first exposure to meditation teachers including Jon Kabat-Zinn and Jack Kornfield. They got him thinking about how he might incorporate mindfulness, wisdom, and compassion into his work.

He also met the organizer of Wisdom 2.0, Soren Gordhamer, and told him what he was working on at Facebook. Gordhamer introduced Bejar to Emiliana Simon-Thomas, a neuroscientist who was then working at Stanford's Center for Compassion and Altruism Research and Education, and Bejar and Simon-Thomas began talking about ways to improve the process for reporting awkward images. They agreed that in order to make the process less binary, they had to make it possible for users to have more nuanced conversations. And since that's hard in the best of times, they would have to automate the process as much as possible. "It's easy to communicate love or joy or happiness, but it's harder to communicate that you're feeling uncomfortable," Bejar said.

Simon-Thomas changed jobs during this time, moving from Stanford to cross-bay rival UC Berkeley, where she became science director at the school's Greater Good Science Center. Meanwhile Dacher Keltner, a social psychologist at the center, joined the effort, and together the team set about reengineering how photos get flagged on Facebook. They knew the current system wasn't emotionally intelligent. In subtle ways, it encouraged the same sort of impulsive reactivity that leads to so much online strife. See a photo you don't like? Report the person who uploaded it. Unfriend them. Block them entirely. Or send them a message. Where in that process was the opportunity for self-awareness, for mindfulness of one's own emotional state?

Before the team got started, only 20 percent of users would send someone a message asking that a photo be taken down. Facebook tried to improve this rate by suggesting some boilerplate language to use: "Hey I don't like this photo. Please remove it." This helped, raising the send rate to 51 percent. But the team believed that a crucial part of the process was missing. They wanted users to take a moment to identify their own emotions before responding. They wanted users to be mindful.

A revised system was soon deployed. Instead of users simply clicking "I don't like this photo," the new system began with a prompt—"I don't like this photo because . . ." This was followed by a list of options, such as "It's embarrassing," "It makes me sad," or "It's a bad photo of me." Just this tweak seemed to make a difference. Soon after implementing it, users were choosing one of these options 78 percent of the time when reporting photos.

If the photo does not violate Facebook's terms of service, the user is taken to a screen that says the best way to get the photo removed is to send the user who posted it a message. Instead of the old "please remove it" text, new language was developed that incorporated the user's response to the question about why he or she didn't like the photo. So when my wife posts a compromising picture of me online, the site now prompts me to send the message: "Hey Alison,

I think this photo is inappropriate and doesn't belong on Facebook. Would you please take it down?"

It's a subtle but significant shift in tone. Instead of being confrontational, the new message asks for understanding. And instead of making it about something the other person did wrong, the new language makes the conversation about how the sender feels. Soon more than 75 percent of people were sending the new mindful messages, without editing them. And half of the offending pictures were being taken down, up from a third before the more compassionate system was put in place.

When Keltner presented these findings at Facebook's second annual Compassion Research Day, he explained what was happening in neurological terms. By pausing to assess his or her own emotional state, the Facebook user is breaking the cycle of reactivity with just one mindful moment. "There are a lot of data that show when I feel stressed out, mortified, or embarrassed by something happening on Facebook, that activates old parts of the brain, like the amygdala," he explained to the engineers in attendance. "And the minute I put that into words, in precise terms, the prefrontal cortex takes over and quiets the stress-related physiology."

Once the company saw that the new reporting and messaging system was working with many of its users, Bejar turned his attention to a demographic group that has a notoriously difficult time managing emotions online: teens. Yale psychologist Marc Brackett was at Facebook's Compassion Research Day and thought he might be able to help. Working with Bejar and colleagues, the team interviewed thirteen- and fourteen-year-olds who had experienced cyber-bullying and zeroed in on the particular emotions they were feeling, and the language they used to express themselves. They then customized a new set of interactions.

When users went to report inappropriate content, the language had changed. Instead of being asked to "report" the action, users clicked a button that said, "This post is a problem." Instead of teens having to click a button saying they felt "harassed," Facebook introduced more precise options, allowing users to say the post "threatened or hurt me" or it was "something that I just don't like." The language may seem less formal, but in fact it is a more accurate reflection of how teens think. And it seems to be working. Forty-three percent of teens who used the new reporting system reached out to a trusted adult when reporting a problem, compared to 19 percent with the old system.

Bejar is now looking further afield. He wants to roll out the new social reporting system to international Facebook users, who sometimes report benign content like a picture of a football team as offensive. (Presumably, these reports are being made by supporters of rival football teams.) His hope is that as people use these features over time, they will learn to modify their behavior and post less harmful content.

The experiment at Facebook is a welcome example of how more mindful technology can ease the suffering of a huge number of people around the globe. It may seem like small beer in a world with such titanic problems, but especially against this backdrop, isn't it worth trying to reduce the amount of pain and angst out there, even if only by a little bit? As Noah Shachtman, a reporter who wrote about mindfulness in Silicon Valley, put it in *Wired,* "It would be easy to be cynical about this effort — to laugh at people who overidentify with a Bollywood starlet or to question why meditation teachers, the masters of directing attention, are working with the social networks that cause so much distraction. But when you sit with Bejar and his colleagues at Facebook as they review these reports — when you see all the breakups, all the embarrassing photos, the tiffs between mothers and daughters — it's hard not to feel sad and awed at the amount of confusion and hurt. More than a million of these disputes happen every week on Facebook. If you had a

God's-eye view of it all, wouldn't you want to handle that pain with gentle hands?"

Facebook's experiment with compassionate engineering holds lessons for companies well beyond Silicon Valley. Though Facebook's technology and scale are unique, the willingness of Bejar and his supervisors to tinker with a highly successful product — trying to imbue it with a little more compassion — is a welcome example that other corporations might follow. It demonstrates that even small changes can make a big impact, especially when motivated by mindfulness. And yet, it is still early days when it comes to bringing compassion into the workplace. Individuals can make a difference, and some companies can find ways to scale the compassionate sentiment. Creating entirely compassionate companies, however, may take some more time. More attainable is to let mindfulness inspire social responsibility. In the next chapter, we'll visit a series of companies that have done just this. And we'll begin in a beachside town in Southern California.

7

Socially Responsible

ONE THRILLINGLY SUNNY DAY, I traveled down Highway 1, the Pacific Ocean shimmering on my right, to the headquarters of outdoor apparel maker Patagonia, just north of Los Angeles. While corporations like General Mills are teaching meditation in the office, and some, like Facebook, are weaving compassion into their products, I wanted to visit some of the executives who are committed to using their organizations as vehicles to put mindfulness into action.

Founded in the 1960s by a French mountain climber named Yvon Chouinard, Patagonia originally made pitons — the spikes climbers drive into the rock face to secure their lines — and other climbing gear for the pioneers navigating the steep rock faces of Yosemite's Half Dome and El Capitan. Chouinard, however, was more than just another hippie living out of his van. The elfin Frenchman had a deep spiritual connection to the land and developed a quiet Zen practice that has informed his business choices for the last fifty years. His breakthrough came when, while climbing, he saw that the pitons were fracturing the rock and making it unstable. Chouinard developed a new class of pitons that didn't harm the rock, and Patagonia was born.

For Chouinard, mindfulness has found its truest personal expression in physical activity. Besides climbing, he spends his time fly-fishing, white-water kayaking, and hiking trails around the globe. "I've learned a lot of lessons from doing these sports," Chouinard told me when I visited the company. Though he is now chairman, having handed over CEO duties to a succession of execs, Chouinard is still a regular presence on campus, overseeing new product development and steering the company's direction when he is not wading through a stream in search of rainbow trout. As we sat in an office overlooking an organic garden and the solar panels on adjacent buildings, Chouinard told me how he employs a sort of mindful intuition to excel in water sports, even at his advanced age. An accomplished kayaker, he learned early on how to roll his boat without a paddle. For him, that was easy enough. So one day, he decided to navigate an entire stretch of rapids on Wyoming's Upper Gros Ventre without a paddle. The water was raging, the rapids were solid Class 4 all the way down, and the water fell one hundred feet each mile. Immersed in the moment, Chouinard made it down unscathed and without rolling over.

"What did that teach me?" he said. "Well, first of all, I had to do everything right. I could turn the boat, but I had to put it on its side and carve it. When a rock was coming up, with a paddle you can just go around it at the last minute. When you don't have a paddle, you have to look way ahead and prepare. And when I went over a drop, I couldn't sit back, I had to go into the drop. I never went over, and I had a perfect run. Perfect. I didn't go from there to never using a paddle, but then that's when I really learned to kayak. I really learned to read the river and not just rely on that tool that is so powerful but covers a lot of bad mistakes."

Recently, he's been taking a similarly intuitive approach to his fly-fishing, catching trout using just a basic rod and line, no reel. "I've caught more fish than I've ever caught in my life," he said. "It's unbelievable. I'll go out with some of the best fly-fishermen in the world and they'll catch six or eight fish in a day and I'll catch fifty. It keeps reinforcing the simplicity thing. Replacing all that stuff with knowledge, experience. The more you know the less you need."

As Chouinard spoke, I heard the distinct echo of Steve Jobs. The focus on simplicity, the elliptical answers — they were the hallmarks of a businessman who was deeply influenced by Zen. And Chouinard's company, like Jobs's, has also developed a culture that reflects its founder's intense personality. Yet for all his personal mindfulness, Chouinard still founded a company that is selling products that are today more fashionable than they are utilitarian, and that contradiction creates some angst for Chouinard. "How do we keep doing this, knowing that we've already outstripped the Earth's carrying capacity, and there's going to be another couple billion people on the planet in thirty to forty years?" he said. "Where does this go? It can be depressing in some ways."

Over the years, Chouinard found ways to bring his personal mindfulness into the operations of his business. Patagonia has done a decent job of minimizing its environmental impact. It pioneered the technique of using recycled soda bottles to make fleece jackets, and many of its products use more recycled material than those of its competitors. And it organizes a robust aftermarket for used Patagonia products. "We're not trying to rationalize what we do, but we think we're doing a better job than most companies now," Chouinard said, striking a glum note. "But what does the future look like?"

A few years ago, Chouinard made the decision that to best prepare for the future, Patagonia needed a younger, more business-savvy steward. So he hired his longtime protégé, Casey Sheahan, to become the newest CEO. Chouinard knew Sheahan when he was just a boy and taught him how to fish. Sheahan went on to a career in the ski industry, then into high-profile jobs at Nike and Merrell footwear, before becoming Patagonia's CEO. Sheahan has since retired, but he remembers the initial shock of transitioning from Nike, a notoriously hard-edged corporation, to Patagonia, whose priorities transcend the bottom line. At one of his first board meetings, Sheahan was outlining his growth plan for the coming quarter and explaining how he would hit his numbers, when Chouinard stopped

him. "He said, 'Don't focus on the actual outcome or the number,'"
Sheahan said. "'What are you going to do to improve the company to
get there? Are you going to be focused on the best-quality product?
Are you going to make sure that we're always leading?'"

With his questions, Chouinard was telling Sheahan that if the
process wasn't sound, if his intentions didn't come from the right
place, the outcome, however profitable, didn't matter. It struck a
chord with the new CEO. Sheahan remembered how when he was
a boy, and Chouinard was teaching him how to fly-fish, the old man
would emphasize a deliberate, immersive technique.

"He got me to work on my casting, and slowing down, and working on an efficient, easy-to-perform cast as opposed to just going out
and trying to hook a bunch of fish," Sheahan said. "So if you focus
on the process and get better at that, you will actually have a happy
outcome. You'll have a better process, and you will catch fish because you're in tune with what's happening in the water and your
surroundings, instead of going out and just trying to catch fish. That
was a powerful lesson for me that was part of an unspoken Zen approach that Yvon carried into the business. It came from his early
climbing days. It was really about not just bagging the peak, but how
you did that."

So instead of chasing quarterly goals, Sheahan doubled down
on the environment-first approach to running the business that Chouinard pioneered. It wasn't easy to let go of the focus on finances
that made him a star at Nike, but for Sheahan, a meditator, whose
wife, Tara, is also a longtime practitioner, the inclination to focus on
taking care of the Earth came naturally. He went about intensifying
Patagonia's commitment to environmentalism, even as the company
continued to grow, all while trying to be a compassionate manager
of his growing workforce.

It wasn't always easy. The first test for Sheahan came shortly
after he took over. It was during the depths of the financial crisis,

sales had plunged, and by his math, he would need to lay off 150 employees. Patagonia hadn't fired anyone since 1991, and this would be an inauspicious way to start his tenure. He came home one night, torn up over the decision before him. Tara asked him a simple question: "Are you making this decision from a place of fear, or from a place of love?"

"Fear, of course," he said.

"What would happen if you made a decision from a place of love?" she said.

"Patagonia is my family," he said. "We'd find a creative solution to reduce overhead without laying people off."

And that's what he did. After a few rocky quarters around the financial crisis, sales began to ramp up to unheard-of levels. The subsequent years have been the most successful ever. "Why is that?" Sheahan said. "It also coincides with the greater awareness we've brought to our impact as an apparel manufacturer. The greater transparency we've brought to our customer about what is going on in our factories, what is in our products."

Today the Patagonia campus, a collection of solar-powered buildings nestled in a valley by the ocean, is a little corporate utopia. Free daycare is offered for the children of employees. Chefs cook organic food in the cafeteria. Dogs lounge near desks. Everyone seems to be on a first-name basis with everyone else. An organic garden flanks the campus. Outdoor meeting spaces are set up for teams who want to converse under the trees. In terms of attracting talent, the company's approach has been an unmitigated success; for every job opening, Patagonia gets about a thousand applications.

And yet in some ways, Patagonia is struggling to come to terms with its own success. One outgrowth of Chouinard's discomfort with the consumerism inherent in his business is a decidedly unusual ad campaign: from time to time, Patagonia runs ads that discourage shoppers from buying their products. "Don't buy this jacket," the ads read — a clever ploy that raises brand awareness, hints at the company's conscience, and adds a taboo allure to a jacket all at once. For Sheahan, the goal was also to get consumers to question their own behavior. "We want people to look at their own lives, and live in an examined way, and again, question whether you really just want that product, or do you really need it because it's cold this winter," he said.

Though Patagonia doesn't refer to it explicitly, the company is doing its part to foster a movement known as "mindful consumption." Like mindfulness itself, mindful consumption is as simple in theory as it is difficult in practice. It asks that we seriously examine the motivations and the implications for our every purchase. It implores us to be honest with ourselves about what we need, as opposed to what we want. And it requires that we investigate the underlying causes and conditions behind each item we buy, each good we consume, and each service we request. "Mindful consumption is premised on consciousness in thought and behavior about consequences of consumption," according to an oft-cited paper by professors at Emory University and California State Polytechnic University on the burgeoning movement.

Mindful consumption works on a number of levels. It shifts the onus of sustainability away from corporations and other faceless actors and puts it squarely on the individual. The goal is to foster a "mindset of caring for self, for community, and for nature, that translates behaviorally into tempering the self-defeating excesses associated with acquisitive, repetitive and aspirational consumption." Mindful consumption also asks that individuals, and businesses, question the very merits of consumption. "In business, and particularly in marketing, consumption has generally been treated as a proxy for market demand, and more of it has been seen as being always better for business," the authors wrote. Even when overconsumption is acknowledged, it is usually presented as a problem that can be solved if only things were greener, more environmentally sustainable. In other words, it's not the impulse to consume that's the problem, it's the fact that consuming harms the environment. But mindful consumption doesn't accept that consumerism is all right so long as it doesn't harm the environment. It questions the very premise of our materialistic culture, demanding that we investigate the motivations behind our purchasing habits. "Mindful consumption is the way to heal ourselves and to heal the world," said Thich Nhat Hanh.

Are we buying that new bag because it's fashionable, the season's latest trend? Or because we actually need a new bag? Do we truly need that new TV, or does acquiring it satisfy the primal urge to consume, fulfilling deep emotional needs with ephemeral material goods? Each purchase has ramifications far beyond the cash register, and being a mindful consumer means considering what goes into the sourcing, production, distribution, and delivery of a good or service, before mindlessly whipping out a credit card. The point isn't that we should stop buying stuff. We need to transact to sustain ourselves, live our lives, and support the economy. But when we do consume, we should aim to do so mindfully, supporting companies that attend not only to the bottom line, but to the well-being of their employees, the planet, and society.

Admittedly, not everyone has the luxury of making mindful choices with every purchase. Those on a tight budget may not be able to afford the organic produce over the conventional, for example. But even those with lesser means can make smart decisions about what they buy, choosing simple, healthful foods instead of junk foods, and choosing to save for the future rather than splurge on fads. Indeed, mindful consumption can at times be more of a challenge for those with more resources. There is massive societal pressure to accumulate stuff for accumulation's sake, to live in a big home because we can, to have a second home and fill that home with more stuff, and to keep spending until we drop. For those with the resources to fulfill these consumerist fantasies, the real challenge is being able to say no.

Practicing mindful consumption can seem like a tedious, exhausting endeavor. Even simple buying decisions — like whether or not to buy a new salad bowl, and which one to buy — can be fraught with ethical uncertainties and unanswerable quandaries. Is it better to spend a bit more and buy a wooden bowl made by artisans in North Carolina? Or to save a little money and get the cheap plastic one at Target? There's no one right answer, of course. And being a mindful consumer doesn't mean only shopping organic, or never buying from a chain store. Instead, it means deeply considering each choice, weighing the competing priorities and implications, and embracing — on an emotional level — the decision. It means being accountable to oneself, and to society, for the impact of our purchasing habits. While it may seem like a daunting commitment to practice mindful consumption, in time such considerations come more easily. Mindful buying becomes an intuitive decision, rather than something to labor over.

"If you ask enough questions, you get down to the root causes," said Chouinard. "And if you ask enough questions, it's like, 'Why are there so many irresponsible companies making shoddy things as cheap as possible?' It's because we're demanding it. The consumer. That's where the buck stops. We're no longer called citizens. We're called consumers. We're the ones asking corporations to make this stuff. We're telling the gas companies that we want cheap fuel, no matter where it comes from, as long as the price is cheap. So we're the problem."

At one point in our conversation, Chouinard went off on a tangent about a new product that particularly enraged him: a plastic banana slicer. Shaped like a banana and made of yellow plastic, the slicer had recently become the focus of thousands of news stories after tongue-in-cheek reviews on Amazon went viral. Chouinard couldn't believe people would actually buy such a thing, made out of a petroleum product, no less, when a knife cuts a banana perfectly well. As he ranted about the banana slicer, I was shrinking inside. I had purchased one not long before, swept up in the media hoopla over the device. Worse, I'd used it only once. It was a mindless decision on my part, and I was suddenly flushed with guilt before this mountaineer sage. But I couldn't bring myself to confess my failings to Chouinard and moved the conversation along. Nonetheless, his message stuck with me, and I've tried to be more deliberate in my purchases since then.

For the founder and principal owner of a successful apparel maker, Chouinard is remarkably down on people buying his products. He genuinely believes that most people who purchase Patagonia items ought not to be doing so, because they are buying from a place of impulse and selfishness, rather than from a place of need. He likens our affinity for shopping to the plight of an addict and says that for meaningful change to occur, not only must Patagonia produce more sustainable clothes, but consumers have to buy less. "It's like being an alcoholic and being in denial that you are an alcoholic," he told me. "Until you face up to the fact that you're an alcoholic, you're never going to get over it. And so we not only have to change, to do the best we can making our goods, but we also have to educate our consumers to consume less." Nor is Chouinard worried that this attitude might put Patagonia out of business. He figures the company is selling to only a fraction of its potential customer base, and even if current fans bought a fraction of what they currently do, the company could continue to grow. "We just want to sell less to our existing customers and have them lead a more examined, simple life," he said.

Because the alternative, Chouinard said, is unsustainable. Rampant consumption will diminish our resources, not to mention leave us spiritually unsatisfied and financially bankrupt. "There's no business to be done on a dead planet," said Chouinard, quoting the conservationist David Brower. "And that's what we're facing."

In recent years, as my mindfulness practice has deepened, I naturally began buying less stuff. This wasn't just because my wife and I live in a small New York apartment. It was because before whipping out my credit card, I paused to contemplate why I was making a purchase, and what all went into the production of whatever it was I was tempted to buy. Though those new shoes would look great, I actually didn't need them. Another suit would have been nice to round out my professional wardrobe, but the truth is, I had plenty. In time, I began buying less and saving more. Our small apartment was less cluttered than it otherwise would have been, and I avoided accumulating more disposable junk of little lasting value. Today, when faced with the choice to buy some nonessential good, I often hear Chouinard's words ringing in my head and decide to put off that purchase, at least for now.

Other big companies are now adopting the principles of mindful consumption to some degree. Not all are outright lobbying people to buy fewer of their products. But like Patagonia, some of its peers are aiming to produce timeless garb that won't go out of style in a few months and is durable enough to last a generation.

As Chouinard knows, Patagonia isn't perfect. Try as it might to minimize its impact on the Earth, it still is depleting resources, albeit at a slower rate than some of its competitors. And though Sheahan has moved on, the work he and Chouinard set in motion continues. Teams at Patagonia are assessing how to minimize packaging — using just a rubber band instead of a bag — and the larger goal is to create a completely recycled and recyclable product line. Patagonia does its part to support other social causes as well. The company is working to restore natural habitats around the globe, promotes fair trade, and is working with suppliers and other partners to reduce the environmental impacts of its supply chain. In his book *The Responsible Company*, Chouinard wrote about his continued effort to make things better, despite the bleak state of affairs, with a perspective informed by decades of mindfulness practice. "We are all still in the earliest stages of learning how what we do for a living both threatens nature and fails to meet our deepest human needs," he said. "The impoverishment of our world and the devaluing of the priceless undermine our physical and economic well-being. Yet the depth and breadth of technological innovation of the past few decades shows that we have not lost our most useful gifts: humans are ingenious, adaptive, clever. We also have moral capacity, compassion for life, and an appetite for justice. We now need to more fully engage these gifts to make economic life more socially just and environmentally responsible, and less destructive to nature and the commons that sustain us."

In the same way that mindfulness quietly cultivates feelings of empathy for ourselves and others, it also motivates us to do good for others out there in the wider world. Social responsibility is a natural extension of compassion. *Metta* meditation practice concludes by wishing well for all sentient beings. Embracing social responsibility is putting that sentiment to work in the world. When we understand that our customers and the environment are suffering in their own ways, too, the natural impulse is to help.

This is easier said than done, especially in the confines of corporations. But it is nonetheless happening at companies large and small. And like Patagonia, some of the most mindful companies I observed were those whose founders or CEOs embodied mindful living personally and strived to reflect those same principles in their business operations. They were the companies that looked deeply at the work they did and strived to do it with compassion for their employees, respect for suppliers and partners, and a keen awareness of their impact on the planet. And if there is one trait that seems to distinguish many of the most mindful companies I encountered, it was concern for the environment.

Mindfulness insists that we take a deep look at the causes and conditions of all phenomena — from our own thoughts and emotions to the weather. Meditation practice expands our awareness not just to ourselves, and the collective, but also to the societal, the environmental. "If your business is causing environmental problems, then because you have practiced meditation you may have an idea of how to conduct your business in such a way that you will harm nature less," said Thich Nhat Hanh. "Meditation can calm your suffering and give you more insight and more right view on yourself and on the world and if you have a collective wisdom, then naturally you will want to handle and conduct your business in such a way that will make the world suffer less."

And indeed, mindfulness appears to make us more inclined toward socially responsible behavior. In a paper from 2010 titled "In the Moment: The Effect of Mindfulness on Ethical Decision Making," Nicole Ruedy of the University of Washington and Maurice Schweitzer of the University of Pennsylvania make the case that sitting down and doing nothing leads to more virtuous behavior.

The crux of their argument is that the more self-aware someone is, the less comfortable he or she will be misbehaving. "Mindfulness raises awareness of one's own thought processes, thus greater mindfulness is likely to make justifying larger infractions more difficult," they wrote. To test their hypothesis, Ruedy and Schweitzer ran a series of experiments. First, using the Mindful Attention Awareness Scale (MAAS), a fifteen-point questionnaire that assesses how present-minded people are, the researchers gauged the inherent mindfulness of ninety-seven participants from a large northeastern university who weren't formal mindfulness practitioners. They found that more mindful individuals were also more likely to be inclined toward ethical decision making. Next, the researchers worked with 135 people and again assessed their trait mindfulness using the MAAS. This time, they devised an experiment in which participants had four minutes to unscramble fifteen anagrams and would be paid one dollar for each correct answer. In a sad commentary on human nature, 55.2 percent of participants cheated. Nor was a lack of mindfulness an accurate predictor of who would cheat and who would not. But there was one wrinkle. "Among the cheaters, mindful participants cheated by smaller amounts than less mindful participants," the researchers found. "This finding suggests that greater self-awareness curtails unethical behavior, possibly by increasing the costs to one's self-concept of acting unethically."

One of the most pressing ethical issues of our time is how we confront climate change. A few fringe voices aside, the scientific community is adamant: human activity is warming the Earth and changing the weather. With that much established, how could a mindful CEO *not* consider his or her company's impact on the planet? "Just as individuals have to wake up, if organizations and businesses don't get more enlightened, we're going to take down the Earth," Tara Brach, the popular mindfulness teacher, told me.

And in the same way that our hearts open up to ourselves when we are mindful, so too do our hearts open up to the land when we are aware of the finitude of our natural resources, and just how easy it is for us to deplete and soil them. "Mindfulness opens up our senses," said Mark Coleman, an environmentalist and mindfulness teacher who often leads retreats in nature. "If we're doing any genuine mindfulness practice, we're embodied, we're more sensorially aware. We have a much deeper attunement to our body and our land."

Being in nature calls forth the same qualities as meditation practice—stillness, curiosity, and peace. That's why, in the same way that I get a bit rough around the edges when I don't meditate for a few days, or even weeks, I get antsy when too much time goes by without taking a walk in the woods. In fact, sometimes simply being in nature is a potent meditative practice. "Mindfulness opens up the heart to gratitude, mystery, and wonder, all things that are revealed in nature," Coleman said.

A mindfulness practice — even one developed and cultivated in the urban jungle — can make environmentalists out of those who have never given much thought to nature's wonders. "As we become more mindful, we are able to see how we're connected, the matrix of life and our place within it," said Coleman. "We see that our actions and other people's actions have real consequences. We see that if a company is really thinking about its social impact, its environmental impact, it can't help but make changes." Yet despite the growing wave of mindfulness in the workplace, Coleman is pessimistic about the prospect of real change in the boardroom. "Until we have a different paradigm that isn't at the beck and call of shareholders, the changes are going to be incremental at best," he said. "Mindfulness does nevertheless make people more aware of their impact."

Coleman is a regular teacher at Spirit Rock Meditation Center, but he also has a growing line of business working with companies that want to bring the spirit of mindfulness into the office. The company he's worked with most closely is Prana, a Southern California maker of gear for climbers and yogis. Like Patagonia, Prana was founded with a mindful ethos. The company has all the attendant trappings of a meditation-friendly office — free yoga and mindfulness classes — but it has also made social responsibility a core part of its mission.

Each day, around 3:00 p.m., someone in the company hammers a giant gong that hangs amid the cubicles. As the ring echoes through the office, work at the company grinds to a halt. People turn off their music, wrap up their calls, and pause their conversations. For a few minutes, all employees just focus on their breathing, taking time to recenter themselves amid the hustle and bustle. Scott Kerslake,

CEO of Prana, told me that the afternoon pause is part of an effort to keep employees attuned to their hearts, minds, and bodies throughout the day.

Prana has been around for more than twenty years, and the orientation toward mindfulness is part of its DNA. Kerslake said the whole sport of rock climbing hinges on one's ability to remain in the moment, present to the body's relationship with the cliff. Not being present can be fatal. Yoga, of course, has its own spiritual roots, ones that go much deeper than the power yoga taught at commercial gyms might suggest. "The connective tissue between yoga and climbing is mindfulness," Kerslake said.

Like Patagonia, Prana does its best to minimize its environmental impact. "We've focused on it right from the beginning. To focus on your own actions and be aware of the ramifications — being aware of cause and effect — that is being mindful," Kerslake told me. "We ask ourselves: What's our impact as a company — in terms of waste, working conditions, the materials we're using for our products?"

As Prana has grown in recent years, benefiting from the boom in yoga's popularity, it has turned to Mark Coleman to help it stay grounded. Kerslake met Coleman when he did a ten-day Insight Meditation retreat at Spirit Rock, and soon after, Coleman was making regular visits to Prana headquarters down the coast. Now, when Kerslake and the team face thorny business decisions, they can consult with Coleman. Recently, the company has been trying to increase the use of organic cotton and other environmentally sound alternatives to synthetic fabrics. "Conventional cotton and rayon are pretty terrible from an environmental perspective," said Kerslake. But "that sometimes bumps up against our financial goals." Such junctures require senior managers to talk frankly with one another, balancing the aspirations of the company with its financial realities.

To help the team make decisions from a place of compassion, Coleman leads the managers through exercises designed to increase empathy. In one, Coleman instructs them to identify with differ-ent constituents — customers, suppliers, factory workers — and put themselves in these new shoes. Try to imagine the lives they lead, and then remember that "just like me," they want to be happy. "Just like me," they want to thrive and succeed. "Just like me," they hope not to experience pain. This practice, a variant of one taught at Spirit Rock and in MBSR courses around the world, is a powerful way to get us outside of our own self-centered narratives and instead begin to make decisions based on the needs of a much broader range of constituencies.

Kerslake knows Prana can still be better. The company uses some undesirable materials and is still making products that are best described as luxuries rather than necessities. "As a man and as a sentient being this is a struggle. It's not an easy thing to deal with," he told me. But as CEO, he sees a valuable opportunity to change people's minds.

"There are few companies that care about the impact of their actions," he said. "That's my motivation behind coming here. It's a little bit of jujitsu. Our role in Prana is to change people's minds, el-evate their understanding of how things are getting done." By em-phasizing fair trade apparel, promoting environmentalism, and changing the paradigm of office life, Kerslake believes he has a chance to positively influence the way his customers and employ-ees engage in consumerism, and work. "We're still crappy at this," he said. "But we're less crappy than a lot of people."

Patagonia and Prana were built mindfully from the ground up. But not all companies have such green DNA. Some companies develop in conventional frameworks but pivot when their leaders grow more mindful. Such was the case with Eileen Fisher — the company, and the woman, grew to embrace social responsibility as the founder deepened her mindfulness practice.

Eileen Fisher, a wisp of a woman with a bob of white hair, began doing yoga in the late 1990s, long after her eponymous clothing company was well established. To complement her stretching, she added a basic mindfulness meditation practice. Initially her commitment was small, just five minutes a day, but the impact was huge and immediate. "It gave me time to stop, to notice, to question why and what I was doing," she told me. Soon, her sitting practice had grown to thirty minutes a day, and she was bringing mindful awareness to other aspects of her personal life, as well. And, as I've found, over time, committed mindfulness practice is apt to change the way we think about environmental sustainability, capitalism, and more.

In time, Fisher began offering yoga, Pilates, and mindfulness classes to her employees. But she didn't stop there. In an effort to bring a more mindful culture into the office, she installed a pair of chimes in every room of company headquarters. Before each meeting, someone rings the chimes and everyone in the room sits together in silence for a few minutes, checking in with their bodies and minds, and bringing a sense of clarity to the start of the meeting. "It's hard to concretely say what a difference it's made, but the feeling of connection is amazing," Fisher said. "That minute to stop is powerful. Everyone is coming from their different worlds and different agendas, and this brings us together."

The company also adheres to what it calls the "Circle Way." Whenever possible, meetings are held in a circle, rather than at a traditional conference table with a leader sitting at the head. The belief is that there "is a leader in every chair." Like other mindful meeting techniques, the Circle Way allows introverts and more junior employees to have a voice. At the company's World Café meetings, people from all over the company come together and brainstorm ideas, irrespective of station or expertise.

Fisher has won the trust of her employees by setting a good example, but also by taking good care of them. At least 10 percent of annual after-tax profits are distributed to staff. And in recent years, Fisher has been transferring ownership of the company to workers through an employee stock ownership plan. Massages are available to all employees during working hours. And while there are managers and a hierarchy, Fisher advocates a looser corporate structure than most other companies with a thousand-plus employees. In all, the company has undergone a radical transformation in the last decade and a half. While mindful meetings are de rigueur at Eileen Fisher today, "when I tried this fifteen years ago people rolled their eyes at me," she told me. Now, a local Tibetan meditation group uses the building during the weekends for silent retreats.

When it comes to the company's impact on the world, mindfulness has made Fisher more sensitive to environmental degradation. In recent years she has made sustainability, already a value of the company, a top priority, shifting manufacturing processes and changing the sourcing of materials. "Every day we try harder to make less environmental damage," she said, adding that they try to use lasting materials like linen and silk whenever possible. "They wrapped mummies in linen," Fisher said. "Silk is stronger than diamonds." Starting in 2004, the company began moving toward organic cotton, after Fisher began to appreciate that conventionally grown cotton is among the most environmentally destructive crops in the world.

In 2012, Eileen Fisher changed the way its silk in China was dyed, reducing the use of chemicals by 45 percent and water usage by 25 percent. And eventually, mindfulness led Fisher to reevaluate her company's overseas production facilities. Though the company has been manufacturing in China since the early 1990s, Fisher in recent years has redoubled her commitment to the workers there. Factories were upgraded, workers were given better salaries and more time off, women's health clinics were set up, and the company now abides by fair pay standards. And now, all full-time employees in China receive entrepreneurial training, so they can, it is hoped, start their own businesses, rather than keep working in a factory. "By working directly with individual business owners and our non-profit partners in China, we have found that we can create positive social change, one factory at a time," she said.

Like Chouinard, Fisher sometimes wrestles with the fact that at the end of the day, she's producing and marketing fashion items, drawing on natural resources and doing her small part to perpetuate consumer culture. But she sees clothing as a fundamental human need, and she tries to make hers durable and timeless. "We all need clothes, even people in the poorest countries need clothes," she said. "It's wonderful to have beautiful clothes that really last." As part of her efforts to reduce the company's long-term environmental impact, she instituted an extensive recycling program, called Green Eileen, where customers can donate old clothes, which are then cleaned and resold, with the proceeds going to charity.

Taken together, the company's growing commitment to social responsibility and employee well-being represents a paradigm for a new kind of mindful company, one committed to not harming the world around it, and to making the people inside it better. "It's not just about how happy we are today," Fisher told me. "We have to look more holistically. We have to make decisions based on more than our bottom line. When I think about what really matters, it matters that each of us find out who we really are and bring the fullness of ourselves to our whole lives."

It turns out this philosophy is no impediment to running a successful company. After sales at Eileen Fisher took a dip during the financial crisis, business has picked back up, employees are energized, and the quality of the clothing being produced is as good as it's ever been. Fisher attributes this corporate resiliency to a staff that is fully engaged with their work on a personal and professional level, believing in both the mission of the company and their role in the process. "When they are fully alive and present, they look at the work in more creative ways and holistic ways and are more energetic," Fisher told me. "They do so much more than any CEO could tell them to do. They act from their own core."

Eileen Fisher was able to pivot from being a relatively conventional clothing company to one that embraced mindfulness from the inside out. The transformation of the company, and its founder, serves as a powerful example for those who believe change isn't possible in entrenched corporate cultures, and an inspiration to other aspiring mindful leaders.

Patagonia, Eileen Fisher, and Prana were all private companies, unburdened by shareholders' expectations of rising quarterly earnings, and free to chart their own course. So what happens when a big, conventional, public company decides it wants to put mindfulness into action — not just by offering it to its own employees, but by making it a robust part of its product offering? For Aetna, the big health insurer based in Hartford, Connecticut, the shift started literally by accident.

On February 18, 2004, Mark Bertolini, a rising star at Aetna, was taking a much-needed vacation day with his family. An expert skier who loved the slopes, Bertolini had brought his wife and daughter from their home in Hartford to the resort at Killington, Vermont. Bertolini was skiing fast. He was comfortable zipping around even the most treacherous terrain and had gotten ahead of the pack. While still moving at a brisk pace, he turned back to look for his daughter, Lauren.

He didn't have the chance to see her. One of his skis caught an edge, launching him into the air. His six-foot-one frame ricocheted off a tree and over a ledge, sending him careening thirty feet down a ravine. Bertolini was motionless when Lauren found him. His body was slumped on the side of a cliff, his neck caught on a tree stump, the only thing preventing him from sliding another thirty feet into an icy river. Bertolini's neck was broken; five of his vertebrae had snapped. His shoulder blade had split down the middle. A tangle of nerves connected to his left arm had been ripped out of his spinal cord. Ski patrol rescued him, and a helicopter flew in to transport Bertolini to Dartmouth-Hitchcock Medical Center in New Hampshire. In the intensive care unit there, a priest administered last rites.

Bertolini pulled through and was able to leave the hospital just a week later. It was a bit of a miracle, and he attributes his recovery in part to his preexisting physical fitness. Less than a month after the accident he presented at an Aetna investor conference, walking with a cane, his left arm in a brace, and his head crooked from the pain. But Bertolini wasn't the same man after the accident. "Prior to my accident I used to run four miles every morning, go to the gym, and I was in really very good shape," he said. "I worked hard and played hard." After the accident, however, his pain was debilitating. Bertolini soon learned he would not regain the use of his left arm. Neuropathy set in, resulting in continuous pain in his extremities. "It was as if somebody were burning my arm with a torch all day long and to this day it feels this way," he said. "It's never stopped." To manage that pain, Bertolini followed doctor's orders and turned to drugs. He took OxyContin, he took Vicodin, and he took Fentanyl. They barely helped, and Bertolini barely slept at night. "I was taking all of it, and everything was just a fog and the pain didn't go away," he said. "The pain just kept coming and coming." Before long, Bertolini was forty pounds overweight, and colleagues began encouraging him to take long-term disability and ultimately quit. "You're lucky to be alive," they said. That's one way to look at it, Bertolini thought, "but I can't live stoned on drugs, sitting at home all day long."

So after a year of unsatisfactory results with conventional treatments, Bertolini went looking for alternative remedies. He started with craniosacral therapy, which improves circulation of spinal fluid. This got him off narcotics in four months. To improve his wrecked flexibility, he grudgingly turned to Ashtanga yoga.

At first, Bertolini thought yoga "was for girls." But after his first class "I couldn't move the next day," his body was so sore. He liked the challenge and threw himself into the practice. Each morning, the vigorous stretching became a welcome replacement for his daily runs, now impossible because of the injuries. He also grew to appreciate the intellectual and cultural history of yoga, reading the Vedas, the Upanishads, and the Bhagavad Gita. Soon he had a meditation practice to complement his daily yoga, and he grew to appreciate and practice mindfulness, sitting in the morning and evening each day. Just as craniosacral massage reduced his pain, and yoga improved his flexibility and energy, mindfulness began to change the way Bertolini viewed the world. "I started realizing that through my practice, through focusing on the inner self, I could control my pain," he said.

Whereas he was once constantly thinking ahead to something he had to do later in the day, which prevented him from actually paying attention to what was going on, he was now alive to the now, "present in the moment." Difficult thoughts and emotions became easier to manage. "Meditation is not about not thinking about nothing, it's about accepting what you think, giving reverence to it, and letting it go," he said. "It's losing the attachment to it. Same thing with pain. You recognize that it's pain — I happen to recognize the biological reality of it — so therefore I'm able to let it go when it happens."

Bertolini's words brought to mind a common adage in mindfulness circles: "Pain is mandatory. Suffering is optional." That is, all of us will experience pain. But *how* we experience it is up to us. Will we let pain define us? Will we react to it, letting it narrow our vision and obscure the richness of our other experiences? Or will we note

it, accept it, explore its curious sway on our psyche, and choose not
to identify with it? Bertolini, at his best, is choosing to experience
the pain, but not to suffer.

Bertolini wasn't lacking ambition or talent before his accident,
but in the years that followed, his mindfulness practice began to
benefit his work life in more subtle ways. In addition to being in less
pain than he might otherwise have been, he was less stressed, even
as his responsibilities mushroomed. During 2008, he would lead
meetings at Aetna as the company tried to chart a course through
the financial crisis. People would ask him, "'Why are you so Zen?'"
he said. His response: "There's no use in getting worked up about
it. What we need to do is be even more present." The company was
$550 million off target for the year, and Bertolini was telling his fel-
low executives to drop the panic response, stop using their Black-
Berrys and laptops during meetings, and pay attention to each other.
"If we're clear and we're present, we'll get through this quicker,"
he'd say. "We'll find the right answers and we'll move ahead." His
steady demeanor paid off. In 2010 Bertolini became CEO of Aetna,
a Fortune 100 company with more than $30 billion in revenues and
more than 20 million members.

For many corporate executives, this would have been the moment to trim the sails and charge ahead. Analysts, investors, and
board members don't like surprises. Best, logic holds, to be conventional and try not to screw up. Instead, Bertolini loosened up. If
mindfulness had helped him so much, why, he reasoned, shouldn't
it help his employees, and even Aetna's millions of customers? Bertolini decided to use his company as a laboratory.

When he first approached Aetna's chief medical officer, Lonny
Reisman, about offering yoga and mindfulness in the workplace, the
response was chilly.

Reisman came into Bertolini's office and said, "Mark, what are
you doing?"

"This is important stuff," the CEO replied.

"Because you're doing yoga, everyone has to do yoga?" Reisman shot back. "That's what everybody's saying."

"Tell you what, Lonny," Bertolini said, appealing to the clinician. "Let's measure heart rate variability. Let's measure cortisol levels if you want to. But let's see how stressed our people are and look at the results."

Reisman consented, and when the results came in, the executives were floored. For all the good things employees said about working at Aetna, most of them were highly stressed. Now could they try yoga and meditation in the office? Bertolini asked.

Shortly after taking over as CEO, Bertolini partnered with the American Viniyoga Institute and a Florida company called eMindful that teaches mindfulness, mostly via videoconference. He wanted to see if his employees could benefit from these practices in the same way he had. To bring some academic rigor to the project, Bertolini turned to Duke University and its Integrative Medicine Program, which has grown adept at tracking the benefits of alternative treatments. Aetna and its partners chose to roll out the training at two locations, company headquarters in Hartford, and an office in Walnut Creek, California, near San Francisco. Two hundred thirty-nine employees were selected to participate, and each was assigned to either a twelve-week Viniyoga training or a twelve-week mindfulness course. Only those who self-reported as highly stressed and had no previous intensive meditation training were accepted.

The yoga program is not what you might expect. Instead of practicing elaborate poses that contort the body, the Viniyoga program focuses on stress-reducing breathing techniques, mental relaxation techniques, and gentle poses designed more for calming the mind than stretching the muscles. The Mindfulness at Work program designed by eMindful takes its inspiration from Kabat-Zinn's MBSR program but has adapted it to focus on work-related stress, work-life balance, and self-care. In the Aetna intervention, the yoga was taught in person on both the East and West coasts, while mindfulness was taught in person in Hartford, and via videoconference to some in Hartford and all of those in Walnut Creek.

Reporting the results of these interventions in the *Journal of Occupational Health Psychology* in 2012, the authors provided a succinct refresher on just how mindfulness works in the workplace. "Mindfulness may reduce stress by allowing individuals to significantly shift their experience by learning to pay attention in the present moment, with a curious and accepting attitude," they wrote. "By training the mind to notice a stream of sensory and perceptual events, one begins to realize how intention and behavior are formed. The careful and repeated practice of this nonjudgmental observation gradually allows individuals to realize that events are actually unfolding processes that can be quite fluid. In other words, even apparently negative events, thoughts, sensations, emotions, and behaviors come to be seen as changeable. While this process is not necessarily conscious even in those learning it, the process does allow individuals to experience the world in a significantly different, and less stressful, way."

The twelve-week courses got under way in the wake of the financial crisis. Layoffs at Aetna were afoot, adding uncertainty to already-stressed workers. But the researchers took pains to make the training accessible, offering classes during lunch breaks. Ease of application was important. "To successfully address this issue for *employees,* worksite stress management programs must be accessible, engaging, and convenient in terms of scheduling, time requirements, and on-site locations, as well as have management support," the researchers wrote.

After twelve weeks the results were in. Compared with the control group, all employees who stuck with either the yoga or the mindfulness reported significant reduction in perceived stress and sleep difficulties. They all also demonstrated improved breathing rates and heart rhythm coherence, a measure of autonomic balance. There was also evidence that these programs might impact the bottom line. Compared with the control group, the employees who saw their stress levels drop had lower overall health care costs, to the tune of $2,000 per employee per year.

Since that initial study, Aetna has offered mindfulness and Viniyoga to more than a third of its employees. Aetna is also offering Viniyoga and mindfulness training to its customers as part of its suite of wellness offerings. eMindful, the company with which Aetna worked, has administered training to more than one thousand employees in recent years. To measure the effectiveness of the training, eMindful asked participants a series of questions before and after the workshops were completed, including "In the last month, how often have you been upset because of something that happened unexpectedly?" and "In the last month, how often have you felt nervous and 'stressed'?" The responses, taken together, were compiled on a Perceived Stress Scale. Before eMindful training, workers averaged 23.5 on the PSS. That is, this was the baseline stress level for employees in the companies where the training took place. After the training the stress levels were measured again, and the average PSS score among those who stuck with mindfulness had dropped to 14.7. Self-reported stress had gone down by a third.

Workers who took the eMindful course also showed similar gains in self-reported measures of time management, perceived strenuousness of their jobs, mental and interpersonal demands at work, and their ability to handle their workloads. Mindfulness, it seems, made life easier for them. It also made them more efficient. Before taking the Mindfulness at Work course, respondents were losing 146 minutes per week in productivity. After completing the program, the amount of lost time was reduced to 77 minutes, resulting in more than an hour's gain in work time per employee per week. Those who participate in the programs there demonstrate substantial decreases in heart rate variability — a common sign of stress — and are productive for 69 additional minutes per month, Bertolini told me.

As Bertolini talked me through the impact of his programs, he smiled easily and gestured freely with his right hand. His left arm was limp, however, the legacy of his skiing injury. I asked him if he still hurt, and he smiled wryly, suggesting I didn't know the half of it. The nerve receptors in his arm were still shooting off, constantly alerting him to the permanent damage done. Yet Bertolini was calm. Though he was in pain, he wasn't suffering.

As Aetna began offering mindfulness to its employees, it zeroed in on poor dietary habits as a main source of illness. With that realization came the opportunity to train employees in mindful eating, a practice that can have immediate impacts on our health and well-being. The result was a company-wide program called "Metabolic Health in Small Bytes" that teaches employees mindful eating habits and educates them about the roots of obesity. This is fertile ground for practice. For many of us, food is something we turn to as a crutch. When we're feeling stressed, sad, or confused, our minds look for something to distract them from the pain, and the powerful dopamine hit we get from certain foods — especially sugar, fat, and salt — triggers our pleasure receptors. Like so many things, however, enjoying indulgent foods is best done in moderation.

Metabolic Health in Small Bytes was piloted with a group of six hundred Aetna employees and showed initial positive results. It is now offered to all of Aetna's roughly thirty-five thousand employees, and thousands have participated. Tandon Bunch, a nurse coordinator for Aetna in Arlington, Texas, was a three-sport athlete in high school, as healthy as they come, and went on to be a cheerleader at Connors State College in Oklahoma. But by her early thirties, wracked by chronic back and neck pain, she had stopped exercising and quickly gained weight. Food became a crutch, and soon she weighed 175 pounds, a full third more than her optimal weight. When Bunch first heard of the Small Bytes program, she was somewhat skeptical. "I didn't see it as strange or mysterious, but I didn't know if it would work for me," she said. Nonetheless, wanting to improve her own health and set a good example for her overweight mother, she enrolled.

One of the first things Bunch learned was how to gauge her fullness level. Her instructor taught her how to monitor how hungry she was, on a scale of one to seven, and even when she was eating to be aware of how full she felt. Before long Bunch realized that, like so many other people, she was often eating even when she wasn't hungry. She ate because it tasted good. She ate out of compulsion to finish her food. She ate because other people were eating. This was especially true when she went out to restaurants. As a way to prevent herself from overeating when out, Bunch now asks for a to-go container at the start of a meal, places some of her meal in there for later, and eats what's left. Unconventional perhaps, and surely not appropriate at certain fine dining establishments, but some of her friends now follow her lead. A third mindful skill she now employs to curb her overeating is discerning whether she is actually hungry or instead simply thirsty. Sometimes we mistake the need for hydration for the need to eat, a subtlety Bunch can now discern more clearly thanks to her practice.

Mindful eating helped Bunch get her weight down to 143 pounds, well on her way to her goal of 135. Moreover, she reports that her overall wellness improved. "I haven't been sick. I haven't had any colds or the little illnesses that people get," she said. "I feel like I look so much better, my clothes fit better. And when you look better, you feel better all the way around."

A classic component of mindfulness training in both monastic and secular settings, mindful eating is a fundamental part of the practice, even if it is easy to overlook. At a purely sensory level, it provides a tremendous opportunity to get out of our heads and into our bodies. When eating, it's easy to experience the world through taste, smell, touch, sight, and sound. As Bunch discovered, it's also an excellent chance to be more mindful of the difference between our needs and our desires, the difference between what's necessary and what is habitual. Studies by researchers at the University of New Mexico showed that modified MBSR programs reduced binge eating. In another study of an overweight population, mindfulness practice reduced compulsive eating and abdominal fat. Thanks to these results, mindful eating is drawing increased scholarly attention.

I often eat lunch at my desk. It's not a great habit, but when it happens, I try to be mindful, instead of just scarfing down my sandwich or salad. I try to slow down, to chew thoroughly, to pay attention to how my mind is behaving. When I manage to pull it off, lunch at my desk isn't so bad after all. Instead of another thirty minutes that blend into the fog of the workday, that time becomes an opportunity for me to get back in touch with my body and hone my ability to be focused in the present moment. It's something many employees at Aetna are experiencing, thanks to Bertolini's commitment to practice. Some thirteen thousand Aetna employees have participated in one of the mindfulness or yoga courses.

But can pursuing the greater good be good for the bottom line? That's the vision of Aetna and other big companies that are led by mindful leaders, and they're beginning to calculate their return on investment when it comes to mindfulness. Take the study Aetna did with Duke. One of the findings was that highly stressed employees incur an additional $2,000 per year in health care costs, compared to their less-stressed peers. Scaled across a large company, this quickly amounts to millions of dollars a year in stress-related charges. And while it's hard to draw a direct causal connection, Aetna is already starting to see results. Health care costs at the company—which total more than $90 million a year—are going down. In 2012, as the mindfulness programs ramped up, health care costs fell 7 percent. That's $6.3 million going straight to the bottom line, partly thanks to mindfulness training, it appears. Not all of that is attributable to meditation, of course. But stress exerts a tax on an organization—in terms of both productivity and health care costs. Reducing stress, therefore, is going to help the bottom line. Aetna figures the productivity gains alone amounted to $3,000 per employee, an eleven-to-one return on its investment. That's an impressive ROI for any program. While mindfulness may not always be 100 percent free, especially when sold as an offering by a large health insurer, it is certainly cheap.

These initial results are enough to inspire Bertolini to press on, despite some reservations about offering meditation as medicine. He's understandably wary of coming off as proselytizing. "Introducing these concepts into the workplace without making it feel like they're learning Buddhism or Hinduism or whatever or a religious thing is a very fine line to walk," he said. "You have to choose your words right." But the upside is too great as he sees it. If he can improve the productivity and health of his employees, all while saving his company money with a low-cost application, that outweighs any reputational risks. "All that we've done isn't that expensive," he said. "It's probably cost us $120,000 a year to do this. If you save one life, who gives a shit about the money? If you prevent four people from becoming diabetic, we've done an enormously powerful thing."

The benefits of a more mindful workforce can't be quantified in dollar terms alone, but sound economic data to back up the anecdotal evidence will certainly help get mindfulness into more offices more quickly. Now imagine if not just Aetna, but all health care companies were incorporating mindfulness into their own corporate cultures and offering it to their customers.

Bertolini demonstrated the power of one executive, motivated by mindfulness, to do right by his employees and customers. It remains one of the biggest corporate experiments with mindfulness gone right. Bertolini may soon have company. Though he was able to effect change on his own, discovering practice as a remedy for his own suffering and taking steps to scale mindfulness within Aetna, other executives are taking deliberate steps to become more mindful. They are being drawn to the practicality of the emerging field known as mindful leadership, and they are seeking out knowledge and training wherever they can find it. And for some, that means heading to a former Christian monastery on the banks of the Hudson River.

8

The Space to Lead

IT'S EASY TO MISS the Garrison Institute. The spires of the former Franciscan monastery are barely visible from the Amtrak, which speeds by at the foot of a hill overlooking the Hudson River. The road that winds through the suburban town of Garrison skirts the property but affords no glimpse of its fortresslike red-brick and stone facade. But as you turn down a gravel drive and pass through an open field, the institute, a grand, rambling building resembling something out of an M. C. Escher drawing, bursts into view.

The monastery was built in 1932 but fell into disuse and disrepair. A decade ago, it was slated to be demolished. But Jonathan Rose, a meditating real estate developer from nearby New York City, came across the property and had a vision to turn it into a refuge where he could deepen his longtime meditation practice and offer teachers a space where they could instruct others. With his wife, Diana, Rose acquired and restored the building, turning it into a retreat center that today hosts a full calendar of mindfulness programs. And it was here, on a steamy summer weekend, that Janice Marturano was presiding over another group of meditators, this time as she led a Mindful Leadership retreat.

Since I had last seen Marturano, she'd left General Mills and founded the Institute for Mindful Leadership, through which she was teaching classes around the country. In many ways it was familiar territory for her. The curriculum was little changed from her time instructing colleagues in Minneapolis. But in the intervening months, it seemed Marturano had changed. She was more confident, and even a bit calmer. A year of teaching mindfulness outside the confines of her own office had given her a new command of the material, and new confidence when offering the material to nervous first-timers.

She also knew how to put them at ease. "This is not group therapy," she told the twenty or so nonprofit executives, who had taken time off from their jobs at organizations like the Girl Scouts. It was a sweltering summer day, and people were sweating inside despite the efforts of air conditioners. "It's just more grist for the mill," Marturano said as the group squirmed. "More things to be mindful of."

Plenty of the students, myself included, nodded off during the first meditation session. It was the end of a long workweek, and a saunalike heat had taken hold outside. Sleepiness is a common and totally understandable obstacle in meditation practice. The only time we ever stop going is when we sleep. So when the mind doesn't have something to occupy it, it automatically goes into rest mode. Sleepiness hits expert meditators and novices alike. But with practice, it becomes easier to harness mindfulness to remain at ease and awake, even when the body is tired.

After we meditated, Marturano had the group brainstorm about the essential attributes of good leadership. The descriptors that were offered—"compassionate," "attentive," "warm-hearted," "encouraging"—were not the same ones you'd use to describe a battlefield general. Words like "driven," "aggressive," and "demanding" didn't make the cut. Marturano then used the conversation as a springboard for a discussion of what she said were some of the main qualities of effective leadership: clarity, focus, and compassion. All of them, she said, can be cultivated through mindfulness.

Clarity, for Marturano, means seeing clearly how things are.

It's about "not having expectations of something other than what is," she said. That is, it is about acceptance, the same sort of mental reorientation that we learned in Chapter 4 so effectively reduces stress. Clarity means understanding that our initial reaction might not be the absolute truth. It means understanding that whatever we're feeling, and whatever is happening, is bound to change. Accordingly, we'd be wise not to cling to our first impressions, instead giving ourselves space to maneuver in what are often complicated situations at home and at work.

Focus, as we saw in Chapter 5, arises when we practice meditation, the repeated effort of bringing our attention back to the breath strengthening our minds as if we were at the gym. For leaders, said Marturano, that's especially important today, when our always-on digital lives mean that even the best manager's attention is constantly divided. Too many workers today are perpetually reacting to what's in their inbox, never taking the time to set their own agendas. "This does not ever allow us to reset," Marturano said. "We ramp up and we stay here."

And compassion, for Marturano, means opening up to the pain that we and those around us are experiencing every day, and having the wherewithal to do something about it. "We are generally not very good at acknowledging the difficulties in our lives, but quite good at denying and ignoring those parts of our lives that are painful," Marturano said. "This is especially true for leaders." As we saw in Chapter 6, compassion can be a transformative force in the workplace. And the power of compassion is amplified when wielded by an executive with real sway over an organization. Mindful leaders, Marturano said, recognize their own pain but don't let their personal struggles negatively impact their interactions with others. Moreover, they recognize the ways in which others are dissatisfied and work to alleviate that pain.

As Marturano told her class at the Garrison Institute, mindful leaders embody many of the core qualities that mindfulness cultivates. They are less stressed and more accepting of what is happening. They are more focused and not easily distracted, staying on task and paying attention to those around them. And they are compassionate, working to improve working conditions for themselves and others. "Leadership presence is a tangible quality," Marturano wrote in her book, *Finding the Space to Lead*. "It requires full and complete nonjudgmental attention in the present moment. Those around a mindful leader see and feel that presence."

Later in the day at Garrison, Marturano offered some tips for leaders as they worked to bring mindfulness into their communications with colleagues. First, she said, mindful leaders should pause to check in with their bodies. If you're bringing tension, anger, or stress to a meeting, work to let it go before proceeding, responding to the situation at hand rather than reacting to your state of mind five minutes ago. Next, be open to what is before you. Bring clarity to the situation, accepting the situation rather than being upset because you expected it would be different. After that, listen deeply. Interrupting prevents people from opening up. Don't try to finish others' sentences. "When you're formulating a response, note when your mind is wandering," she said. "It's usually like doing battle in meetings. We're always looking for an opening to get our point in." Finally, speak the truth with the intention to do no harm. That is, be honest and compassionate.

The weekend went on like this, a mix of meditation sessions, discussion, and instruction, as Marturano's students tried to cope with the heat. In a testament to their own dedication, and Marturano's skillful teachings, they all stuck it out, participating in what is one of the most popular avenues into mindfulness today: mindful leadership training.

• • •

A whole cottage industry is springing up around mindful leadership. Retreats promise to turn ho-hum managers into intuitive gurus. Some, like Marturano's, are taught by well-credentialed teachers, while others are of dubious provenance.

The need is clear. As responsibilities grow, so do the range and magnitude of problems we are expected to solve. Instead of just performing one task, a middle manager might oversee a small team of workers. Moving up, as a division head, might entail overseeing several managers with their own teams. With each promotion, the scale and complexity increase. "Leaders across domains express a common refrain of being in 'uncharted waters' where old models, routines, and assumptions are called into question with no clear pathways on which to navigate," said Jeremy Hunter, a professor at the Peter F. Drucker and Masatoshi Ito Graduate School of Management at Claremont Graduate University who teaches mindful leadership. "As a result, there are enormous stresses on individuals, institutions, and organizations who are called upon to meet, and effectively adjust to, increasingly discordant, unpredictable, and extreme events."

Clarity, focus, and compassion, however, can help ease this burden. By becoming more accepting, less distracted, and increasingly altruistic, leaders can more effectively manage their own time and expectations and work toward beneficial outcomes for themselves and others.

Bill George, a Goldman Sachs board member, is an advocate of the practice and teaches mindful leadership at Harvard Business School. "The use of mindful practices like meditation, introspection, and journaling is taking hold at such successful enterprises as Google, General Mills, Goldman Sachs, Apple, Medtronic, and Aetna, and contributing to the success of these remarkable organizations," George said. "These competitive companies understand the enormous pressure faced by their employees—from their top executives on down. They recognize the need to take more time to reflect on what's most important in order to create ways to overcome difficult challenges. We all need to find ways to sort through myriad demands and distractions, but it's especially important that leaders with great responsibilities gain focus and clarity in making their most important decisions, creativity in transforming their enterprises, compassion for their customers and employees, and the courage to go their own way. Focus, clarity, creativity, compassion, and courage. These are the qualities of the mindful leaders I have worked with, taught, mentored, and interviewed.

"As you take on greater leadership responsibilities, the key is to stay grounded and authentic, face new challenges with humility, and balance professional success with more important but less easily quantified measures of personal success," George advised. He acknowledges that this is much easier said than done but argues that mindful leadership offers a set of tools that allow us to stay highly effective on the job, without compromising our integrity. "When you are mindful, you're aware of your presence and the ways you impact other people. You're able to both observe and participate in each moment, while recognizing the implications of your actions for the longer term. And that prevents you from slipping into a life that pulls you away from your values."

This tension — between the demands of an important job and a clear set of personal values — can derail even the best leaders. As I traveled the country meeting mindful workers, I encountered many executives who, after they began meditating, simply quit their high-paying jobs. Which is why it is all the more remarkable to find deep practitioners who also remain devoted to their work — especially when they're at the top of one of the biggest carmakers in the world.

When I caught up with Bill Ford in the greenroom of an auditorium in San Francisco, he looked shaken. Ford, heir to the eponymous automotive dynasty and the former chief executive and chairman of the company, had just walked off the stage where, in front of a thousand people, he had come out of the closet as a meditator. Wearing jeans, a crisp dress shirt, and an expensive-looking blazer, Ford reclined on a white leather couch, nursing a bottle of water, as he explained to me how practicing mindfulness meditation had changed his life, and his family's company.

Ford's journey began with his own commitment to environmentalism. Growing up in northern Michigan, he spent time outdoors in all seasons, the forests and frozen lakes reminiscent of Scandinavia. As a boy, Ford latched on to the caretaker at an old fishing club his parents belonged to, following him through the woods, learning about the trees and fish. "That sparked an early interest in all things nature," he said. But it wasn't until he got to college that he realized that much of the world was being pillaged and polluted by the very industrial complex that had created his family's wealth. He returned home after finishing his studies, saw a strip mall where there had once been a beautiful meadow, "and I'd think, 'Gee, how'd that happen?'"

Ford studied liberal arts and philosophy, becoming one of the more contemplative members of the family dynasty and a committed conservationist. At the same time, he had been groomed to go deep into the family business, and he eventually rose to run the company. And even then, he kept reading philosophy, kept thinking about the natural world. Reconciling his vocation and his contemplation was a personal challenge. Often, his environmental views didn't square with the work his company did. In an old-line industrial company that was doing the bare minimum to comply with environmental regulations, how could he be true to his values?

When he joined Ford, he was told to stop associating with environmentalists and keep his views to himself. "I was considered a Bolshevik in the company," he said. Environmentalists were equally suspicious, believing he was a wolf in sheep's clothing. Ford was struggling internally. "How could I maintain my sense of humanity while still working there?" he would ask himself.

Then one day in the early 1990s he came across a book by Jack Kornfield, the mindfulness teacher, called *A Path with Heart*. Kornfield was among the first Westerners to bring mindfulness meditation to the masses in the United States, and in *A Path with Heart*, he lucidly explained how mindfulness meditation works, not only to relieve stress and improve focus, but also to help people become more emotionally receptive, more empathetic. "It literally changed my life," Ford said of the book. After reading it, Ford called up information and asked for Kornfield's home phone number. Once he got Kornfield on the phone, he explained who he was, and his dilemma. Then, after an initial call, Ford flew out to Spirit Rock for an in-person meeting. From that point on, Kornfield was Ford's teacher.

Ford the environmentalist continued to wrestle with Ford the industrialist. How could these two sides of his life coexist? he wondered. At times, Ford thought about walking away from the auto company, inherently a massive polluter. But by encouraging Ford to practice mindfulness of his own internal conflicts — analyzing his competing priorities and finding a way to balance them — Kornfield helped Ford get in touch with his intentions as a leader. And in time, it became clear that the scion was indeed committed to the family business.

But Ford knew he had to change it. Ford made it his mission to turn the company from an unredeemingly environmentally destructive corporation into one that was at least helping to change things little by little, even if it couldn't be perfect. "If we didn't get on the right side of this we would end up like the tobacco industry," Ford remembered. His fear was that in twenty years, people wouldn't want to work for Ford, and he would be ashamed to tell his friends about his work.

The change would take time and effort. When Ford joined the company, he saw other executives who "had lost their humanity." The corporate culture was fueled by ego and bluster, and leaders in the company let work dominate their lives. There was the manager who would end a meeting only when he had finished his cigar, no matter if the team had made it through the agenda thirty minutes prior. There was the executive who thought it was a sign of weakness if you left a meeting to go to the bathroom. And there was the manager who, when Ford asked him to lunch, said the next opening on his calendar was three years out. If this was what a life in the C-suite did to a man, Ford wanted no part of it.

That's when Ford started frantically calling Kornfield, who reminded him that while it was important to work hard in all the conventional ways — hitting revenue targets, effectively managing employees — what's most important is setting a good example that others can emulate. If he would be more mindful, those around and beneath him would be, too.

Ford had to tread lightly. He knew he was part of an emerging generation of mindful leaders but was also sensitive to the fact that not everyone in Detroit is ready for an open discussion of such things. "Being an environmentalist and a practitioner, I think they would have locked me up permanently," Ford said of his unlikely standing as a meditator who cares about climate change and oversaw one of the world's largest automakers. "But there is a new generation coming through. It's true in manufacturing, it's true in banking, it's true in almost every field."

This new openness among executives is a marked departure from the corporate culture of even a couple of decades ago, when sensitive types would have been run out of the building. "There was this notion not only that you had to work, but that you couldn't even admit that you had interests outside of work or a family, or something like this that was important to you," Ford said of a former incarnation of his namesake company. "That drove a lot of people into heart attacks. If they didn't have a heart attack they were massively unhappy. I'm pretty pleased that there's a new generation that is much more receptive to all this coming through."

But in time, he became more comfortable wearing his compassion on his sleeve. In 1999, early in his tenure as chairman, he looked out his office window and saw smoke billowing from the company's nearby River Rouge complex. He grabbed his coat and ran out the door. A deputy tried to stop him. "Generals don't go to the frontlines," the subordinate protested. Ford said, "Demote me," and hurried off.

A gas explosion had torn through the plant, killing six and injuring dozens. It was one of the company's darkest days. When company lawyers learned he had gone to the site of the accident, they were horrified, worried his presence might further expose the company to litigation. The lawyers protested again when, in the aftermath of the explosion, Ford forged a relationship with the families of the six victims, with whom he remained in touch years later. "That's what's wrong with so many of our corporations," Ford said of his lawyers. "It's one thing to meditate on compassion, but it's another thing to act on it."

Ford's behavior around the Rouge explosion was just one part of his push to create a more transparent, accountable company. "There's such a greater level of transparency in our company, and that extends. Once you have transparency into the business, you also have transparency into the people running the business." Ford pointed to Susan, the public relations executive sitting at his side. "It used to be that someone in Susan's job was to let as little out as possible. And it's because everything had to be shaped perfectly. And that's of course crazy, because none of us are perfect."

That attitude now extends to the conference room, as well. "There's much greater transparency in the business, it's much less hierarchical," Ford told me. "It used to be that everyone in the room was extremely aware of where everyone in the room was along the corporate hierarchy. I'm not naive; people are still aware. But it's not the limiting factor that it used to be. People will voice opinions and they'll speak up, so it's a much healthier organization."

Ford did not go so far as to offer mindfulness training in the office. "That's more of a personal journey," he said. Instead, he tried to use his influence to soften the edges of a once-hardened corporate culture, and to foster some awareness around environmental issues where previously there was none.

He would, however, talk to other executives about how mindfulness and self-awareness have changed his life. "I talk more about ethics and values and sense of community, because those are things that everyone can relate to. As soon as you start bringing in terminology that they're not familiar with, they shut down, or they think you're on a different planet. But those terms are universal, and I think everyone can get it."

During the financial crisis, Ford faced the biggest challenge of his career. Auto sales plummeted, his competitors had to be bailed out by the government, and he worried that he might be the one to preside over the downfall of his family's company. During those fraught months, he talked to Kornfield often for advice and continued his sitting practice. Every day when he woke up during the crisis, he would spend time meditating, setting the intention that whatever happened during the day, he would face it with a sense of compassion and loving-kindness.

As Ford oversaw layoffs, some of the fired employees would write the CEO letters. But instead of berating him, the workers thanked him for giving them the opportunity to work at Ford. He broke into tears as he read these but took some measure of solace that, no matter how bad the economy had gotten, Ford employees were still proud to work there. Ford hadn't become a tobacco company.

Those letters spoke to what Ford said was an innately positive culture at the company. Employees at all levels were active when opportunities to volunteer in the community came up, so he started the company's Volunteer Corps, which allows them to do community service on company time. "I wanted to institutionalize the spirit that was already there, of compassion," he said. "If all you're working for is stock options and paychecks, that's not enough."

Setting up the Volunteer Corps was part of Ford's commitment to culture at the company, and in the communities where the company operates. He made it a priority to bring clean water to towns near factories in the developing world, and improving education in towns in the United States. "Wherever we can help, we should," he said. "I'm a firm believer that we get back ten times what we give. The goodwill we engender, not just with the people we help, but with our own employees – it's a huge payoff. You could call it ethics. You could call it compassion. You could call it values. It all ends up in the same place pretty much as far as I'm concerned."

That sounded a lot like karma, and midway through our conversation I asked him if he considered himself a Buddhist.

After some hesitation and a glance at Susan, the PR lady, he said, "Probably. Yes. But it's not the religious piece that draws me to it. It's really the philosophy of Buddhism that I find really interesting. And I actually don't think of it as a religion, although it clearly is for many people. For me it's really a philosophy and a way of life."

Unprompted, and seemingly eager to discuss it more, Ford then launched into a discourse on the distinctions between the various schools of Buddhism. "I'm also not sure that a lot of the Eastern philosophy really fits in today's Western society," he said. "So therefore, you ask, 'Am I a Buddhist?' I'd say yes, but I'm not sure what type. Tibetan Buddhism has a lot of cool things, but it's so complex. All the deities? I mean, forget it. A lot of the Mahayana tradition is way too stylized and I don't get it. And then I think of the Theravada tradition, and a lot of it's very austere. It's probably closer to what I relate to, because it's easier to grasp. But going out and begging for food is not easy to relate to in Western society. So I don't consider myself a disciple of any particular school. The principles are what I relate to." It was one of the most unexpected spiels I'd ever heard from a corporate executive, revealing the depth of Ford's contemplative streak, and his crackling intelligence.

Before Ford retired as CEO of the company, he had a dark vision of life after his tenure at the top. "One of the saddest things I've seen is an ex-CEO," he said. "No one is telling them how great they are, the company plane is grounded, the adulation has stopped. They have no other identity. That really struck a chord with me."

During the financial crisis he would lay awake in bed, worrying he might become another casualty of the executive suite. But as he did that, he truly pondered "what it would be like to lose absolutely everything, including a large part of my own identity." What if the company folded, and he lost his job, and the family coffers were drained, and he was just another nobody?

"But I realized, through practice, that it really wasn't my identity," Ford said. "It was a lot of trappings, and it's stuff I care deeply about and people I care deeply about. But I realized through practice that the core of me would be just fine. And that the people I loved and cared about would still love and care about me. That sounds fairly trite, but I also know that had I not been practicing for a little bit of time, I think I would have understood that intellectually, but I know I wouldn't have felt it right here," he said, pointing to his heart. "I realized that losing everything really didn't mean losing everything."

Responsive, motivated by a sense of what's right, and empathetic with his employees, Bill Ford embodies the traits of mindfulness and managed to do so at the upper echelons of American capitalism. It would have been easy for him to simply charge through life as the heir to an automotive dynasty, never questioning the status quo. Instead, Ford, a longtime meditation practitioner, developed these qualities through countless hours on the cushion, and plenty of challenging introspection. These practices made him clear, focused, and compassionate — qualities he embodied, making him a great leader at his company and in the community.

Mindful leadership is taking root at big multinational corporations like Ford, and also at tiny organizations with much smaller staffs. And while the essential qualities of a mindful leader are the same, leadership itself can manifest in a variety of unique and surprising ways. For example, similar to the way that social responsibility is an extension of compassion, mindful leaders can find ways to empower others to become more compassionate. Even if they don't institute meditation training in the office, mindful leaders can foster compassion in others, creating a ripple effect. It happened when Bill Ford established the Volunteer Corps, and it happened in a Southern California food company started by a famous actor, too.

Around Christmastime in 1980, Paul Newman and his friend and neighbor, the writer A. E. Hotchner, decided that instead of buying their friends commonplace gifts for the holidays, they'd hand out a delicious salad dressing made from a recipe they had perfected over the years. It was a whimsical pursuit for Newman, one of the greatest actors of his generation — star of *Butch Cassidy and the Sundance Kid* and *Cool Hand Luke* — yet they found the experience of producing a healthful product that their friends might enjoy deeply rewarding. Working from Newman's basement, the men filled empty wine bottles with the mixture, slapped a crude label on each, and distributed them to their nearest and dearest. A few weeks later, most of their friends came back, begging for more.

It turned out there was a market for their recipe, and Newman and Hotchner set about founding Newman's Own. The for-profit company launched in 1982, producing salad dressings and soon moving on to offer pasta sauces, pizzas, and other goods. But rather than use the profits, which came quickly, to pad the pockets of company executives and investors, Newman's Own had a different mission from the outset. All profits, the founders agreed, would be given away to charity. To date, Newman's Own has given away more than $350 million to a range of causes.

Paul Newman wasn't into mindfulness, per se. He was simply, wonderfully, a generous, compassionate man who realized that lending his name to a for-profit company could do some good in the world. Yet when it came time to expand, Newman began working with someone who did have a deep understanding of mindfulness.

In 1992 Newman's daughter Nell approached her father about starting a line of Newman's Own made purely from organic ingredients. Newman agreed, giving her enough money to get started on the condition that the money be repaid to the foundation once she was profitable. Nell Newman wanted to focus on organic snack foods, offering people sweet and satisfying alternatives to the ubiquitous overly processed junk that fills the center of the supermarket. To get Newman's Own Organics off the ground, she turned to her friend Peter Meehan, a longtime meditator.

I was introduced to Meehan through alumni of the Antioch College Buddhist studies program. In 2000, when I attended that program, in Bodh Gaya, I got my first in-depth look at mindfulness. Meehan had taken the same course, with some of the same teachers, twenty-one years earlier, in 1979, the first year of the program. For Meehan, the most important practice he brings to the office is being mindful of his intentions.

Seeing clearly why he's making certain business decisions is a practice in its own right. With self-awareness about the implications of his actions for others, he is less likely to make unethical decisions. "The power of intention is profoundly important in life, in practice. It is fundamentally a core of right livelihood," he said, referring to the Buddhist principle of making a living without harming others.

One reason Meehan gravitates toward the practice of mindful intention is because it's easier to communicate to people who don't have a practice. Remaining alert to our intentions is as much an exercise in intellect as it is a feat of concentration. It engages the same rational, questioning mind that so often gets us into trouble but inclines it toward a more virtuous pursuit—continuous examination of the causes of our present state, and the implications of our future actions. Meehan said that a focus on motivation and intention, more than meditation, is easy to communicate to colleagues. "It's comfortable for people," he told me. "I'm not asking them to follow their breath, which is hard to do at a meeting or on the phone."

In his meditation training, Meehan has worked with a heightened awareness of intentions. On one retreat, after doing walking meditation—slowly pacing, so that the smallest sensations in his toes became as vivid as a slap to the face—his teacher asked him if he had noticed his intention to stop walking. Why had he stopped? Did he notice that choice? Or had he just mindlessly stopped walking, unaware of his intentions? "You start to see how granular it can be in those settings, and how grand it can be in some settings," he said.

Given Newman's Own's unique approach to philanthropy—namely, to give away all profits—Meehan has an easy time getting in touch with his intentions. So long as he's doing something work related, be it going over company financials, reviewing marketing plans, or managing his production chain, Meehan is contributing to the greater good. "By the simple act of us going to work, all these great things happen," Meehan said.

Early in the company's history, Newman's Own Organics took an innovative approach to allocating its philanthropic dollars. At first Paul Newman himself called the shots. But once the company started generating its own sizable profits, Newman handed responsibility over to Meehan. For a while, he made decisions about which organizations would receive his company's charity dollars. But after some time, Meehan decided to pass the baton. "None of this would be possible without the pretzel maker in North Carolina or the cookie maker in the Midwest," he said. So he began a program that gave his producers a say in how profits were handed out. Then, after a few years, some of the charities to which he had been giving began nominating their colleagues to have a say. The power of charity was rippling out, as people who had been touched by the power of giving were compelled to share it with others. "It was a powerful lesson," Meehan said. "It's better to give than receive."

Like other mindful leaders from Chouinard to Ford, Meehan is keenly aware that his business has a sometimes detrimental impact on the world around him. He remains troubled by the fact that the millions of dollars Newman's Own Organics has given to charity are all the result of excessive consumption of snack foods. But the solution, he said, is to "tie good results to it." If you're going to promote consumption, find ways to use the spoils from that behavior to do something positive in other arenas, he said. "You don't have to be a nonprofit," Meehan said. "You just have to have the right intention as a for-profit company."

For Meehan, exercising compassion as a mindful leader meant finding ways to distribute the fruits of his company's labor, benefiting a diverse group of causes, and also empowering others to discover the power of giving. For other mindful leaders, compassion is more overt and is best embodied when communicating with colleagues. Which is why one day, an unusual post appeared on the official LinkedIn blog.

• • •

LinkedIn, the social networking site for professionals, had gone public earlier in the year, making millionaires and billionaires of its employees and executives. This would typically be the time when a company like LinkedIn doubles down on its growth, using its newly filled coffers to roll out an aggressive expansion plan. After all, it is trying to catch up with cross-valley rival Facebook, which had also recently gone public. The two companies compete for users' time, advertisers' dollars, and engineering talent every day. But instead of emphasizing competition and growth, the blog post, by chief executive Jeff Weiner, was simply titled "Managing Compassionately."

Weiner wrote that compassion is the one management principle that he strives for above all others, even though it is consistently hard to achieve.

Compassion is not the same thing as empathy, he wrote.

> *Though oftentimes used synonymously in western culture, the contrast between the two is an important one. As the Dalai Lama explains, if you are walking along a trail and come along a person who is being crushed by a boulder, an empathetic reaction would result in you feeling the same sense of crushing suffocation and render you unable to help. The compassionate reaction would put you in the sufferer's shoes, thinking this person must be experiencing horrible pain so you're going to do everything in your power to remove the boulder and alleviate their suffering.*

Weiner wrote that he tries to bring the same kind of compassion in action to his work. When disagreeing with a colleague, for example, it's only natural to see the world through our own eyes. But instead of instinctively reacting based our own self-centered calculations of what's best, Weiner wrote that "it can be constructive to take a minute to understand why the other person has reached the conclusion that they have. For instance, what in their background has led them to take that position? Do they have the appropriate experience to be making optimal decisions? Are they fearful of a particular outcome that may not be obvious at surface level?" Listening compassionately, Weiner said, means making the effort to understand, and even identify, with your adversary. At the same time, he suggests bringing a heightened scrutiny to the origins of one's own ideas and emotions. He calls this "being a spectator to your own thoughts."

"Asking yourself these questions, and more importantly, asking the other person these questions, can take what would otherwise be a challenging situation and transform it into a coachable moment and truly collaborative experience," he wrote.

A few months after that blog post went up, Weiner explained the origins of his thinking on compassion. In the midst of the dot-com bubble he read *The Art of Happiness,* by the Dalai Lama, where he first learned the parable of the man being crushed by a boulder. That inspired him to begin weaving compassion into his daily life, trying to listen mindfully and become less emotionally reactive.

One day he realized that a colleague was managing poorly, bringing not one ounce of compassion to his relationships with employees. The colleague was undermining another member of their team at every turn. "They would do so with disparaging remarks or jokes that were made at that person's expense in a large group setting or staff meeting," Weiner said. "It made everyone uncomfortable, and I'm not sure the person doing it recognized the damage that it was doing." Finally Weiner confronted his colleague. "The next time you feel like making a joke at that person's expense or expressing anger or frustration, you should find a mirror and do it to yourself. Because at the end of the day that person's in the role because you want them in the role." Weiner suggested the colleague either play to the person's strengths, or find the person a new job.

A couple of weeks later the colleague came back and said he was changing the way he worked with his employees and would try to manage with more humility. But as Weiner listened, he realized he wasn't exempt from blame. Weiner, at times, was undermining his own team members. "As he was telling me this, I realized I was doing the exact same thing to someone on my team," he said. "It's something a lot of inexperienced executives do. It's a very human thing to project your own perspective onto others. The tendency will be to expect people to do things the way you do them. It's very natural." But it's not the right way to manage, he said. "You need to take a moment to put yourself in their shoes, to understand why they come with what they come with. What is their background, what is their baggage? From that moment going forward I decided that would be a first principle of management — managing compassionately."

This more compassionate style of management isn't at odds with LinkedIn's responsibility to its shareholders. "We're a very purpose-driven organization," he said. "Our vision is to create economic opportunity for every professional. We're going to create revenue if we do that well. We're going to create long-term shareholder value if we do that well." In fact, Weiner said that LinkedIn's approach to creating value — by creating opportunity for its members to make money — is aligned with his principle of managing compassionately.

When it comes to compassion in the office, Weiner acknowledged that "it's not enough to just state it as a vision." You have to reinforce it day to day. At LinkedIn, this goes so far as incorporating assessments of whether leaders are managing compassionately into their performance reviews. The company offers classes in mindfulness meditation to employees. When team members disagree, they're encouraged to explore the other's perspective and understand why someone is holding a view so unlike their own. Weiner now uses the promise of a compassionate workplace as a way to sell LinkedIn as a great place to work. "Culture and values have become perhaps our most important competitive advantage," he said.

• • •

If all our bosses were a bit more mindful — accepting, focused, compassionate — we all might be a bit happier under their supervision. And for those of us who are leaders ourselves, being mindful on the job would likely lead to greater job satisfaction personally, and happier employees reporting to us.

But as leadership training becomes one of the most popular avenues through which mindfulness is taught, there is concern in certain camps that something essential is being lost. Though Marturano, Ford, George, and Meehan cultivated their mindful leadership through years of meditation, many are coming to the practice with a more utilitarian outlook, believing it might be simply an exercise to improve management skills. Whether or not that is the case, the very suggestion that mindfulness might be used not in the service of personal transformation, but in the service of profits, is upsetting some purists. In the next chapter, we'll travel to the frontlines of the brewing fight for the soul of mindfulness.

9

McMindfulness

TWO GOOGLE EXECUTIVES were seated onstage before a crowd of hundreds in a hotel ballroom in San Francisco, speaking to a crowd at a conference celebrating the burgeoning popularity of mindfulness and meditation in the workplace, and in Silicon Valley in particular. Both wore all white, giving them the vague air of religious leaders, and one sat cross-legged, his feet folded beneath his butt in the plush chair. They were discussing "Three Steps to Build Corporate Mindfulness the Google Way," explaining how admission into the company's popular mindfulness course, Search Inside Yourself, had become one of the hottest tickets on campus. But before they could get very far into the talk, interlopers took the stage.

With swift, almost choreographed movements, two dreadlocked protesters unfurled a banner that read EVICTION FREE SAN FRANCISCO, a nod to the housing shortage that is being exacerbated by well-paid tech workers driving up area prices. A third conspirator whipped out a bullhorn, turned to the crowd, and shouted: "Wisdom means stop displacement! Wisdom means stop surveillance! San Francisco's not for sale! San Francisco's not for sale!"

The Googlers looked on with amusement and then irritation, as the protest continued for a couple of long minutes. The crowd stirred, unsure how to react. Eventually, the activists were ushered offstage, but not before a burly security guard tried (and failed) to wrestle the banner away from them. The confrontation was captured on camera and promptly uploaded to YouTube. And the jarring video, showing a tug of war between a black-clad bouncer and a pixyish activist at a conference about meditation, quickly went viral.

In the aftermath, one Googler on the stage did his best to defuse the situation. "Check in with your body and see how it feels," he said. "See what it's like to be around people with heartfelt ideas that may be different than what we're thinking." But the mood in the air had shifted. A note of discord had been injected into the ostensibly tranquil gathering of mindful leaders. Mindfulness was under assault.

The protest, a potent clash of the Bay Area's dueling counter-cultures, was a watershed moment for the mainstream mindfulness movement. It brought to a head, in very public fashion, the growing backlash against corporations and organizations that are seeking to use mindful awareness practices to improve not only personal well-being, but also workplace productivity, and even profits, too. After the fact, one of the protesters, Amanda Ream, a Buddhist and a union organizer, explained why she disrupted the conference. "Just like the gentrification of a neighborhood where new, wealthy people displace people who have lived there longer, the dharma is undergoing a process of gentrification in San Francisco today," she said, taking pains to keep mindfulness in touch with its Buddhist roots. "Lost is the bigger picture of the teachings that asks us to consider our interdependence and to move beyond self-help and addressing only our own suffering. The dharma directs us to feel the suffering of others."

What began with some initial skepticism that mindfulness could be effectively taught in a corporate setting has quickly blossomed into a full-blown revolt. The fury is coming from all sides and isn't reserved just for what many feel is the oxymoron that is "corporate mindfulness." Traditionalist Buddhists are concerned that a culture committed to reducing suffering is being appropriated in the name of capitalism. Skeptical secularists are fuming that seemingly spiritual practices are being introduced in the workplace. And the religious right is protesting what it views as a Trojan horse for Eastern mysticism. Among the most vocal critics, ironically, are proponents of mindfulness who believe that in the rush to popularize it, some essential qualities of the practice are being lost.

Willoughby Britton, the Brown professor who is rightly wary of some studies that purport to prove meditation's unqualified benefits, also points out that mindfulness today is more the province of science than of religion. "The main delivery system for Buddhist meditation in the modern West isn't Buddhism; it is science, medicine, and schools," she said. "There is a tidal wave behind this movement. MBSR practitioners already account for the majority of new meditators, and soon they are going to be the vast majority. If Buddhists want to have any say, they better stop criticizing and start collaborating, working with instead of just against. Otherwise, they might get left in the dust of the 'McMindfulness' movement." But as much as skeptics level specific charges of meditation run amok, it seems there is a more general sense of discomfort with just how mainstream mindfulness has become.

Things are apt to get worse before they get better. As more and more people practice mindfulness in one way or another, or at least purport to, the very word itself is in danger of getting watered down. Simply applying the label of "mindfulness" now seems like enough to elevate otherwise commonplace products and services into the rarefied air of the vaguely spiritual, and potentially more marketable. Weight Watchers is promoting mindful eating. Sodexo, a $15 billion provider of food service, has launched a line of healthful services called "Mindful." A company that makes "Mindful Mints" claims that its candy reduces stress. By slapping the word *mindfulness* on new products and services simply to make them fashionable, these corporations are making the word itself somewhat impotent. "Mindfulness" is at risk of becoming the new "organic." Indeed, there's even a butchery called "Mindful Meats," run by conscientious folks, but not meditators. It seems as if the more popular mindfulness becomes, the less it means.

I'm sympathetic to the skeptics, who worry that a noble practice is being quickly corrupted by modern marketing. But having witnessed mindfulness in action for fifteen years, it is clear to me that rarely, if ever, does exposure to meditation make someone a worse person. On balance, the folks who become more mindful tend to be happier, healthier, and kinder. Nevertheless, it is worth addressing the various critiques of mainstream mindfulness, if only to put them to rest.

One line of criticism holds that mindfulness, when divorced from the Buddhist tradition that spawned it, is incomplete and can actually be harmful. Simply using mindfulness as a technique to improve performance and make more money, the argument goes, is more about building up the ego than it is about breaking down the self. It's a fear stoked by comments like the ones made by Arianna Huffington, who has been unabashed in her belief that mindfulness is an enormously practical tool. "There's nothing touchy-feely about increased profits," she said. "This is a tough economy. Stress reduction and mindfulness don't just make us happier and healthier, they're a proven competitive advantage for any business that wants one." True as that may be, her comments are catnip for critics assailing the mingling of capitalism and contemplation. And for traditionalists, those are fighting words.

David Loy and Ron Purser, two professors of Buddhist studies, wrote a much-read article titled "Beyond McMindfulness" that has become a rallying cry for critics. It was published, of all places, on the *Huffington Post*. "The rush to secularize and commodify mindfulness into a marketable technique may be leading to an unfortunate denaturing of this ancient practice, which was intended for far more than relieving a headache, reducing blood pressure, or helping executives become better focused and more productive," they said.

McMindfulness, as they see it, is a commercialized, sanitized, and whitewashed version of the practice. Loy and Purser suggest that promoting mindfulness without emphasizing the ethical foundation of the practice is a Faustian bargain. "Rather than applying mindfulness as a means to awaken individuals and organizations from the unwholesome roots of greed, ill will and delusion, it is usually being refashioned into a banal, therapeutic, self-help technique that can actually reinforce those roots," they said.

To be sure, there are some high-profile examples of mindfulness proponents who have treated meditation like just another accessory to their lavish lifestyles. Bob Stiller, founder and former chief executive of Green Mountain Coffee, was once featured on the cover of *Forbes* as he meditated, his company valued at more than $6.5 billion. Stiller launched a mindfulness program at Green Mountain's Vermont headquarters, trained his leaders in mindful listening, and rolled out a mandatory Mindful Stretching program for the company's hundreds of factory workers. At the same time, however, Stiller himself struggled to embody mindful living. Green Mountain's surging stock had made him a billionaire, thrusting the entrepreneur into the highest realms of American capitalism. He retired as CEO in 2007 and began spending more time in Florida, an easy choice, climatologically, compared to Vermont. Most of his wealth was paper wealth, however, reflecting the value of Green Mountain stock. But when Stiller needed cash, he didn't sell stock. Instead, he began borrowing heavily against its current value. Company records show he had pledged 46 percent of his vast stock fortune as collateral against loans in 2008, a figure that soared to 78 percent in 2012.

Among other indulgences, all this borrowing was funding a growing taste for trophy real estate. He bought a pricey three-bedroom home on the luxurious Intracoastal Waterway in Palm Beach, Florida. Perhaps his most lavish purchase was a $17.5 million apartment in Manhattan's Time Warner Center. The sprawling space, with expansive views of Central Park, had been previously owned by New England Patriots quarterback Tom Brady.

In early 2012, Green Mountain reported weaker-than-expected quarterly earnings. Analysts grew skittish about the company's prospects, and the stock plunged, wiping out much of Stiller's paper wealth. This, in turn, compromised his line of credit. When investors borrow against stock, banks require them to keep a certain percentage of what they've borrowed in their accounts, what is known as a margin. And when Green Mountain stock fell, Stiller's bank demanded that he bolster his accounts, a so-called margin call. In mid-2012 his financial advisers at Deutsche Bank forced Stiller to sell $123 million worth of Green Mountain stock. The sale was a blow not only to his investments, but to his influence over the company he built, taking his stake down from almost 10 percent to just 5.4 percent. His board had no choice but to act. Citing the company's "internal trading policies," it stripped him of his title as chairman and publicly scolded its onetime leader.

That wasn't the end of Stiller's woes. Just days later, Stiller sold a 12 percent stake in Krispy Kreme Doughnuts, collecting $50 million to help bolster his rocky finances. "A lot of people don't understand that I have no other income other than selling stock or borrowing against it," he said at the time. "I went for a year where I couldn't sell any shares. Lavish is all relative."

Practicing mindfulness, clearly, is no antidote to materialism. Even as we grow more attuned to our bodily sensations and emotional and mental landscapes, we don't automatically leave our vices behind. In fact, mindfulness at times can simply make some of our less savory mind states all the more vivid. As we attend to whatever is happening, we find that where we had hoped there was love and compassion, there is instead lust and dissatisfaction. These are life's messy realities. Some of the very same people who promote self-lessness, compassion, and even mindfulness may themselves turn out to be materialistic and deeply insensitive. Bob Stiller may indeed have brought a measure of wellness to his workforce, and he may not have harmed anyone in the process of accumulating — and spending — his enormous wealth, but he clearly wasn't able to manage his own voracious appetite for trophy real estate, among other extravagances. As a result, he brought harm to himself, his family, and his colleagues.

But why would someone who spent so much time getting in touch with himself be so beholden to material goods? How could someone so seemingly spiritual in fact be so materialistic? There are no easy answers to these questions, and Stiller himself hasn't offered a comprehensive explanation for his materialistic proclivities. Mindfulness is no panacea for all our failings. But nor, as Loy and Purser might have it, was mindfulness the reason Stiller indulged his materialistic cravings. He was buffeted by the same longings that plague us all, the same wants and hungers that sometimes cloud everyone's decision making and get us in trouble. The only difference was that, as a billionaire, he had the bank account to indulge his desires. Practicing mindfulness doesn't automatically make us immune to such personal failings. Rather, all it can do is make it more likely that we will spot them when they start to arise, giving us the chance to do the painful work of slowly changing our habits. Unfortunately for Stiller, any modicum of self-awareness came too late.

Stiller's fall to Earth isn't so unusual. Ancient history and the recent past — in the East and West alike — are littered with stories of materialistic holy men. The veneer of spirituality has long been a guise for misbehavior and the accumulation of vast personal wealth. Holy men throughout the ages have adorned themselves in pricey baubles and luxurious silks. Even today, some of the most popular gurus in America have demonstrated a penchant for bling that strikes many as being out of touch with their mantra of inner peace. Bikram Choudhury, the litigious yoga teacher, cuts the figure of an oligarch, driving around Beverly Hills in a Rolls-Royce and sporting a gold-encrusted Rolex. A Thai monk with a taste for Louis Vuitton luggage and private jets had his assets frozen by authorities in 2013. These are the unfortunate outliers among hundreds of thousands of diligent meditators. And in our sensationalized media climate, they are apt to get as much attention as, or more than, say, the very robust mindfulness practice that Stiller implemented at Green Mountain headquarters. Critics may point to these cases of meditators gone wild and claim that because a few supposedly mindful hedonists are unable to keep their desires in check, all mindfulness is a sham. This, of course, is shoddy logic. On balance, mindfulness practice reins in our materialistic impulses.

An alternative, but no less disruptive, scenario occurs when people begin meditating, only to find it causes them to question their very identities. They begin to understand the impermanence of all things, including themselves, and become deeply disturbed. Some even become depressed, experiencing the "dark night of the soul," or a sudden loss of any sense of meaning to life. "I'm seeing people who came to meditation through MBSR or who are not Buddhist but are meditating 'to be happy,'" said Willoughby Britton, the Brown University professor. "They are following their breath or doing a mantra. And then they eradicate their sense of self. They freak out. That is a pretty common experience in my study."

Britton cautions that embarking on a serious introspective journey is no walk in the park, and that while the benefits can be ample

and obvious, there are risks, too. "The fact that adopting meditation may be very disruptive to your life, that you might require
supplemental therapy, or that you might be a little less functional
and lower performing while stuff gets kicked up and you are working through," she said. "That is not really in the current marketing
scheme."

There's more to the warning label. If mindfulness doesn't make
you materialistic or manic, it might just brainwash you. Critics of
mainstream mindfulness also contend that as corporations adopt
meditation practices, they will co-opt it, using it to subdue employees into mindlessly following instructions. "Up to now, the mindfulness movement has avoided any serious consideration of why
stress is so pervasive in modern business institutions," Purser and
Loy wrote. "Instead, corporations have jumped on the mindfulness
bandwagon because it conveniently shifts the burden onto the individual employee: stress is framed as a personal problem, and mindfulness is offered as just the right medicine to help employees work
more efficiently and calmly within toxic environments. Cloaked
in an aura of care and humanity, mindfulness is refashioned into a
safety valve, as a way to let off steam — a technique for coping with
and adapting to the stresses and strains of corporate life."

It's a seductively nefarious vision: corporations brainwashing
their minions with meditation, turning them into more efficient,
profitable drones. But as I traveled the country, observing mindfulness programs at various offices, the most flagrant offenders I saw
were guilty not so much of teaching meditation as a means to subju-
gate employees as they were of simple incompetence.

One snowy afternoon I drove up to the world headquarters of athletic apparel maker Reebok, outside Boston. During the lunch
break, a few dozen employees assembled in a conference room for a
monthly mindfulness class led by Richard Geller, who runs a small

consulting firm called MedWorks, as in "meditation works." In addition to Reebok, his clients include IBM and Papa Gino's pizza.

On this day Geller, a slight man with a soft voice who also has a business writing technical manuals, was paying a regular visit to one of his longtime clients, preparing to offer a one-off introduction to mindfulness that was slated to run for sixty minutes. A bit before noon he set up shop in a large conference room decorated with posters and jerseys featuring National Hockey League players from the Pittsburgh Penguins and the Edmonton Oilers, the oversize menacing faces of enforcers glowering down at a few dozen meditators who had come in search of serenity.

As I asked Geller what was in store, he grew nervous and began rambling. "I teach in a completely nonreligious manner," he said. "I use the same style that I used to teach technical practice, because this is the corporate world. I like my clients and future clients to view me as a vendor of something useful. It's very difficult to teach in the corporate environment. It's still a hard sell. People remember the Beatles and Maharishi on the Johnny Carson show, and they have other stereotypes in their minds. Some of them are accurate, because meditation did come from yogis in caves thousands of years ago. So it's a big leap to get them to purchase my services." Geller himself perpetuated some of the New Age stereotypes. As students trickled in, he flipped on a boom box that began piping out Native American flute music.

With the students seated and the music off, Geller gave them a primer on meditation. "It is perhaps more relevant today than it was thousands of years ago when it was invented, given how much our minds are bombarded with sensory information," he said. "You've been breathing since you were born, but it's not something you normally notice that often. Your breath is the most interesting thing in the world. Nothing else matters. Feeling those little bodily sensations, the air coming into the nose, down into the lungs."

Geller then instructed students in the body scan technique. "For this one shoes are optional. I like to take mine off," he said, awkwardly removing his loafers mid-sentence. "It starts with feeling your feet. It allows energy to flow up and down your spine, which doesn't always happen but is very nice when it does." He instructed students to relax their bodies bit by bit. "The mind is wide awake. The whole body is our object, your center of attention."

He finished with instructions on how to employ these techniques during the workday. "Sitting meditation, eyes open, is very helpful at work. You can do it at tense meetings; unbeknownst to everyone else in the room, you're sitting there meditating. You might find the idea and solve the problem everyone else is grappling with because you're calm. Those stress chemicals aren't shooting through your bloodstream." And that was it. There was no discussion about using awareness of fleeting bodily sensations as a means to witness impermanence in action. No mention of decreasing our emotional reactivity. This wasn't class one of an eight-week MBSR course. No one asked any questions. The Reebokers shuffled out the door, looking mildly perplexed, and went back to designing athletic apparel.

Geller seemed well intentioned, and his limited instructions may well help those on their lunch break enjoy a brief moment of connection with their bodies. But absent any explanation of the insights that mindfulness can spark, the whole affair was rather underwhelming. It was as if Geller and the management at Reebok believed that just by showing up to a single meditation class, the workers might be cured of whatever ailed them. When instead, mindfulness training in the workplace is but the first step of a long, personal journey.

And yet, this is a scene that is likely to be played out with increasing frequency in the years to come. Geller's meager offering is but one example of the great rush to peddle mindfulness training to anyone who is willing to pony up the bucks for an hour-long session that might appease worn-down workers hankering for any semblance of stress relief. In short order, it has become a crowded marketplace, full of products with dubious provenance and questionable efficacy.

eMindful, the company that administers Aetna's mindfulness training, has done some good work. By sending trainers in person to the health insurer's offices in Connecticut, it was able to make hundreds of employees fluent with mindfulness practices, reducing stress and improving overall morale at the company. But eMindful's primary offering consists of online classes administered by floating heads through a video chat session.

One morning I logged on to WebEx and joined an eMindful training led by Dawn Barie, a sprightly blond psychoanalyst from the Washington, DC, area. I was hopeful at first. Barie seemed nice enough, and her soothing voice, piped through my MacBook Pro speakers, was a gentle complement to my first cup of coffee. Twenty-six other professionals from around the country had logged on for the class as well, and after Barie conducted a quick survey via the WebEx group chat box, it was clear that most had never before practiced mindfulness. One man piped up and said he was "a bit anxious with all of the tasks due today, so trying to just enjoy being here."

Barie began with some basic sensory awareness exercises. She asked us to tune in to the sensations in our bodies, to note any apprehension we were feeling. I went along with it, slipping into practice. But before long, Barie had lost me. She never quite seemed to make eye contact, the result of the awkward videoconferencing technology. She wore a pair of big black headphones, a jarring reminder of the virtual classroom. My Wi-Fi connection, a bit slow that morning, occasionally cut in and out, freezing her mid-sentence. Moreover, all the other marvelous functions of my computer silently demanded my attention. There was e-mail to check, Twitter to scan, Facebook to peek at, a whole Web to surf. It's hard enough practicing mindfulness while sitting with your eyes closed in a quiet room, free from distractions. Expecting novices to be mindful while interacting with a device engineered for multitasking is a fool's errand.

When I tuned back in to Barie, she had begun leading a "visioning exercise." We were instructed to imagine walking along and seeing a good friend across the street. We wave to the friend, but the friend ignores us. "How did that make you feel?" Barie asked.

The answers from the virtual classroom were predictably meek.

"Maybe he didn't have his glasses on so he couldn't recognize me," someone named Shar chimed in via Web chat.

"I felt invisible," said another.

Barie's visualization exercise didn't seem to inflict any psychic damage on my disembodied classmates. But nor was it mindfulness.

Then, as if the WebEx course didn't create enough distance between teacher and students, Barie loaded up a video of someone doing yoga on her screen and played it over the WebEx. There we were, staring at a live stream of someone else's computer monitor, showing a video of a stranger doing yoga. If that represents the future of mindfulness, the critics are right to be concerned.

Kelly McCabe, CEO of eMindful, started the company in 2007 after a career on Wall Street that included stints at Lehman Brothers and a brush with J. P. Morgan chief executive Jamie Dimon. What she thought was going to be an instant hit was initially a dud. "I thought companies would be all over this," she said. Instead, eMindful barely stayed afloat for the first few years. The financial crisis was in full swing, and McCabe was offering a decidedly unique product. It wasn't just that she was trying to sell mindfulness; she was doing it in a virtual classroom. As McCabe pitched her nascent course, the rejection letters piled up. Finally, in 2009, Aetna signed on as an anchor client, and business has steadily increased since then.

Those initial rejections seem to have colored eMindful as a company, however. McCabe is reluctant to challenge students' worldviews too aggressively. Instead, she believes that a softer touch is called for. "That stuff comes up on its own," she said. "You can't do the practice and watch what your mind is doing without these things coming up — questions like 'What am I doing with my life? Why am I doing something if it makes me unhappy?'"

But there's another reason why eMindful's offerings are such lightweight affairs: McCabe is wary of scaring off her clients. It's one thing if mindfulness makes employees happier and healthier and more enamored with their jobs. However, it could quickly become a problem if they start challenging hierarchies and questioning the rationale for certain business decisions. A safer course for mindfulness trainers, it seems, is to avoid challenging the status quo, teaching meditation instead as a simple relaxation technique. Because after all, the company is paying for this training, and repeat clients can't be scared off.

Another line of attack on mindfulness today holds that it is being used to improve performance in unethical lines of work. Though the critics' screed on this point veers into the conspiratorial at times, Purser and Loy accurately point out the difference between those who simply practice attention-enhancing techniques and those who embody a fuller mindfulness. "The mindful attention and single-minded concentration of a terrorist, sniper assassin, or white-collar criminal is not the same quality of mindfulness that the Dalai Lama and other Buddhist adepts have developed," they wrote.

David Forbes, a professor at the City University of New York, is also skeptical of mainstream mindfulness. "People are working so hard to make it secular. In education and schooling, it is just about attention and self-regulation and control, and calming yourself," he told me. "But for what? What do you stand for? What are your ethical values?" Forbes is particularly concerned about the use of mindfulness in training the military.

"It's not just for PTSD; they're training soldiers to kill better," he said. "I'm all for getting everyone to be more self-aware. But there is a danger in using mindfulness to not feel angry, when maybe they should be angry about something." Forbes conjures up a sinister image: that of the mindful sniper, using his newfound skill of mental control to fix his scope on a target and slaughter with Zen-like efficiency. This phantom menace alone is enough to turn some people off the idea of bringing mindfulness anywhere near the military. But setting aside the fact that there's no record of any mindful snipers having been deployed to Iraq or Afghanistan, there's another reason why such fears miss the mark. Even if there were snipers versed in mindfulness, in the moment of the kill, the sniper, by definition, wouldn't be acting mindfully.

"That's not mindfulness," said Saki Santorelli, who runs the Center for Mindfulness in Medicine, Health Care, and Society at the University of Massachusetts. "The sniper may be highly attentive, highly focused. But if you think of mindfulness purely as an attentional stance, it's too simple. Harming, killing — that's not so useful, that's not so infused with mindfulness."

Instead, mindfulness in the military is generally being used for an altogether different task: healing. In one sense, mindfulness has been a core teaching of the U.S. military for decades now. "We should base our decisions on awareness rather than on mechanical habit," reads a passage in *Warfighting*, the U.S. Marine Corps book of strategy. "That is, we act on a keen appreciation for the essential factors that make each situation unique instead of from conditioned response." What is that state of intuitive awareness being described, free from preconceptions, if not mindful awareness? And today, mindfulness is being brought to the military by a woman named Elizabeth Stanley, who knows the military as well as anyone.

Nine consecutive generations of Stanley's family have served in the military, and she was deployed in Germany, Korea, and the Balkans. Yet Stanley emerged from her years in the service depressed and struggling with PTSD. As she moved ahead, picking up an MBA from MIT and a PhD from Harvard, Stanley traveled a now-familiar route: after trying unsuccessfully to medicate away her pain with drugs, she found some measure of relief in yoga and was soon practicing meditation.

In the years after 9/11 Stanley went on a number of intensive meditation retreats, honing her own capacity for deep concentration, nonreactivity, and compassion. Soon she was bringing this to bear in her work at Georgetown University, where she is a professor at the Edmund A. Walsh School of Foreign Service. Then in 2007 the Defense Advanced Research Projects Agency (DARPA) approached her about bringing mindfulness training to warriors. Today, she has trained hundreds of soldiers and Marines with Mindfulness-based Mind Fitness Training, or M-FIT, an adaptation of the MBSR course tailored to the unique stressors of combat.

The notion of meditating warriors strikes many as a contradiction: what place is there for a practice that espouses loving-kindness in the most effective fighting force on the planet? Won't meditating warriors lose their edge? Or conversely, might they use mindfulness to become more effective killing machines, misusing the practice in profoundly damaging ways? For Stanley, such simplistic thinking is symptomatic of the massive cultural gulf between the civilian elite and the military. Caricaturing soldiers as impressionable youth who will abandon their training upon exposure to meditation underestimates their seriousness of purpose. At the same time, coloring them as stone-faced killers looking for any edge on the battlefield is a gross simplification. Brushing aside such reductive thinking, Stanley argues that members of the U.S. military are just like other members of the U.S. workforce: complicated, sometimes confused, generally well intentioned, and frustrated, dissatisfied, and anxious, too. And she makes a simple and articulate case for the sound use of mindfulness in the military: troops who are in less pain will inflict less pain on others. "My intention is to reduce suffering," Stanley said. "But compassion doesn't pick favorites. If you reduce suffering in our forces, you are by definition reducing suffering in anyone whom those troops are coming in contact with down range."

An easy way to understand what Stanley is talking about is to imagine the experience of a soldier on the ground in, say, Iraq. If he's like the average American troop there, he's about twenty years old, hasn't graduated from college, and probably hasn't benefited from much emotional regulation training. Yet we ask a tremendous amount from these young men. We expect them to be calm under pressure, to exercise wise judgment in the field, and to exercise extreme discipline when deploying force. On top of all the normal stressors inherent in any job—demands from superiors, long hours, sometimes uncomfortable working conditions, difficult colleagues—troops have the added disruptions of the threat of injury or death, the moral weight of potentially using lethal force, long and repeated deployments, and the blurred lines between combatants and civilians.

"We're putting them in environments where the only way to succeed is to have incredible nonreactivity, to have Emotional Intelligence, to be able to read social and body cues, to show respect and humility," Stanley told me. "All of these are facets that require incredible situational awareness, not just of the people there, but of yourself and of the reactions you're having."

She's not advocating nonviolence, an unrealistic goal when working in the military. But she says compassion has a fierce side as well. "Sometimes the most compassionate act is in self-defense, pulling a trigger," she said. Stanley is suggesting that those entrusted with defending the country take the extra step of becoming emotionally aware while they are bearing arms. This is especially important now, as our military relies on technology more than ever before.

"One of the cultural consequences of our nation's overreliance on technology, and the undervaluing of the role of the human in security issues, is a misunderstanding of how the human body and mind work, and a divorcing, falsely, of performance and mission accomplishment from well-being," Stanley said. In other words, we might win military battles on the ground, but our troops are still coming back emotionally defeated.

Research is starting to bear this out. The army commissioned a series of Mental Health Advisory studies to investigate soldiers who had harmed civilians or personal property or pets while on patrol in combat zones. The data showed that soldiers who had mental health issues were three times as likely to lash out as those with a clean mental health history. This, to Stanley, is all the more reason to train combatants in mindfulness. If they can better manage their own emotions, they might be able to prevent making mistakes in the field. "People who are in emotional pain have less capacity to manage their impulses and reactivity," Stanley said. "Their pain is going to be exploding onto the scene around them. If you kill a noncombatant, you are only increasing the cycle of violence. You want to try to interrupt that cycle of suffering."

A 2008 study by Stanley examined two detachments of Marines headed for Iraq, one of which received mindfulness training and the other did not. As the deployment wore on, some who had received the training but were initially skeptical began calling Stanley back home, asking for tips. Others turned to brothers in arms, requesting support as they tried to reestablish a practice. Over time, the Marines who continued to practice mindfulness during their tour demonstrated the ability to regulate their attention more effectively, becoming less distractible and more focused, and also were able to regulate their emotions, experiencing fewer negative emotions and more positive emotions than their peers who did not practice.

Not all the Marines were onboard with the training. "Do not

fuck with my time off," said one. "We don't get enough and this shit took some of it away." Another: "This is yoga and meditation, don't like it." But many of the Marines who began to practice appreciated the instruction, wishing only that it was part of their regular training and not taught during their free time. Marine Major Jeff Davis, who led the pilot study among the Marines, initially worried that the training would "create someone less disposed to action or more disposed to over-thinking." But in the end the opposite proved true. Mindfulness, he said, "made the person more attentive, and when they did decide to act, they had a clear idea of what they were going to do and had a clarity of purpose."

Stanley has her critics. When Tony Perkins, head of the Family Research Council, a right-wing Christian group, heard that the armed forces were using mindfulness to promote relaxation and resilience, he blew a fuse. "The military seems intent on driving religion out and replacing it with wacky substitutes," Perkins said on his morning talk radio show. "They've added atheist chaplains, Wiccan worship centers, and now, meditation classes. But none of them are as effective or as constructive as a personal relationship with God." This is typical of the often knee-jerk reactions some people have to mindfulness despite the growing body of scientific evidence proving its efficacy, and more importantly, despite claims from soldiers and veterans who extol its virtues. One can only imagine what a little mindfulness might do for Tony Perkins.

Another factor muddying the conversation today is that because mindfulness is, to some people, synonymous with meditation, they can assume that anyone who meditates is practicing mindfulness. This is not the case.

There are many forms of meditation, and different practices have different aims. With mindfulness, the intention is to become accepting of things the way they are, even difficult situations, and the result is often a more peaceful, compassionate disposition. Other popular forms of meditation have different goals. In particular, Transcendental Meditation is experiencing a renaissance these days, thanks in part to a cadre of celebrity endorsers including comedian Jerry Seinfeld, celebrity chef Mario Batali, and the film director David Lynch.

Transcendental Meditation is one of a variety of meditative traditions that emphasize concentration practice. For some who practice TM, as it's known, silently reciting their individual mantra is a powerful way to let the outside world fall away and to tap into elusive reserves of energy and focus. Ray Dalio, the billionaire hedge fund manager behind Bridgewater Associates, says TM is one secret to his success, allowing him to be more creative and less beholden to the status quo. "It's a heck of a return on an investment for twenty to forty minutes a day," he said of his practice. "I think it's the single most important reason for whatever success I've had." Dalio is, by all accounts, a charismatic and deeply intelligent man. And he's quite philanthropic, giving away millions to noble causes. But Bridgewater is known as an unforgiving place to work — ruthless, overwhelming, and relentlessly focused on the bottom line, with a culture that borders on the cultish. Moreover, hedge funds reward financial engineering, not the production of useful goods and services. Could we say Dalio is mindful of his employees' well-being if that's the kind of company he runs? And while he may do some good with his money, it's worth asking what effect hedge funds have on important issues like growing inequality. How do they skew and manipulate the financial system? Do they create equitable opportunities for all investors, not just those with the most sophisticated algorithms and the best insider information?

Dalio's TM practice may lend him the veneer of spirituality, and his meditations may indeed help him focus and be more creative. But TM doesn't emphasize the cultivation of insight, as mindfulness does. Nor does it stress the importance of reducing suffering in one-self and others. There's nothing wrong with TM. By all accounts, it can do a lot of good for a wide range of people. But it would be a mistake to confuse it with mindfulness.

If only it were so easy. Conflating mindfulness with other meditative practices is inevitable, and the irony of a materialistic meditator is just too rich to ignore. Over time, there is a risk that this misunderstanding will erode support for broad applications of mindful practices. As critics conflate authentic practice with the broader universe of self-improvement techniques, it will be all too easy for some cynics to write off mindfulness altogether. Indeed, in a world that is broken in so many other ways, why should we expect mindfulness to retain any sort of integrity? As the philosopher George Santayana said, "American life is a powerful solvent. It seems to neutralize every intellectual element, however tough and alien it may be, and to fuse it in the native goodwill, complacency, thoughtlessness, and optimism."

Not even mindfulness is immune to the forces at work in the contemporary marketplace of ideas. In some situations, it is apt to be oversimplified and taken wildly out of context. "These things are common to many of the religions that have come to the West," Lama Surya Das, an American teacher of Tibetan Buddhism, told me. "They get commercialized, watered down, diluted, and mixed with social trends." Surya Das expresses some of the same reservations as Loy, Purser, and Forbes. "We need to be concerned," he said. "Yoga without spirituality is just physical culture. There's no sense of union. Mindfulness is becoming denatured. There's a lot more to it than health and lowering your blood pressure, or sharpening your mind to perform better, like a Navy SEAL sniper. Concentration without the insight is not that helpful." The parallel to yoga is particularly apt. Like mindfulness practice, yogic techniques have been around for thousands of years, emphasizing breath work and spiritual development. In recent decades, however, as yoga has grown popular in the West, much of the original motivation has been lost, and yoga has instead become a glorified stretching routine.

Meditation in America may be destined to be diluted, commercialized, and co-opted. But it doesn't mean that mindfulness, even in a secularized, popularized form, can't have a major positive impact on the lives of thousands or even millions of people. For now, at least, there is scant evidence to suggest that mindfulness is being used as a tool of repression of schoolchildren, workers, and soldiers, as the most alarmist scenarios would have it. True, some programs in the corporation might not go as deep as they should. And there's reason to hope that teachers will instruct children how to examine the root causes of their own emotions, not simply how to behave better in class. Given how much our work can drive all of us crazy, it would be irresponsible to keep mindfulness training away from certain organizational settings simply out of fear that it might somehow be denatured. And still, there is a more fundamental problem inhibiting the spread of authentic mindfulness: supply and demand.

Around the country, companies and organizations are hearing about the benefits of mindfulness and seeking out training. Yet all too often, their searches come up short. There are woefully few offerings for companies that are looking to bring mindfulness training into the office. Most of the successful ones today — and most of those featured here — are homegrown. In part, this is because it's still early days. It's only been a few years since mindfulness has been mainstream enough to be offered inside a corporation, and the market has simply not caught up with the public's appetite. But another holdup to the scaling of authentic mindfulness training is the lack of any common set of standards, any coordination, or any unified effort by the main voices in the field.

A human resources manager who is interested in bringing meditation training into the office but unsure of where to begin is confronted with a sea of disparate offerings, with little clue as to which is better than the next. You could just as easily end up with Richie Geller, playing Native American flute music at lunch break, as you could with Janice Marturano, teaching her rigorous version of mindful leadership. And even if you did get Marturano, her offering might not be the right fit. In addition to programs for executives, there should be accessible offerings for midlevel employees and factory workers, too. And yet there is little in the way of a coordinated effort by the mindfulness community to set guidelines and standards, or to advance any sort of unified agenda. There is no central repository of information on the subject, and no certifying body that legitimizes the field. The fact remains that thirty years after Jon Kabat-Zinn started a revolution with MBSR, there is still no national movement that ties it all together, no one group that is organizing, promoting, and providing continuing education for the mindfulness community. I figured if there was one place that ought to be pioneering such an effort, it was the place that started it all.

On a humid summer morning, I arrived at the Center for Mindfulness in Medicine, Health Care, and Society, part of the University of Massachusetts Medical School near Worcester. Here, in a low-slung building abutting a verdant park, is the group that has done perhaps more than any other to promote mindfulness. Initially led by Jon Kabat-Zinn, but headed for many years by his close friend Saki Santorelli, the center has trained more than twenty thousand people in Mindfulness Based Stress Reduction on-site and certified hundreds of teachers who offer the same curriculum around the globe. An annual conference hosted by the center gives mindful researchers the opportunity to present their latest findings. Affiliated scholars publish their own papers, and Kabat-Zinn and Santorelli remain active on the academic circuit. What's more, a growing program at the center is focused on introducing mindfulness training into professional environments.

Yet as I spent a day with Santorelli and his team, it became clear that for all their diligent work for the mindfulness movement, they had little control over where it was headed. More importantly, they seemed to have little expectation that they will be able to exert such control. They will continue teaching students in Worcester and training trainers who can teach MBSR around the globe. Kabat-Zinn and Santorelli even taught MBSR in China, a powerful endorsement given that government's disdain for anything remotely spiritual, and Buddhism in particular. But when it comes to coordinating any broader movement beyond their own laudable efforts, Santorelli and his crew seemed uninterested.

There's a missed opportunity here. After months of observing mindfulness at work around the country, I was impressed by the diversity of practice, and the lengths to which some were going in order to promote authentic practice in unlikely settings. Yet at times, I felt the range of teachings, certifications, retreats, and purchasable trainings was *too* diverse. For someone who is new to mindfulness, figuring out where to begin might well be baffling. Had I not spent time in India and maintained a regular practice that hasn't changed much in a decade, I'd be confused, too. And for the company that is looking to bring mindfulness to the office, who's the right vendor? When my own employer, the New York Times Company, wanted to offer mindfulness training, the HR managers in charge lamented the dearth of accessible, affordable programs for corporations. And while MBSR is among the most popular methods, there are numerous other groups that do equally good work. The UCLA Mindful Awareness Research Center has its own curriculum. Spirit Rock and Insight Meditation Society have a long history of introducing people to Buddhist meditation and are working on secular offerings.

Google and other companies have found effective ways to bring the practice to the office. Organizations like Mindful Schools have made great strides in adapting the teachings for the classroom. And Liz Stanley and others know how to make mindfulness accessible to government bureaucracies. The list goes on. Yet for all the fertile opportunities for collaboration, these groups are working in near isolation, letting the powerful solvent of American life dilute, and sometimes distort, the practice.

I floated the idea of a sort of National Organization of Mindfulness to Santorelli and others. It could be an umbrella group that would incorporate the folks in Worcester, UCLA's Mindful Awareness Research Center, Insight Meditation Society, and Spirit Rock, to name a few. With leaders from the field around the same table, a common set of standards for training and teaching could come together. A national nonprofit could certify good programs and act as a hub with resources for those interested in the fast-emerging practice. A common core of sorts could provide a bedrock for training, and differing tracks could specialize in training for individuals, businesses, schools, and the like. Teachers and programs could be certified, giving those new to the mindfulness world some confidence that whomever they were hiring was qualified. And continuing education credits, as is done in other professions, could ensure that teachers remain on their game. But while many agreed that such an organization might be nice, no one has yet stepped up and tried to fill the void. "Those professional organizations run the risk of tamping down a lot of creativity," Santorelli said. "They can exist to perpetuate themselves."

It's an understandable concern. Any such effort would require tremendous work, and a fair amount of bureaucracy. Plus, standardization presents its own risks, crowding out a lot of creative people who might have deep practices and virtuous motivations, yet for whatever reason don't fit into a more formal organizational structure. But absent a well-organized movement to nurture and promote high-quality teaching, the next few years are apt to leave many people who are looking for mindfulness training stuck with inferior offerings, or empty-handed altogether. In the meantime, the door is open for an explosion of charlatans and hucksters peddling mindfulness to the masses. Because the fact remains that as much as mindfulness is going mainstream, the marketplace for information, education, and training on the topic is a disorganized, confusing, and ineffective mess.

We may still be a ways off from millions of card-carrying members of the National Organization of Mindfulness hosting meditation sessions in every office across the country. That shouldn't stop us from setting out some best practices when it comes to engaging with mindfulness ourselves and introducing the practice to a broader audience. Because like it or not, mindfulness is now mainstream. On balance, that's a big step in the right direction. People are becoming less stressed, more focused, and more compassionate. Organizations and companies are embracing social responsibility and cultivating more humane leaders. And mindfulness is spreading gracefully, without damaging the integrity of any of the world's great religions. Buddhists who are worried that their timeless tradition is under threat would do well to remember that Buddhism has been persecuted for centuries and remains a lively and diverse tradition. As one popular saying goes, "The dharma takes care of itself."

True, mindfulness training in corporations can confirm the worst suspicions of the skeptics. It is pacifying workers, the rap goes, making them corporate lemmings who blindly follow the instructions of their greedy overlords. But the eMindful Web session wasn't nefarious. It was simply a first step on a much longer journey. Richie Geller's workshop at Reebok wasn't a brainwashing exercise. It was just an initial taste of a substantially larger meal. Not everyone who begins practicing mindfulness will embark on a lifelong quest to promote happiness for all and heal the planet. As I saw on my travels, there is a wide spectrum to the quality of the offerings. Many programs — like those at General Mills, Aetna, and Eileen Fisher — are comprehensive, emphasizing not only stress reduction and productivity, but also kindness and compassion. Others are lacking. But I never saw mindfulness training in the workplace having a negative impact.

What's most important is that people are practicing mindfulness for the right reasons. "I don't see it as a pacification technique, where you're suppressing people's rightful discontent," Sharon Salzberg told me, as we discussed teaching mindfulness meditation in the workplace. "It gives us lots of opportunity to see things in a different way. And then we can make clearer choices about what we want to do or help create. Maybe people will wake up to the fact that they need to leave."

Another way to say it is that mindfulness shouldn't be a selfish pursuit. Though practicing may help us perform better on the job, achieve more harmonious workplaces, lead better, and even make more money, it's important to remember that these are happy side effects of the practice, not the ends in themselves. The true purpose of mindfulness is to cultivate compassion for ourselves and others, to free ourselves from this perennial dissatisfaction that makes us feel as if nothing is ever good enough. "The main function of mindfulness is actually insight," Salzberg said. "It's not just to enjoy your tea more as you're drinking it mindfully. It's not just to have a better day, although that's wonderful. At some point people need to have that sense that mindfulness is about insight, and you can have a better cup of tea as well."

• • •

Loy, Purser, and a chorus of McMindfulness fear-mongers can be hyperbolic in their critiques. At times, their accusations — that capitalism is co-opting mindfulness — can border on the conspiratorial. But they raise important questions and are right to be concerned about the increasing superficiality of mindfulness. Rather than dwell on their critiques, however, it's comforting to know that some of the most accomplished mindfulness teachers in the world appear to be onboard with the practice's burgeoning popularity.

Thich Nhat Hanh, the Vietnamese monk who has spent his life bringing the practice to the West, said that as long as business leaders practice "true" mindfulness, it's OK if they also enjoy the benefits of being more effective at work and helping the business perform better. Simply practicing mindfulness, he said, will fundamentally change their perspective on life, opening their hearts, cultivating compassion, and naturally inspiring them to reduce suffering in themselves and others. He went on to provide a simple way to distinguish between mindfulness and McMindfulness.

"If you consider mindfulness as a means of having a lot of money, then you have not touched its true purpose," he said. "It may look like the practice of mindfulness but inside there's no peace, no joy, no happiness produced. It's just an imitation. If you don't feel the energy of brotherhood, of sisterhood, radiating from your work, that is not mindfulness."

10

The Future in Microcosm

THE FIRST WISDOM 2.0 CONFERENCE, a gathering of mindful techies, took place in 2010 at the Computer History Museum in Silicon Valley. Just a couple of hundred people attended the event, which featured engineers, entrepreneurs, and meditators talking about the challenges of being mindful in a digitally saturated world. "As much as we're connected, it seems like we're very disconnected," Soren Gordhamer, founder of the conference, told me when I covered it for the *Financial Times*. "These technologies are awesome, but what does it mean to use them consciously?" What transpired was a thoughtful discussion about how to be mindful in an always-on world, and what role technology might have in teaching mindfulness. It was among the first glimmers that mindfulness was breaking through to the mainstream, and it was about to take off.

Three years later, Wisdom 2.0 had quadrupled in size. As mindfulness had grown more popular around the globe, workers in Silicon Valley had taken to the practice with particular zeal. The conference now occupied a massive steel and glass pavilion called the Concourse Exhibition Center, located in the Design District of San Francisco, a neighborhood of industrial lofts and warehouses that is home to lots of start-ups. Some 1,700 people attended, more than twice as many as twelve months earlier. Over the next four days, a who's who of speakers from the mindfulness community, Silicon Valley, and the broader business world would take the stage and explain how meditation had changed how they live and work. Teachers like Jon Kabat-Zinn and Jack Kornfield were there. Contemplative neuroscientists like Judson Brewer had come from their posts in East Coast academia. Tech luminaries were in attendance, including Twitter founder Evan Williams and LinkedIn CEO Jeff Weiner. A-listers from corporate America had shown up, too, including Arianna Huffington and Ford Motor Company chairman Bill Ford, who used the venue to come out as a meditator. Padmasree Warrior, chief technology officer of Cisco, spoke about "applied wisdom in business life." Irene Au, former director of user experience at Google, talked about "cultivating empathic design." There were even two members of the House of Representatives, Tim Ryan from Ohio and Tulsi Gabbard from Hawaii, who explained how they hoped mindfulness might benefit their constituents. Like technology itself, Wisdom 2.0 seemed to be following Moore's Law, doubling in power at a predictable rate. And what was once an event about mindfulness and technology had become only nominally about tech; Wisdom 2.0 now encompassed a much broader discussion about how to expand the qualities cultivated by meditation throughout the professional world. While mindfulness is being practiced in workplaces around the globe, Silicon Valley, it was clear, had claimed the mantle as the epicenter of this burgeoning movement.

Inside the Concourse Exhibition Center, it looked as if Burning Man had come to the Bay. There were perforated wooden domes featuring built-in benches, looking like steampunk creations on the playa. Huge screens displayed the Wisdom 2.0 logo: a brain plugged into a lotus flower. There was also lots of bad art around—gauche paintings of pseudospiritual imagery made with neon acrylics, a mishmash of fiberglass Buddha sculptures, inflatable white stars hanging from the ceiling. Hipsters dressed like lumberjacks did yoga in the aisles. At dozens of round tables participants organized their own "unconferences," coming up with spontaneous panels such as "Workplace: The New Zendo," "Translating Mindfulness into Business Language," and "Why Can't Exxon, Chevron and the Rest of the Frackers Wake Up?" In between sessions, VIPs huddled in the roped-off backroom of the Mindful Lounge, a meeting space sponsored by *Mindful* magazine. Up a flight of stairs, an area was sponsored by Google and used for business meetings. Muscled security guards in black T-shirts guarded access to the backstage area, keeping the riffraff away from the conference elites. Even at a gathering ostensibly about letting go of the ego, it seemed that some age-old hierarchies were firmly in place.

Nonetheless, there was an earnest buzz in the hall as entrepreneurs, engineers, venture capitalists, and executive coaches mingled with meditation instructors and gurus from around the globe. I ran into people I knew from both worlds — sources I had talked to regularly while covering Silicon Valley businesses years before, and mindfulness experts I had gotten to know while writing this book. It was a convivial atmosphere, and each spontaneous meeting in the hallways felt like a serendipitous moment, with new and important connections being forged near the complimentary green tea stations.

At one of the first panels, Gordhamer asked Jon Kabat-Zinn, the granddaddy of mindfulness, why he was there. "I'm here for one purpose only, but I don't have any idea what it is," Kabat-Zinn said. "I have a lot of different ideas about what it is, but there's something about the mystery of it that is very seductive. This is not a conference, and maybe it's not a show. But maybe it's a showing up. There is some kind of magnetic attraction that has brought us all here, from near and far."

Kabat-Zinn went on to say that with so many people plagued by information overload, it was important to distinguish between attending a conference like this simply to fill the mind with more information, and showing up with a willingness to change the way we live our lives. "I see this as maybe the manifestations already of the early phases of what I would call a global renaissance of awakening, of true wisdom. And let's just recall for ourselves that we are in the information age. This is not called Information 2.0. This is called Wisdom 2.0," he said. "And that is a huge stretch for us, how we are going to deal with all this information that is so overwhelming us that we are perpetually self-distracting . . . What we're talking about is diving deeply into the full dimensionality of our own being and understanding how to allow that dimensionality to emerge through multiple avenues, multiple intelligences, multiple rhythms."

If that didn't entirely make sense, it didn't have to. The crowd lapped it up. The next day Arianna Huffington took the stage wearing a sculpted emerald dress. Ever the chameleon, she has over the course of her career pivoted from Republican to Democrat and from commentator to entrepreneur. After selling *Huffington Post,* the political blog network she founded, to AOL for $315 million, she pivoted once more and has devoted herself to spreading the gospel of health and well-being, including mindfulness. "For me this is Disneyland," she said. "I can't have enough of these conversations, which also happen to be the most important conversations you can be having right now."

Huffington has no illusions that people will suddenly put down their smartphones and stop surfing the Web. She knows that technology is a deeply ingrained part of our lives and will only become more so in the years to come. She also knows that our digital distraction is a recipe for unhappiness. "Multitasking is one of the great ways that we are cheating ourselves from being fully present," she said. Huffington's concern, then, is looking for ways to fight fire with fire. "How can we use technology to help us disconnect from technology?" she asked. Her answer, besides trying to cultivate a modicum of mindfulness in the *HuffPo* offices with meditation teachers and nap rooms, is to flood her eponymous websites with articles promoting the virtues of contemplative practices, and to develop apps that encourage meditation. "We will look back at this as a historical moment, when many things aligned," she told the crowd. And while Huffington mingled with her fans after the talk, it was impossible to shake the air of celebrity worship around the event. After a while, she was whisked back to the VIP lounge where the speakers reclined on leather couches and enjoyed fruit plates.

With its mix of feel-good psychology, celebrity cameos, and savvy marketing, Wisdom 2.0 has become the de facto public face of this burgeoning movement, the essential conference for the mindful set. It offers up plenty of fodder for the McMindfulness critics, who view events like this as anathema to the introspective essence of the practice. (It was at a Wisdom 2.0 event that the protesters unfurled their banner attacking Google.) And at times, the conference was hobbled by the same sort of big-tent inclusiveness that waters down the potency of any broadly defined left-wing movement—think a spiritually minded Occupy Wall Street, with its mishmash of social, political, and environmental causes. The conference was ostensibly about mindfulness, compassion, and other contemplative traditions, yet there were precious few opportunities for practice. Kabat-Zinn's words echoed in my head. It seemed everyone knew they were supposed to be here, but had no idea why.

But there's plenty to like about it all. Gordhamer is good-natured and a serious meditator, and many of the speakers at Wisdom 2.0 have authentic practices and sound motivations. I've spoken at his events, too. And altogether, the Wisdom 2.0 team has pulled off a remarkable feat. They have taken what was only a few years ago a fringe movement of closet meditators and gotten some of the biggest names in corporate America to profess their allegiance to it. They have done the unthinkable, making meditation mainstream. "There are lots of flighty New Age crystal conferences that I wouldn't want to go to, and then there's a ton of business conferences that I do attend as part of my job," said Bradley Horowitz, a Google executive and committed meditator who was speaking later in the day. "But there's not a lot of places where you can go and hear Jeff Weiner and Bill Ford talk about how they focus their attention on attention."

Wisdom 2.0 is thriving in Silicon Valley for good reason. These days, it seems no tech company is complete without its own in-house meditation program. Adobe, Apple, Asana, Cisco, eBay, Facebook, Genentech, Intel, Juniper Networks, LinkedIn, Twitter, and more all offer mindfulness in the office in one way or another. Jon Kabat-Zinn leads an exclusive retreat for technology leaders once a year. Thich Nhat Hanh, the Vietnamese monk who makes mindfulness a foundation of his hugely popular teachings, is now a regular in the valley, presiding over tea ceremonies in the area attended by tech company chief executives like Marc Benioff of Salesforce.com. "When I talk to Google and the other companies, I will tell them to use their intelligence and goodwill to help us create the kind of instruments to come back to ourselves, heal ourselves," said Thich Nhat Hanh. "We do not have to reject or throw away all these devices but can make good use of them." Thich Nhat Hanh says he wants technology to help people reduce their stress and temper their anger and believes Silicon Valley has the wherewithal to help that happen. "Staff at Google want to know how to transform their suffering just like all other living beings," he said. "They can understand the teaching and practice well and can spread this and they have the means to do that." Silicon Valley, it seems, is the frontline of mindfulness at work.

It's no surprise. This is California, after all, where so many progressive movements have taken root. Name a cause—the antiwar movement, immigration reform, feminism, gay rights, medical marijuana. Each has found early, ample, and enthusiastic converts in the Bay Area. So it is only natural that mindfulness finds its base there, too. Indeed, there's something special about Silicon Valley's power to shape the future. This region is synonymous with innovation. It's not a stretch to think that the companies that are trying to disrupt information, advertising, and media are also attempting to hack office culture. This open-mindedness is no doubt, in part, why spiritual teachers like Suzuki Roshi settled in the Bay Area, and why Steve Jobs felt comfortable being an overtly Buddhist CEO. "The valley has always been at the intersection of these two phenomena," said Bradley Horowitz, the Google executive. "If you look back to the first Eastern mystics who came over, it's very much a part of Northern California culture." As religious studies scholar Huston Smith wrote in the foreword to *Zen at Work,* the autobiography of an early IBM employee who led a double life as a Zen priest, Silicon Valley is "the future in microcosm."

Today that idealism is part of the very DNA of some technology companies, which, as business and cultural pioneers, are helping mindfulness spread as fast as a viral video of a sneezing panda. What takes root in California often inspires imitators far and wide, and it looks to be no different when it comes to meditation. "It can be tempting to dismiss this as just another neo-spiritual fad from a part of the country that's cycled through one New Age after another," the journalist Noah Shachtman wrote in *Wired.* "But it's worth noting that the prophets of this new gospel are in the tech companies that already underpin so much of our lives. And these firms are awfully good at turning niche ideas into things that hundreds of millions crave."

Take, for example, billionaire Twitter founder Evan Williams. Williams was never going to be the most obvious CEO. While many of today's business leaders climb to the top through a mix of charisma, confidence, and bravado, Williams was always the shy, thoughtful type. His early successes were notable but kept him mostly below the radar. A company he founded, Pyra Labs, developed an early publishing platform called Blogger. Even after Google acquired the company in 2003, Williams didn't become a tech celebrity. But a few years later, with a little company called Twitter, he had a true breakout hit.

I remember the first time I interviewed Williams in 2010, at Twitter's inaugural conference for developers who used its API. The company was becoming a mainstream fixture by this time, and Williams had faced the glare of the flashbulbs many times in recent months. But when I sat down with him and cofounder Biz Stone, in a staging area at the Palace of Fine Arts in San Francisco, Williams spoke in a near whisper. My recorder barely picked up the audio. The man behind one of the greatest broadcast mediums ever invented seemed reluctant to be heard.

When I caught up with Williams a few years later, at the office of his latest company, Medium, he was almost a different man. Still tall and lanky, with an unexpressive face and big, placid eyes, Williams nonetheless had a new air of confidence about him. Some of this, perhaps, was attributable to the success of Twitter, which had gone public, making Williams enormously wealthy. But part of it also seemed to be a newfound calm and ease. Perhaps wealth had bolstered his sense of self-worth. Or perhaps it was the fact that he had begun meditating.

Williams, founder of the ultimate short-form messaging service, was taking a different tack with Medium than he had with his earlier hit. The company, which offers a simple user interface for publishing long-form writing, seems to be Twitter flipped on its head. The company attracted easy venture capital money, and the downtown San Francisco office of Medium has all the trappings of today's Silicon Valley start-up. A hive of millennials in jeans and T-shirts buzz around an airy open floor plan stocked with organic food and potent coffee. Yet it is not the cool factor, the résumé of its founder, or the early traction that is the defining characteristic of Medium's culture. Instead, it is that at this very early stage — with just a couple of dozen employees — Medium is a mindful company, embracing the value of deep listening, a less hierarchical organizational structure, and even silence.

Raised on a farm in Nebraska, Williams has retained his midwestern humility. He dropped out of college and says he still feels insecure about his educational pedigree, his own version of "imposter syndrome." As he founded a series of successful companies, this translated into an awkward, and often ineffective, management style. Williams was very good when it came to giving feedback on product design, but less skilled at getting the most out of his team. "My Achilles' heel was always relating to people," he said. "I was good with a small group because within my inner circle I could treat everyone like peers, but when the company grew, I found that rather stressful. I'd fake it, and of course people sense that. It hurt my effectiveness."

Williams, always curious and never afraid to tinker, had dabbled in meditation over the years. But only recently, as a growing number of Silicon Valley entrepreneurs turned to mindfulness, did he try it in earnest. What was at first a somewhat solitary pursuit began to take shape as Williams started working with Jonathan Rosenfeld, an executive coach who incorporates mindfulness into his training. That initial taste led to a burgeoning daily practice. Now Williams uses an app called Lift to keep track of his daily meditation. Developed by his friend, sometimes business partner, and fellow meditator Tony Stubblebine, Lift has caught on with a new generation of digerati who are enthralled with the "quantified self" movement, in which every activity, calorie, and moment is tracked and measured using new technology. And Williams is bringing meditation to his colleagues, too. In the company's early days, Medium employees were already going on retreat together. The team attended two offsites in Marin County, each of which included long periods of silent mindfulness meditation. Since then, Williams has turned to Will

Kabat-Zinn, son of MBSR pioneer Jon Kabat-Zinn, to lead weekly meditations in the office. The courses were so popular that Will Kabat-Zinn started offering back-to-back sessions, so everyone in the office could attend.

For Williams personally, mindfulness has changed the way he's performing at work. No longer the reluctant manager, he has grown more adept at managing his growing staff, embodying many of the qualities of a mindful leader. "It's affected me a great deal, and as a leader of the company my energy is different and I relate to the company in a different way," Williams said. Mindfulness has also made him more comfortable in his own skin. "The DNA of a company comes from the founder's personality," he said. "If I'm less anxious, everybody's less anxious." He's realized that he doesn't have to be a Type A leader, that he doesn't have to be a great public speaker. Thanks to the self-awareness cultivated through mindfulness, Williams has embraced a more serene approach to his business life. It's not that he has stopped working hard, or that he isn't trying to grow the company in specific and ambitious ways. But moment to moment, he's become more accepting of what's happening with the business and, most importantly, with himself. And by not striving so hard to act in inauthentic ways, he has freed himself to be more attentive to the things he's actually good at—like product design. "It doesn't give you skills you don't have, but it lets you tap your potential," Williams said of mindfulness.

For his employees, Williams sees mindfulness as a needed counterweight to a culture that is notorious for burnout. "Start-up culture historically and stereotypically is this hard-driving, work 24/7, sleep under the desk, fairly macho culture where mindfulness seems very out of place," he said. "But we're hiring you for your brain, and this makes your brain better. From a very selfish perspective we want you to do this. You won't be seen as doing nothing if you're meditating here."

To drive home this point with Medium employees, Williams penned an internal memo titled "Meditation: Improving Action Through Inaction." In it, he reiterated that "we encourage you to take time during the workday to do nothing. That is, close your eyes and sit quietly without distraction . . . we hope you'll learn the value of doing nothing." But Williams also wrote that "personal happiness, however, isn't the reason that we provide the opportunity to do nothing. Guided meditation might be a perk, but we also think of it as a calculated investment. To be more mindful is to be more present in your life. In cultivating the art of 'non-doing,' you will also learn to act (and work!) more deliberately." Williams went on to tout the value of being unconditionally present in the workplace ("The practice focuses not on changing who you are or what is happening around you but on 'paying precise, nonjudgmental attention to the details' of daily life; meditation alters how you inhabit the world as it already exists") and used the familiar analogy of meditation as exercise for the brain before making some salient points about practicing mindfulness at work. "Mindfulness makes you a better person in ways that simultaneously make you a better team player: people who meditate also show increased activity in a section of the brain associated with empathy," he wrote. "Whether you're a product designer or a backend systems engineer, the ability to relate to others might very well be integral to increasing user engagement or rooting out the recent site regression." It was an impassioned call to inaction by one of the most successful entrepreneurs of our time, and he ended by tying mindfulness to the very mission of the company itself.

"Our goal at Medium is to create a platform that encourages users to read and write online in a more mindful way," Williams wrote. "Yet we also live our lives online; taking a break from working often involves continued sensory overload and indiscriminate — or mindless—media consumption. Meditation might just make Medium better and more beautiful by making you, the people who build it, more mindful in every aspect of your lives."

If this is the new face of mindfulness in corporate America, the McMindfulness critics have little to fear. Williams is emphasizing real meditation practice as a means to cultivate mindful awareness, has transformed his own leadership style for the better, and is creating a humane environment where his employees can thrive. Medium may not have set out to stop global warming or end world hunger, but it's doing important work in its own field and planting the seeds for a more mindful technology industry. And as Thich Nhat Hanh said, simply by practicing meditation, Williams and his employees are growing more compassionate, which will in time inspire them to become kinder to themselves, and more socially responsible toward others.

Silicon Valley companies want nothing more than to be the most popular kid at the party. They chase users before revenues and value buzz over business models. They also don't want to be left behind. Fear of missing out is a powerful motivator. So when Twitter founders and Googlers make headlines by publicly embracing mindfulness training, it isn't long before many of their corporate peers follow suit. There's nothing wrong with this, of course. But at times, it's unclear if technology companies are adopting mindfulness so rapidly because they actually believe it will make their companies better, or if they are doing it because everyone else seems to be doing so. Either way, mindfulness training is spreading like a computer virus through the technology campuses of the Bay Area.

At Adobe's San Francisco office, in a retrofitted brick warehouse that once stored supplies for miners during the Gold Rush, mindfulness is all about productivity enhancement. Code-named Project

Breathe, Adobe's mindfulness initiative was pioneered by Scott Unterberg, a senior program manager for the company's cloud computing division. To employees, Unterberg pitches mindfulness as a chance to "recharge your batteries" during the day, tapping into a rich well of sustained focus and energy instead of getting jacked up on coffee. "Instead of drinking a latte, getting amped, going into caffeine tailspin, and being so wired by the end of the day that you can't be productive, you can take a break, clear your head, and keep going," he told me when I visited Adobe one summer.

Demand for Project Breathe is high. Hundreds of employees have participated, academics are lining up to track the results, and the program is expanding to encompass a guest speaker series. I dropped by Adobe's San Francisco office just in time to join the weekly Wednesday afternoon meditation. Two dozen employees from across the organization had gathered in a narrow concrete room. Perched on colorful cushions, the engineers dropped into silence at the chime of a bell. We sat for five minutes, a bell rang, the group exchanged pleasantries, and then the bell rang once more, ushering in a fifteen-minute period of silence. The bell rang a final time, smiles floated around the room, and then the employees headed back to their iMacs. It was a pleasant interlude in the middle of a busy day. No talk of changing the way our brains work. No mention of decreasing our emotional reactivity. Just a quick recharge before returning to the cubicle. To the human resources department that had to sign off on Project Breathe, this uncomplicated approach is no doubt part of the appeal. Happier employees are more productive employees, and healthier employees are less expensive. Hundreds of Adobe employees have participated, and the program is growing fast.

And at Intel, the chip maker, a similar effort is under way. Lindsay Van Driel, a manager at the company, developed the program with a local yoga and meditation instructor, after being inspired by

the burgeoning movement in Silicon Valley. With a mix of meditation and discussion, Awake@Intel resembles MBSR more so than
Project Breathe at Adobe. Marne Dunn, a digital literacy strategic
program manager at Intel, began taking the Awake@Intel course
and now helps teach it. She said it has allowed her to better manage her self-criticism. "The main benefits are aroused awareness of
myself and how critical I am of myself and not allowing negative
self-talk," she said. "It was a matter of being frustrated that I wasn't
getting anywhere and I wasn't being heard. I was finding when you
have negative stuff going on, you're projecting that."

Soon after it was launched, Intel had spent more than $75,000
on the program and was scaling it up, spreading it to offices around
the world. More than 1,500 employees have participated, and initial
results are encouraging more investment. Awake@Intel students
said they were happier and more creative, and were better able to
focus and be more collaborative with their colleagues. "If we show
people pages and pages of our feedback, there's nothing that anyone can say that takes away the validity of that experience," said Van
Driel.

From LinkedIn CEO Jeff Weiner's campaign to become a more
mindful leader, to Facebook's experiments with compassionate engineering, mindfulness is changing Silicon Valley in ways large and
small. And still, Awake@Intel, Project Breathe at Adobe, and a number of other similar programs at the likes of Salesforce.com, AOL,
and others all exist in the shadow of the course that has set the bar
for programs for teaching mindfulness at work. The one led by a
gnomish multimillionaire from Singapore. The one with the most
startling ambitions. The one, of course, at Google.

The sprawling Googleplex, home of the world's most influential
technology company, in the perennially sunny south San Francisco
Bay, has grown famous over the years as much for its culture and

perks as for the products it creates. Beside the tyrannosaurus skeleton and the yellow brick road are a community garden and a café serving free organic food. An entire service economy thrives within the campus, complete with dry cleaner, bike repair shop, and personal trainers. The workers who enjoy these corporate luxuries are the same engineers who scan the world's books, advance artificial intelligence, and design self-driving cars. It is this strange mix of material luxury and intellectual rigor that makes Google one of the world's most sought-after employers. *Fortune* has named it the best place to work four times, including in 2011 and 2012. Part of Google's magnetism comes from the missionary zeal of its founders, who set out to organize all the world's information and make it universally accessible, all while making the company a good global citizen. And though the company hasn't always lived up to its lofty aspirations — invading people's privacy at one turn, snuffing out competitors at the next — it hasn't lost touch with its idealism. Talking to Googlers, you still get the sense that they really believe they can solve the world's problems.

Now Google is taking its corporate mantra, "Don't be evil," and turning it inward. With Search Inside Yourself, a course in mindfulness and Emotional Intelligence that is among the most popular offerings on campus, Google seeks to intervene in the lives of its employees with techniques that foster compassion, love, and altruism. Not only is Google trying to do no harm, but at least some of its employees have much more audacious goals. As Chade-Meng Tan, the founder of the program, told me, "We're trying to create the conditions for world peace in this lifetime."

Meng is a forty-something-year-old man of Chinese descent with a toothy smile, pockmarked cheeks, and a mop of black hair. He is always grinning and quick to crack a thickly accented joke, but his joviality belies his deep intelligence. He was Google employee number 107, and that kind of seniority — and wealth — means he can now do just about anything he wants. A few years ago he gave himself the job title of "Jolly Good Fellow" and began serving as the unofficial ambassador to dignitaries visiting its Mountain View campus. When ex-president Jimmy Carter comes to Mountain View, Meng greets him. When Taylor Swift comes to visit, Meng is there with a smile. But this high-profile schmoozing is just the star-studded window dressing for Meng's real mission at the company. While his fellow Googlers work to engineer new algorithms, Meng has embarked on his own project, *social engineering*. He is the founder of Search Inside Yourself, perhaps the most finely tuned program on the planet for bringing contemplative wisdom into the workplace. And in a few short years he has made Google — already the epicenter of the technology world — the epicenter of the mindful work movement as well.

I arrived at Google on a warm afternoon to attend the last session of the two-month course. A couple dozen Googlers — a mix of high-achieving engineers, product managers, and salespeople — had squeezed into a sun-drenched classroom with walls painted in Google's signature primary colors. At the head of the class was Meng, sitting cross-legged on a barstool, as if he were levitating. Nearby was Rich Fernandez, the Watson to Meng's Sherlock Holmes.

The theme of the day's class was "Effective Leadership Skills." It sounded like the kind of dry syllabus you might find at nearby Stanford Business School. But instead of teaching Googlers how to become hard-nosed managers, squeezing every last drop of productivity out of their intimidated underlings, Meng talked about compassion. In a company like Google, he said, simply looking out for yourself will take you only so far. Organizations are complex, interdependent systems that require not only cooperation, but often self-sacrifice. As a colleague, you should understand that your own success depends on the success of your teammates. Instead of trying to do the least amount of work possible while still getting the

job done, try offering your services to a colleague in hopes that together, your team might be more efficient. And as a manager, instead
of working your reports so hard that they are burned out, seek to
manage them effectively, pacing their workload so they can maintain a baseline efficiency.

"There's a false dichotomy between getting shit done and being
loved," he said. "We usually choose 'getting shit done' because we
have to pay the mortgage," Meng said. "But being loved is good for
your career. When you are loved, people will work harder for you."
To back up his point, he cited the work of James Kouzes and Barry
Posner, authors of *Encouraging the Heart,* a classic tome of management theory. "Leadership is not an affair of the head," they wrote.
"Leadership is an affair of the heart."

Drawing on some of the foundational principles of mindfulness
and compassion, Meng went on to explain that for Googlers to excel
at their jobs, they needed to be not only proficient and productive,
but also compassionate and lovable. "Why are we in a Google class
talking about compassion?" Meng rhetorically asked the two dozen
students. "Because compassion is essential to leadership." The
Googlers were rapt.

After Meng's introductory talk, he turned things over to Fernandez. Fernandez, a beaming forty-five-year-old with a closely mani-
cured beard, wore jeans and a bright blue Google Maps T-shirt that
read I AM HERE. ("It's not about maps," he told me before class.)
Fernandez flipped through a series of slides on a digital projector as
he talked about the importance of empathy, open-mindedness, and
even political tolerance. One slide showed a massive gorilla hugging
a tiny kitten. Another slide featured a ferocious-looking dog slob-
bering kisses onto a timid cat. For a generation of Googlers hooked
on Internet memes, this was valuable cultural currency. The slides
also provided some welcome levity as Fernandez prepared to dive
into what he and Meng said were the principles of effective leader-

ship. The first was to lead with compassion, citing the working definition of Thupten Jinpa, the Dalai Lama's translator: "a mental state endowed with a sense of concern for the suffering of others and aspiration to see that suffering relieved."

After Fernandez's riff on compassion, Meng launched into a discussion about management consultant Jim Collins's hierarchy of leadership. At the bottom of Collins's pyramid is the highly capable individual, who makes contributions through hard work and talent. Higher-order workers are defined by working toward group objectives, finding efficiencies, and leading a team while setting high standards. The top of Collins's pyramid is the Level 5 executive, who "builds enduring greatness through a paradoxical combination of personal humility plus professional will." It's a counterintuitive truth: some of the most effective leaders are in fact some of the humblest people you'll meet. Instead of being confident of their own perspectives to the exclusion of others' opinions, they solicit advice and make others feel welcome. Instead of bullying colleagues into submission, they work to make them feel unthreatened and included. In other words, they exhibit traits that look an awful lot like compassion. "The reason we are practicing compassion is because it leads to Level 5 leadership," Meng said. "And happiness. And world peace."

Before students had time to digest this lesson, Meng moved straight on to teachings about how compassion can be practiced and learned. Compassion is no different from playing the piano or solving math problems, Meng argued. "All the highest qualities of the mind can be trained," he said. "They are habits." To get the Googlers started, he introduced them to *tonglen*, an ancient Tibetan practice that cultivates compassion. The technique involves visualizing oneself taking on the pain of others as you breathe in, then exhaling wishes for happiness and well-being for all sentient beings. The purpose, Meng said, is to develop an inclination toward unconditional love for all beings. "It creates the habit of seeing goodness in everyone, even the assholes," Meng said. "If you know someone, and he's a dick, you'll still see that he's a dick, but you'll also see goodness in him." The students practiced *tonglen* for several minutes, taking deep belly breaths that filled the room with sweet-sounding sighs. In a question-and-answer session that followed, one female engineer asked Meng about joy, which she said she had been feeling lately, in part because she had begun meditating.

Meng launched into a lecture on *piti,* the Pali word for the rapturous concentration found in deep meditative states. This led to a discussion of self-compassion, and how we can cope with our own unhappiness more effectively. "Pain happens to everyone and always will," Fernandez said. "Suffering is something else. It comes from grasping onto that pain and making it a part of our identity. You can experience pain without suffering. Things are impermanent by their nature."

If this approach seems a bit scattershot, it is. Search Inside Yourself crams a ton of learning into a short amount of time, trusting that its high-achieving students are up to the task of taking in some radical ideas and transforming their lives in short order. Meng figures even small doses of potent practices can be effective. Indeed, researchers know that an eight-week MBSR course can rewire the brain, reduce stress, and ameliorate depression. But can the basic principles of mindfulness be communicated in a weekend course? Or a day? Or three hours? Meng and the team behind Search Inside Yourself are trying to find out, looking for what they call the "minimum effective dose" that can incline people toward more mindful lives. There's growing evidence that even short bursts of mindfulness practice can have a big impact. Boston University researchers showed that as little as three and a half hours of mindfulness was enough to make substantive changes in the structure of the brain.

"We're iterating," Fernandez said. "We're trying new things out. Sometimes they work. Sometimes they don't work. This is Google."

It's typical Silicon Valley thinking: efficiency and speed, even when it comes to enlightenment. Training your mind and changing your brain may take serious time and effort. But if there are shortcuts, leave it to the folks at Google to find them.

Over the course of Search Inside Yourself, Googlers who are lucky enough to be included also get primers on Emotional Intelligence, MBSR and the work of Jon Kabat-Zinn, the health perils of stress, the physiology of an amygdala hijack, and neuroplasticity. "What we think, what we do, and most importantly what we pay attention to can change the brain," Meng tells his students. Thousands of Googlers have taken the course, which is available to all employees on a first-come, first-served basis. Meng is working to train new co-instructors to meet demand. The waiting list is often several hundred people long.

At times, Search Inside Yourself comes off as one part Deepak Chopra and one part Harvard Business School, and lectures are peppered with stories straight from the Buddhist canon, as well as citations of academic research. Its pedigree, however, is unparalleled. Meng developed Search Inside Yourself with Mirabai Bush, a longtime practitioner and one of the first teachers to bring mindfulness to the workplace, and Daniel Goleman, the Emotional Intelligence pioneer. And more than any other in-office program out there, Search Inside Yourself does a comprehensive job of blending meditative practice, intellectually rigorous teachings, and genuinely practical techniques that have the potential to transform the many hours we spend at work.

Now, with Search Inside Yourself running at full speed, Meng has set his sights beyond his own company. He wants to see if Google's unique blend of mindfulness and Emotional Intelligence training can catch on elsewhere in corporate America. In true Silicon Valley fashion, he didn't commission market research or hire a consultancy to see if the idea would fly. Instead, he launched a startup that will either take off or flop.

The Search Inside Yourself Leadership Institute (SIYLI, its acronym, is pronounced "silly") was founded with the intention to offer the curriculum to other big companies. Early results have been encouraging. Corporations across the country have signed up, bringing in accredited teachers from SIYLI to offer up Meng's unique blend of mindfulness and EQ to employees. Tech companies Plantronics and VMware were early customers. Defense contractors and other East Coast multinationals have done abbreviated courses. Accounts with Farmers Insurance, SAP, Autodesk, and more suggest that SIYLI holds appeal across a wide spectrum of the business world. At Plantronics, the first full customer, "it changed the tenor of conflict resolution in meetings," said chief strategy officer Barry Margerum. "Those that went through the classes are employing different ways of speaking when they need to express their feelings," he said. "It's less confrontational, more open, and people are more careful when they speak."

Google's efforts with Search Inside Yourself and SIYLI are an extension of its corporate DNA. When Google went public in 2004, cofounder Larry Page penned a letter to investors, warning them that this was not your average company. There's the famous line, of course: "Don't be evil." Page expounded on this, writing that "we believe strongly that in the long term, we will be better served — as shareholders and in all other ways — by a company that does good things for the world even if we forgo some short term gains." But the very next section of the letter went even further, declaring it was Google's intention not only to *not* be bad, but to also proactively be a force for good. Page even used the word *mindful,* a prescient note that forecasted the work of Search Inside Yourself. "We aspire to make Google an institution that makes the world a better place," Page wrote. "In pursuing this goal, we will always be mindful of our responsibilities to our shareholders, employees, customers and business partners."

Ten years later, Googlers today tend to be disarmingly earnest when preaching the corporate mission. When I asked Meng why mindfulness was so popular in Silicon Valley, and why Search Inside Yourself was so popular at Google, his reply was typically sincere. "The corporate spirit here is to radically change things for the better, to take radical steps for improving the world," Meng said. "At Google we created something useful and are giving the crown jewels away for free. Search Inside Yourself is along those lines. What if we can do something groundbreaking here — teaching Emotional Intelligence, and mindfulness at work — then give it away, so the world becomes a better place? It's a very altruistic and idealistic culture."

Fernandez echoed these sentiments: "At the level of the people who work here every day, we have the aspiration to have the happiest and most productive and innovative workplace." And Google chairman and former chief executive Eric Schmidt sings the same song. When Meng wrote a book about Search Inside Yourself, Schmidt blurbed, "This book and the course it's based on represent one of the greatest aspects of Google's culture — that one individual with a great idea can really change the world."

Meng, never one to shy away from speaking his mind, was even more forceful in his characterization of Silicon Valley. "Northern California is becoming the spiritual capital of the world," he said, going on to frame the mindfulness revolution in the history of Buddhist teachings across the ages. "What we are doing is the fourth turning of the wheel of the dharma (a term to describe different Buddhist epochs). The first was Buddha, then Mahayana (the schools that include Zen), and then Vajrayana (the Tibetan tradition). Now this."

Search Inside Yourself and SIYLI are quintessential representations of mainstream mindfulness today. Grounded in scientific literature, emphasizing the benefits of stress reduction and improved productivity, all in a lighthearted, easygoing tone, the program succeeds in making the difficult work of confronting our rambunctious minds — and trying to decrease our emotional reactivity — seem like an entirely manageable endeavor. One part stress reduction, one part performance enhancement, one part compassion, and one part profit motive, mindfulness as it's being practiced at Google, and throughout Silicon Valley, is a window into the wider world of mindfulness at work today and, as Huston Smith said, the future in microcosm.

It's not perfect. Critics may label it McMindfulness and quibble with the motives of the practitioners and the authenticity of the techniques. But if, through practice, employees become a little less stressed out, if relations between coworkers become just a bit more harmonious, if companies are inspired to behave just a little better — that will be a good thing indeed. Besides, it might be the best thing going right now. Until a National Organization of Mindfulness starts certifying teachers and making them widely available around the country, efforts like Search Inside Yourself and SIYLI are needed more than ever.

Even the best in-office program can do only so much good, though. Being mindful at work is not the responsibility of our employers. It is our responsibility. It is not a human resources function. It is an intimate personal journey. And it is not something that happens only at the office, from nine to five; it is a round-the-clock effort that demands the full attention of our hearts and minds. Our work lives are no longer confined to the office. Most professionals check their e-mail at home, fuss about to-do lists over the weekend, and return to work Monday feeling as if a couple of days off was merely a momentary respite from the overwhelming continuum of their jobs. With mindfulness, we can change that dynamic. When each moment of our lives is an opportunity for practice, work is not some tedious burden that saps our energy and dictates our lives. Instead, work is yet another opportunity to be mindful.

Much of this work starts at the personal level. If we truly want to experience a new way to work, we must begin with ourselves. It doesn't matter if your office has built-in meditation rooms or if your company's founder is motivated by wholesome intentions; if you're not doing your own part to become a more mindful worker, the rest of that will scarcely matter. As I discovered fifteen years ago in India, a critical foundation of mindfulness is diligent meditation practice. This comes in various forms. For some, it may be a daily sitting routine. For others, it may be walking meditation at the office. Still others may focus on loving-kindness meditation. Regardless of the technique, a commitment to the practice is critical if we are to pursue mindful work.

I go through different routines depending on what else is happening in my life. Sometimes I'll wake up in the morning and hit the meditation cushion. Other times, especially when mornings are busy, I'll go to weekly sitting groups with other mindful workers in New York. And sometimes, when the daily meditation practice falters, I'll simply take time to get in touch with my bodily sensations, thoughts, and emotions in more fleeting moments throughout the day. Walking down the long hall that leads from my desk to the restroom, I'll be aware of the sensations as I walk, rather than letting my mind wander to the next story I have to write. Riding the elevator up to the cafeteria, I'll tune in to the weird experience of my body being lifted through space. Techniques like these have been effective for 2,600 years or so and still work their magic today. The same practices that pioneers like Jack Kornfield, Sharon Salzberg, and Joseph Goldstein brought back to the United States some forty years ago are just as powerful now. The same techniques practiced by Steve Jobs in isolation are no less potent when done in the office, many decades later.

And though the practice remains the same, we now have new insights into just what is happening when we invite ourselves to be transformed by meditation. Our amygdala response is tempered, preventing us from going into fight-or-flight mode at the first sign of conflict. The gray matter in our prefrontal cortex, an area of the brain associated with higher-order thinking and pro-social emotions like compassion, empathy, and love, is growing stronger. Our minds and bodies are becoming healthier. It can help us improve our immune response, heal faster, and even lose weight.

Mindfulness won't transform our entire economic system on its own. Creating a world with more equitable distribution of wealth, less corruption and greed, and a sustainable future will take not only mindful awareness, but also a whole lot of new policy, as well as the undoing of habits and systems as old as history itself. Perfection is more than should be expected from a simple meditative technique. Though mindfulness has been changing lives for millennia, it has not eradicated poverty or ended wars, and it would be folly to expect it to do as much now, especially given the magnitude of the challenges we face.

Instead, mindfulness can change us from the inside out. It can make us compassionately accepting of imperfection. It can shift us from reaction to response, from greed to gratitude, from fear to forgiveness. And it can do the same for business. When mindful workers occupy positions from the C-suite to the factory floor, there's a real opportunity for individuals, groups of workers, and companies to change for the better. Workplaces can become more humane, products can become more sustainable, consumers can make better choices. And slowly, mindfulness can start to change the culture, and capitalism, one dollar at a time.

Whatever kind of work we do, the practice of mindfulness can bring new depth to our jobs. For office workers, it might reduce stress, making drab days in cubicles more bearable. For athletes or emergency workers, it may improve concentration, giving them an edge in the midst of frenzied action. For executives, it might open up the space to lead more effectively. And with good luck and hard work, a quiet revolution can take place in the workplaces of the world. Every one of us has the power to foment that change inside ourselves. To start, just follow your breath.

Acknowledgments

THESE PAGES WOULD BE BLANK were it not for the inspiration, support, and wisdom of many guides.

Robert Pryor of Antioch University led me to the source of these incredible traditions. My first real teacher, Anagarika Munindra, remains top of mind and deep in my heart. S. N. Goenka taught me how to sit, really sit. And Chökyi Nyima Rinpoche still reminds me how lively the teachings can be.

Sharon Salzberg, first as an author I read, and now as a friend, was so generous with her wisdom and compassion. Joseph Goldstein was both welcoming and patient as I found my way through the material. Mark Epstein was unfailingly encouraging. Daniel Goleman, fellow Timesman, guided me as I discovered all that writing a book did and didn't need to be. Robert Thurman reminded me that wisdom is sometimes crazy. And a deep bow to Jon Kabat-Zinn, who first suggested I write *Mindful Work*. Teachers I know less well but whose instructions provided invaluable inspiration include Guy and Sally Armstrong, James Baraz, Tara Brach, Eugene Cash, Jack Kornfield, Phillip Moffitt, and Rodney Smith.

At the *Financial Times,* where this project started, special thanks to Gillian Tett, who supported the idea from the start, and Sue Matthias, editor of the *FT Weekend Magazine,* who took a chance on an offbeat story. Richard Waters set the ball rolling by hiring me. And Andrew Edgecliffe-Johnson, my friend and neighbor, continues to teach me much about work and family.

At the *New York Times,* big ups to Andrew Ross Sorkin and Jeff Cane, first for bringing me onboard, then for letting me see this through. Colleagues on DealBook, especially Michael J. de la Merced, put up with my side project amid an always-busy beat. Matt Richtel gave me pro tips on how to get stuff done. Dean Murphy gave me the space to be a mindful M&A reporter. And Jill Abramson and Susan Chira made it clear I didn't need to be a closet meditator at the *Times.*

It was at the UC Berkeley Graduate School of Journalism that I learned how to practice my craft. Though Lydia Chavez didn't think I should have been accepted in the first place, she nonetheless taught me how to report, report, report. Marcia Parker made me understand that business journalism need not be boring. Deirdre English taught me a thing or two about leadership, not to mention magazines. And Michael Pollan and Russ Rymer taught me how to write, and think, long.

Over the past few years, many sources became friends. Jud Brewer, Mirabai Bush, Rich Fernandez, Alan Fleischmann, Hanuman Goleman, Tara Bennett-Goleman, Soren Gordhamer, Amy Gross, Jeremy Hunter, Janice Marturano, Melvin McLeod, Chade-Meng Tan, Jessica Morey, Jonathan Rose, Tim Ryan, Jeff Walker, Pamela Weiss, and many others showed me just how diverse mindful work can be. I'm at least one-tenth of a percent happier for knowing Dan Harris, and this book is at least 10 percent better thanks to his input. And Jim Gimian and Barry Boyce were gracious sounding boards, cheerleaders, and coconspirators.

I was blessed with an all-star team as this came together. Amanda Urban at ICM believed I could write a book before I even had a topic, then helped me craft a pitch and steer me to one of the best editors out there. Eamon Dolan was both gracious and tough, at once encouraging but also skeptical, pushing me out of my comfort zone and then reining me in — in short, all the things a good editor should be. His team at Houghton Mifflin Harcourt punches well above its weight, and most importantly, Eamon and HMH publish books that change people's minds. It's a delight to have a place on their bookshelf.

Bill and Susan Morgan weren't very communicative over the past few years, seeing as they were on silent retreat the whole time, but their practice helped point me in the right direction nonetheless. Other dear friends who keep me grounded include Chris Abraham, Megan Berner, Andrew Curry and Effie Kapsalis, Raman Frey, Josh and Mollye Fryday, the Lader family, Aimee and Minh Le, John Peabody, Brian Pollack, Eric Simons, Ian and Ceylan Thomson, Oliver Uberti, and Malia Wollan.

Seth Boyd and Melanie Berner were unfailingly supportive, and their orange tabby cat, Horace, purred loudly as I worked on this manuscript in the woods of New Hampshire. Karen Boyd gives me room to be myself and gave me a room to write this book. And Marc and Linda Boyd help us keep it together and remind us how to have fun. Ruth Felt remains a dear friend and mentor after all these years. Christine Garvey's kindness knows no bounds.

When I was a kid, my dad, George Gelles, told me I should be a writer. He was right, and he went about teaching me how to edit. Since then, he's shown me what it means to be serious about one's craft, and the value of practice. My mom, Bonnie Pitman, is the most inspiring person I know. Setbacks that would have leveled weaker spirits just made hers grow stronger. She sets an example with her voracious curiosity and joy that I try to follow every day, and I know this will count as something new. They spoil me with their love.

Ali, you make me happier than a ten-day meditation retreat. I desire nothing more than your company, which makes me suffer less. Were all that not enough, you brought us Frances Rose Gelles, who is already my greatest teacher in this world.

May you all be happy.

Instructions

BASIC MINDFULNESS MEDITATION is a simple practice. Getting started can be hard. If you're new to it, try starting with just five minutes a day. Don't worry if it's difficult at first, or if you get sleepy when you meditate. Becoming an expert meditator overnight isn't what matters. What matters is that we make the effort to become more mindful of our bodies, thoughts, and emotions.

- Find a posture that is comfortable for you. Sitting upright, with your back straight, is ideal. You can sit in a chair, or on a cushion on the floor, but make sure your spine is erect.
- Close your eyes and take a few deep breaths, settling into your seat. Feel the weight of your body. Relax your jaw, neck, shoulders, arms, and legs. Let your breath come and go naturally, gently, without any effort.
- Notice the sensations throughout your body, from your head to your toes. You might feel warmth, coolness, pleasant sensations, or even some discomfort. Just be aware of these sensations for now, without changing your posture.
- When you're ready, pick one sensation — such as the feeling of your breath passing in and out of your nostrils — and give it your entire attention. Let other sensations recede to the periphery of your awareness, and focus on just this sensation.
- As you rest in awareness of the breath, notice how complex the act of breathing really is. The lungs expand and contract,

causing the torso to rise and fall. Air is passing in through the nose, tickling the nostrils, whooshing in and out.

- Choose one spot, perhaps the indentation above the lips but below the nose, and notice what the breath feels like as it passes by that small patch of skin. Stay with that sensation, resting your attention there as you breathe in, and out.

- After a few breaths, or maybe just one breath, your attention will probably wander. You may notice other sensations in the body, things happening around you, or just get lost in thought, daydreaming about the past or present, possibly judging yourself or others.

- When this happens, simply notice what it is you were thinking about or what was distracting you. Acknowledge it, let it go, and gently return your attention to the breath, noticing each inhalation and exhalation.

- After a few breaths, inevitably, the mind will resume its wandering. When this happens, begin again. Noticing the cause of your distraction, and regaining control of your attention — countless times — is the heart of the practice and, with time, yields enormous rewards.

- When you're ready — after ten minutes, thirty minutes, or an hour — open your eyes. Though your formal meditation practice may have ended, your mindful awareness can continue throughout the day.

Resources

ONLINE

There's no dearth of writing about mindfulness on the Web, and it's not always easy to separate the wheat from the chaff. Here are a few good places to start, maintained by meditators who know what they're talking about:

Greater Good

Run out of UC Berkeley, the Greater Good Science Center sponsors research into social and emotional well-being and also publishes articles and videos about mindfulness, compassion, gratitude, and happiness.
http://greatergood.berkeley.edu

Mindful

The publishers of *Mindful* magazine maintain a lively website with news about the latest research into mindfulness, and stories of its application at work and in everyday life.
http://www.mindful.org

Mindfulness Research Guide

Compiling the latest scientific and academic research into mindfulness, this guide, and its companion monthly newsletter, provides comprehensive updates on the field.
http://www.mindfulexperience.org

Wisdom 2.0

The biggest mindfulness conference in the market, Wisdom 2.0 makes videos of all its programs available online for free.
http://www.wisdom2summit.com

TRAINING

A growing number of outfits offer mindfulness training in the workplace, though still not nearly enough to meet the surging demand. Here are a handful of training programs whose heads and hearts are in the right place.

Appropriate Response

Offering in-depth courses that focus on cultivating mindfulness in the office, Appropriate Response's signature offering is the Personal Excellence Project, which has been used by Salesforce.com and Genentech, among others.
http://www.appropriateresponse.com

The Center for Contemplative Mind in Society

With a focus on higher education today, the center did some of the earliest work to bring mindfulness into the workplace and continues to offer retreats and training.
http://www.contemplativemind.org

Center for Mindfulness in Medicine, Health Care, and Society

The organization founded by Jon Kabat-Zinn continues to do pioneering work and has branched out into teaching mindfulness in the workplace.
http://www.umassmed.edu/cfm

eMindful

The group that partnered with Aetna has a wide range of offerings to teach mindfulness in the workplace, some more effective than others. http://www.emindful.com

Institute for Mindful Leadership

Janice Marturano has taken her work from General Mills and created a curriculum that is broadly applicable to leaders in any field. http://instituteformindfulleadership.org

The Potential Project

Run out of Denmark, with programs around the world, this group has a growing business teaching mindfulness practice inside big corporations. http://www.potentialproject.com

Search Inside Yourself Leadership Institute

An offshoot of Google's in-house program, SIYLI brings mindfulness — Silicon Valley style — to other offices around the country. http://www.siyli.org

Wisdom Labs

Founded by Search Inside Yourself instructor Rich Fernandez, Wisdom Labs is offering holistic wellness programs to companies large and small, with a curriculum emphasizing mindfulness at work. http://wisdomlabs.com

RESEARCH

Academics and scientists are investigating the effects of mindfulness on the brain, the body, and our behavior. While this work is happening at hundreds of universities around the globe, a few institutions stand above the rest.

The Center for Compassion and Altruism Research and Education

Run out of the Stanford University School of Medicine, CCARE promotes research and dialogue with the aim of cultivating compassion and promoting altruism among individuals and society at large.
http://ccare.stanford.edu

Center for Investigating Healthy Minds

Richard Davidson's outfit at the University of Wisconsin, Madison, conducts research on mindfulness, compassion, kindness, and altruism.
http://www.investigatinghealthyminds.org

Center for Mindfulness in Medicine, Health Care, and Society

While it has branched out to teaching mindfulness in the workplace, the Center for Mindfulness also promotes significant research and hosts an annual conference that brings together the brightest minds in the field.
http://www.umassmed.edu/cfm

Duke Integrative Medicine

The center conducts research and offers training in a bid to place Western medicine in dialogue with alternative techniques including mindfulness.
http://www.dukeintegrativemedicine.org

UCLA Mindful Awareness Research Center

Sponsoring research and offering training and retreats, MARC works to promote mindfulness through education and research from its base in Los Angeles.
http://marc.ucla.edu

RETREAT CENTERS

Garrison Institute

Just outside New York City, the Garrison Institute hosts a range of secular and Buddhist teachers in a spectacular former Christian monastery.
http://www.garrisoninstitute.org

Insight Meditation Society

The first retreat center opened in the United States to teach mindfulness meditation, IMS, based in western Massachusetts, offers year-round programs, some lasting just a few days, some lasting a few months.
http://www.dharma.org

Omega Institute

Located in upstate New York, Omega offers mindfulness, yoga, and sustainable living courses.
http://www.eomega.org

Spirit Rock

The sister institution of IMS, located just north of San Francisco, Spirit Rock is also a more traditional retreat center, offering longer retreats as well as daily programs for beginners.
http://www.spiritrock.org

BOOKS

There's a growing library of excellent books on mindfulness and meditation. Here are a few of my favorites.

Boyce, Barry, ed. *The Mindfulness Revolution*. Boston: Shambhala
    Publications, 2011.

Brach, Tara. *Radical Acceptance*. New York: Bantam Dell, 2003.

Chade-Meng Tan. *Search Inside Yourself: The Unexpected Path to Achieving Success, Happiness (and World Peace)*. San Francisco: HarperOne, 2012.

Davidson, Richard, and Sharon Begley. *The Emotional Life of Your Brain: How Its Unique Patterns Affect the Way You Think, Feel, and Live — and How You Can Change Them*. New York: Plume, 2012.

Epstein, Mark. *Going to Pieces Without Falling Apart: A Buddhist Perspective on Wholeness*. New York: Broadway Books, 1998.

Goleman, Daniel. *Focus: The Hidden Driver of Excellence*. New York: Harper, 2013.

Harris, Dan. *10% Happier*. New York: It Books, 2014.

Kabat-Zinn, Jon. *Coming to Our Senses: Healing Ourselves and the World Through Mindfulness*. New York: Hyperion, 2005.

———. *Wherever You Go, There You Are: Mindfulness Meditation in Everyday Life*. New York: Hyperion, 1996.

Kornfield, Jack. *A Path with Heart: A Guide Through the Perils and Promises of Spiritual Life*. New York: Bantam, 1993.

Marturano, Janice. *Finding the Space to Lead: A Practical Guide to Mindful Leadership*. New York: Bloomsbury, 2014.

Ryan, Tim. *A Mindful Nation: How a Simple Practice Can Help Us Reduce Stress, Improve Performance, and Recapture the American Spirit*. Carlsbad, CA: Hay House Publishing, 2013.

Salzberg, Sharon. *Faith: Trusting Your Own Deepest Experience*. New York: Riverhead Books, 2002.

———. *Real Happiness: The Power of Meditation*. New York: Workman Publishing Company, 2010.

Notes

Introduction

Page

1 *Their guest of honor:* Jonathan Rotenberg, "June 6, 1981: The Day I Met Steve Jobs," HighTechHistory.com, http://hightechhistory.com/2012/01/11/june-6-1981-the-day-i-met-steve-jobs/.

1. This Mindful Moment

19 *"I thought I'd bounce back":* David Gelles, "The Mind Business," *Financial Times,* August 24, 2012.

21 *At the 2013 World Economic Forum:* "Can 'Mindful' Meditation Increase Profits?," BBC.com, January 29, 2013.

22 *An article on "mindful leadership":* Bill George, "Mindfulness Helps You Become a Better Leader," Harvard Business Review Blog Network, October 26, 2012.
From 2004 to 2013: Google Trends, http://www.google.com/trends.

23 *"paying attention in a particular way":* Jon Kabat-Zinn, *Wherever You Go, There You Are: Mindfulness Meditation in Everyday Life* (New Work: Hyperion, 2005), 4.

25 *"The ultimate promise of mindfulness":* Jon Kabat-Zinn, "Why Mindfulness Matters," in *The Mindfulness Revolution,*

edited by Barry Boyce (Boston: Shambhala Publications, 2011), 58.

26 *"as steady as a stone"*: Karl Weick, *Making Sense of the Organization.* Vol. 2, *The Impermanent Organization* (New York: John Wiley & Sons, 2012), Chapter 6.

28 *After a seven-week course:* Institute for Mindful Leadership, "Research," 2011, http://instituteformindfulleadership.org/research.

29 *Just 47 percent of Americans:* "Job Satisfaction: 2012 Edition," *The Conference Board,* http://www.conference-board.org/publications/publicationdetail.cfm?publicationid=2258.
    "In the financial crisis": Kabat-Zinn, "Why Mindfulness Matters," 59.

30 *"No one is* compos sui*"*: William James, *The Principles of Psychology* (New York: Cosimo, 2007), 424.

2. How the Swans Came to the Lake

34 *"If you observe your mind"*: Mirka Knaster, *Living This Life Fully* (Boston: Shambhala Publications, 2010), 11.

35 *The first mentions of qualities akin to mindfulness:* J. J. Miller, "Three-Year Follow-up and Clinical Implications of a Mindfulness Meditation-Based Stress Reduction Intervention in the Treatment of Anxiety Disorders," *General Hospital Psychiatry* 17 (1995): 192.
    "It is through the establishment of the lovely clarity of mindfulness": Jack Kornfield, "Doing the Buddha's Practice," *Shambhala Sun,* http://www.shambhalasun.com/index.php?option=content&task=view&id=3101&Itemid=247.
    In 1840 Ralph Waldo Emerson: Rick Fields, *How the Swans Came to the Lake* (Boston: Shambhala Publications, 1992), 54.

36 *"live deliberately"*: Stefanie Syman, *The Subtle Body: The Story*

of Yoga in America (New York: Farrar, Straus and Giroux, 2010), 27.

37   *"he forecast an American Buddhism":* Rick Fields, "Thoreau the Buddhist," *The Review of Arts, Literature, Philosophy and the Humanities,* http://www.ralphmag.org/thoreau-swansJ .html.

38   *"Thoreau's two years at Walden Pond":* Jon Kabat-Zinn, *Wherever You Go, There You Are: Mindfulness Meditation in Everyday Life* (New York: Hyperion, 1994), 24.

39   *"I said, 'I'm going to cut out'":* "Buddhism & the Beat Generation," *Tricycle,* Fall 1995.

41   *"Boomer Buddhists":* Stephen Prothero, "Boomer Buddhism," in *Mindfulness in the Marketplace: Compassionate Responses to Consumerism,* edited by Allan Hunt Badiner (Berkeley: Parallax Press, 2002), 161.
     9.4 percent of respondents said they meditated: National Center for Complementary and Alternative Medicine, "Meditation: An Introduction," http://nccam.nih.gov/health/ meditation/overview.htm.

42   *"You know how it is with stories":* Panel discussion at the New York Academy of Sciences, February 6, 2013.

44   *"Healing From Within":* Bill Moyers, *Healing and the Mind,* PBS, 1993.

50   *"Monsanto became more open":* "Why Mindfulness and Meditation Are Good for Business," Knowledge @ Wharton, http://knowledge.wharton.upenn.edu/printer_friendly .cfm?articleid=3218.

51   *"Toynbee may have noticed something":* David Loy, "Why Buddhism Needs the West," *Tricycle,* Spring 2009.
     Though mindfulness can't be considered Buddhist: Thanks to Jon Kabat-Zinn for that analogy.

3. The Science of Sitting

58 *In 1983, R. Adam Engle:* Jill Suttie, "The New Science of Mind," *Shambhala Sun,* March 2012, 54.

62 *When he returned to Cambridge:* Barry Boyce, "Taking the Measure of Mind," *Shambhala Sun,* March 2012, 42.

64 *substantially thicker than that of non-cabbies:* Eleanor Maguire, Katherine Woollett, and Hugo J. Spiers, "London Taxi Drivers and Bus Drivers: A Structural MRI and Neuropsychological Analysis," *Hippocampus* 16 (2006): 1091.
A study of violinists: Thomas Elbert et al., "Increased Cortical Representation of the Fingers of the Left Hand in String Players," *Science* 270, no. 5234 (1995): 305.

65 *whether meditation changed the brain's physical structure:* Sara Lazar et al., "Meditation Experience Is Associated With Increased Cortical Thickness," *Neuroreport* 16, no. 17 (2005): 1893.

66 *"brain regions involved in learning":* Britta Hölzel et al., "Mindfulness Practice Leads to Increases in Regional Brain Gray Matter Density," *Psychiatry Research: Neuroimaging* 191 (2011): 36.
"It is fascinating": Sue McGreevey, "Eight Weeks to a Better Brain," *Harvard Gazette,* January 21, 2011, http://news. harvard.edu/gazette/story/2011/01/eight-weeks-to-a-better -brain/.

68 *emotional regulation cultivated by meditation:* Gaelle Desbordes et al., "Effects of Mindful-Attention and Compassion Meditation Training on Amygdala Response to Emotional Stimuli in an Ordinary, Non-meditative State," *Frontiers of Human Neuroscience* 6 (2012): 292.

70 *Studies on mindfulness funded by the National Institutes of*

Health: Jeff Warren, "Enlightenment: Is Science Ready to Take It Seriously?," *Psychology Tomorrow,* November 2012. *"A Quest for Compassion":* Greg Miller, "A Quest for Compassion," *Science* 324, no. 5926 (2009): 458.

72   *"That is not the purpose of science":* Linda Heuman, "Meditation Nation," Tricycle.com, April 25, 2014, http:// www.tricycle.com/blog/meditation-nation.

4. Less Stressed

82   *"Most people are first drawn to the practice":* Jon Kabat-Zinn, *Coming to Our Senses: Healing Ourselves and the World Through Mindfulness* (New York: Hyperion, 2005), 72. *Sixty-nine percent of employees:* American Psychological Association, "Fact Sheet: Workplace Stress," http://www.apa .org/practice/programs/workplace/phwp-fact-sheet.pdf.

83   *stress levels have increased:* "Who's Stressed in the US? Carnegie Mellon Researchers Study Adult Stress Levels From 1983–2009," Eurekalert.com, June 11, 2012, http://www. eurekalert.org/pub_releases/2012-06/cmu-wsi061112.php.

84   *"We're basically the descendants":* Noah Shachtman, "Enlightenment Engineers," *Wired,* June 2013.

85   *"mount an aggressive approach":* Arianna Huffington, "Mindfulness, Meditation, Wellness and Their Connection to Corporate America's Bottom Line," *Huffington Post,* March 18, 2013, http://www.huffingtonpost.com/arianna-huffington/ corporate-wellness_b_2903222.html. *"demands and pressures of the recent past":* American Psychological Association, "Stress: The Different Kinds of Stress," http://www.apa.org/helpcenter/stress-kinds.aspx.

86   *the meditators reported that they were less stressed:* Michael

Chaskalson, *The Mindful Workplace* (Chichester, West Sussex: Wiley-Blackwell, 2011).

87 *significantly more flu antibodies:* Richard Davidson et al., "Alterations in Brain and Immune Function Produced by Mindfulness Meditation," *Psychosomatic Medicine* 65 (2003): 564.

a meta-analysis of studies: Paul Grossman et al., "Mindfulness-Based Stress Reduction and Health Benefits: A Meta-Analysis," *Journal of Psychosomatic Research* 57 (2004): 35.

spotlight on the stress hormones: "Mindfulness From Meditation Associated With Lower Stress Hormone," *UC Davis News and Information,* March 27, 2013, http://www.news.ucdavis.edu/search/news_detail.lasso?id=10538.

mindfulness increased happiness: Willem Kuyken et al., "Effectiveness of the Mindfulness in Schools Programme: Non-Randomised Controlled Feasibility Study," *British Journal of Psychiatry,* August 2013: 203.

88 *those who practiced were less stressed:* Jill Ladwig, "Study Shows Mindfulness Training Can Help Reduce Teacher Stress and Burnout," *University of Wisconsin–Madison News,* August 28, 2013, http://www.news.wisc.edu/22069.

In 2007 a group of employees: Cara Geary and S. L. Rosenthal, "Sustained Impact of MBSR on Stress, Well-Being, and Daily Spiritual Experiences for 1 Year in Academic Health Care Employees," *The Journal of Alternative and Complementary Medicine* 17, no. 10 (2011): 939.

study of how mindfulness can improve health: David Creswell et al., "Mindfulness Meditation Training Effects on CD4+ T Lymphocytes in HIV-1 Infected Adults: A Small Randomized Controlled Trial," *Brain, Behavior and Immunity* 23 (2009): 184.

89 *a large group of patients with psoriasis:* Jon Kabat-Zinn et al., "Influence of a Mindfulness Meditation-Based Stress Reduction Intervention on Rates of Skin Clearing in Patients With Moderate to Severe Psoriasis Undergoing Phototherapy (UVB) and Photochemotherapy (PUVA)," *Psychosomatic Medicine* 60, no. 5 (1998): 625.

93 *It is early morning in Waterbury:* "SWRP 72412," YouTube.com, July 25, 2012, http://www.youtube.com/embed/9AuCmqZfubg?rel=0.

96 *Michael Krasner, a professor:* Pauline Chen, "How Mindfulness Can Make for Better Doctors," *The New York Times,* October 15, 2009.

97 *employees at a bank in Johannesburg:* Abdool Karrim Ismail et al., "Towards Gaining a Competitive Advantage: The Relationship Between Burnout, Job Satisfaction, Social Support and Mindfulness," *Journal of Contemporary Management* 10 (2013): 448.

98 *"Depression is often kept going":* Therese Borchard, "How Does Mindfulness Reduce Depression? An Interview with John Teasdale, Ph.D.," EverydayHealth.com, November 11, 2013, http://psychcentral.com/blog/archives/2014/01/19/how-does-mindfulness-reduce-depression-an-interview-with-john-teasdale-ph-d/.

5. More Focused

104 *"A person should be able":* Chögyam Trungpa, *Work, Sex, Money* (Boston: Shambhala Publications, 2011), 19.

106 *various attention tests:* Adam Moore and Peter Malinowski, "Meditation, Mindfulness and Cognitive Flexibility," *Consciousness and Cognition* 18 (2009): 176.

107 *a group of human resources professionals:* David Levy et

al., "The Effects of Mindfulness Meditation Training on Multitasking in a High-Stress Information Environment," Graphics Interface Conference, 2012, https://faculty. washington.edu/wobbrock/pubs/gi-12.02.pdf.

109 *Jackson described how he used meditation:* Phil Jackson, *Eleven Rings* (New York: Penguin Press, 2013), 17.

112 *"Athletes in general":* Mason Fries, "Mindfulness Based Stress Reduction for the Changing Work Environment," *Journal of Academic and Business Ethics* 2 (2009), 8.

113 *Pete Carroll, the coach of the Seattle Seahawks:* Alyssa Roenigk, "Lotus Pose on Two," *ESPN the Magazine,* August 2013.

114 *Tim Frazier, who was a point guard:* Ilene Raymond Rush, "Athletes Using Meditation to Improve Performance," *The Philadelphia Inquirer,* March 17, 2014.

116 *"Concentration bolsters mindfulness":* Sharon Salzberg, *Real Happiness at Work: Meditations for Accomplishment, Achievement, and Peace* (New York: Workman Publishing Company, 2013), 45.

120 *There are more cell phones:* Joshua Pramis, "Number of Mobile Phones to Exceed World Population by 2014," DigitalTrends.com, February 28, 2013, http:// www.digitaltrends.com/mobile/mobile-phone-world -population-2014.

121 *"Unlike other animals":* Matthew A. Killingsworth and Daniel T. Gilbert, "A Wandering Mind Is an Unhappy Mind," *Science* 330 (2010): 932.

123 *energy levels and emotional states:* Patricia Poulin et al., "Mindfulness Training as an Evidenced-Based Approach to Reducing Stress and Promoting Well-Being Among Human Services Professionals," *International Journal of Health Promotion & Education* 46, no. 2 (2008): 35.

125 *seemingly beneficial lifestyle changes:* Michael Mrazek et al.,
     "Mindfulness Training Improves Working Memory Capacity
     and GRE Performance While Reducing Mind Wandering,"
     Psychological Science 24, no. 5 (2013): 776.
     A team led by Harvard researchers: Hölzel et al., "Mindfulness
     Practice Leads to Increases in Regional Brain Gray Matter
     Density."
     researchers in Dalian and Beijing: Yi-Yuan Tang et al., "Short-
     Term Meditation Training Improves Attention and Self-
     Regulation," *Proceedings of the National Academy of Sciences*
     104, no. 43 (2007): 17152.

6. Compassionate

130 *Ryan was moved to write a book:* Tim Ryan, *A Mindful Nation:
     How a Simple Practice Can Help Us Reduce Stress, Improve
     Performance, and Recapture the American Spirit* (Carlsbad,
     CA: Hay House Publishing, 2012).

132 *"You actually slow down":* "Conversations on Compassion:
     Congressman Tim Ryan," YouTube.com, September 7, 2012,
     https://www.youtube.com/watch?v=eo4vQVekCf8.

134 *researchers at Northeastern University:* David DeSteno, "The
     Morality of Meditation," *The New York Times,* July 5, 2013.

135 *The phenomenon was recently studied:* Kristin Neff and
     Christopher Germer, "A Pilot Study and Randomized
     Controlled Trial of the Mindful Self-Compassion Program,"
     Journal of Clinical Psychology 69, no. 1 (2012): 28.

139 *"We do not always view compassion":* Salzberg, *Real
     Happiness at Work.*
     "I worried that in competitive career fields": Dan Harris, *10%
     Happier* (New York: It Books, 2014).

144 *Before the team got started:* Jason Marsh, "Can Science Make

Facebook More Compassionate?," *Greater Good,* July 25, 2012.

146 *"It would be easy to be cynical":* Shachtman, "Enlightenment Engineers."

7. Socially Responsible

153 *"Mindful consumption is premised on consciousness":* Jagdish Sheth, Nirmal Sethia, and Shanthi Srinivas, "Mindful Consumption: A Customer-Centric Approach to Sustainability," *Journal of the Academy of Marketing Science* 39, no. 1 (2011): 21.

154 *"Mindful consumption is the way to heal":* Thich Nhat Hanh, *The World We Have: A Buddhist Approach to Peace and Ecology* (Berkeley: Parallax Press, 2008).

158 *In his book* The Responsible Company: Yvon Chouinard and Vincent Stanley, *The Responsible Company: What We've Learned From Patagonia's First 40 Years* (Ventura, CA: Patagonia Books, 2012).

159 *"If your business is causing environmental problems":* Jo Confino, "Google Seeks Out Wisdom of Zen Master Thich Nhat Hanh," *The Guardian* (London), September 5, 2013. *In a paper from 2010:* Nicole E. Ruedy and Maurice E. Schweitzer, "In the Moment: The Effect of Mindfulness on Ethical Decision Making," Russell Ackoff Fellowship of the Wharton Risk Center Working Paper #2010-07-02, July 2010, http://opim.wharton.upenn.edu/risk/library/WPAF2010-07-02_NR,MS.pdf.

165 *Eileen Fisher:* Barry Boyce, "She Wears It Well," *Mindful* magazine, December 2013.

166 *"By working directly":* "Social Consciousness," EileenFisher.com, http://www.eileenfisher.com/EileenFisherCompany/

CompanyGeneralContentPages/SocialConciousness/
madeinchina.jsp.

167 *Mark Bertolini:* Diane Levick, "A Closer Look at Aetna's Next
CEO," *The Hartford Courant,* August 26, 2007.

172 *a succinct refresher on just how mindfulness works:* Ruth
Wolaver et al., "Effective and Viable Mind-Body Stress
Reduction in the Workplace: A Randomized Controlled Trial,"
Journal of Occupational Health Psychology 17, no. 2 (2012): 246.

173 *Self-reported stress had gone down:* Data provided by
eMindful, March 14, 2013.

174 *The result was a company-wide program:* "Aetna Launches
New Programs Designed to Help Reduce Metabolic
Syndrome Risk Factors," *BusinessWire,* April 15, 2013.
Tandon Bunch: Case study provided by Aetna.

176 *modified MBSR programs reduced binge eating:* Bruce Smith
et al., "A Preliminary Study of the Effects of a Modified
Mindfulness Intervention on Binge Eating," *Journal of
Evidence-Based Complementary & Alternative Medicine* 11,
no. 3 (2006): 133.
reduced compulsive eating: Jennifer Daubenmier,
"Mindfulness Intervention for Stress Eating to Reduce
Cortisol and Abdominal Fat Among Overweight and Obese
Women: An Exploratory Randomized Controlled Study,"
Journal of Obesity, 2011.

8. The Space to Lead

182 *"Leadership presence is a tangible quality":* Janice Marturano,
*Finding the Space to Lead: A Practical Guide to Mindful
Leadership* (New York: Bloomsbury, 2014).

183 *"a common refrain of being in 'uncharted waters'":* Jeremy

Hunter and Michael Chaskalson, "Making the Mindful Leader: Cultivating Skills for Facing Adaptive Challenges," in *The Wiley-Blackwell Handbook of the Psychology of Leadership, Change and Organizational Development,* edited by H. Skipton Leonard, Rachel Lewis, Arthur M. Freedman, and Jonathan Passmore (Chichester, West Sussex: Wiley-Blackwell, 2013).

"The use of mindful practices": Bill George, "Developing Mindful Leaders for the C-Suite," Harvard Business Review Blog Network, March 10, 2014, http://blogs.hbr.org/2014/03/developing-mindful-leaders-for-the-c-suite.

184   *"the key is to stay grounded and authentic"*: Bill George, "Mindfulness Helps You Become a Better Leader," Harvard Business Review Blog Network, October 26, 2012, http://blogs.hbr.org/2012/10/mindfulness-helps-you-become-a/.

186   *a book by Jack Kornfield:* Jack Kornfield, *A Path with Heart: A Guide Through the Perils and Promises of Spiritual Life* (New York: Bantam, 1993).

"It literally changed my life": "Wisdom 2 Bill Ford, Jack Kornfield," YouTube.com, February 24, 2013, https://www.youtube.com/watch?v=9W0Wy8-06t4&feature=kp.

195   *an unusual post:* Jeff Weiner, "Managing Compassionately," LinkedIn.com, October 15, 2012.

9. McMindfulness

201   *"the dharma is undergoing a process of gentrification"*: Joshua Eaton, "Gentrifying the Dharma: How the 1 Percent Is Hijacking Mindfulness," Salon.com, March 5, 2014, http://www.salon.com/2014/03/05/gentrifying_the_dharma_how_the_1_is_hijacking_mindfulness/.

202 *"The main delivery system for Buddhist meditation"*: Heuman, "Meditation Nation."

203 *"There's nothing touchy-feely"*: Huffington, "Mindfulness, Meditation, Wellness and Their Connection to Corporate America's Bottom Line."
   a much-read article: Ron Purser and David Loy, "Beyond McMindfulness," *Huffington Post,* July 1, 2013, http://www.huffingtonpost.com/ron-purser/beyond-mcmindfulness_b_3519289.html.

204 *he had pledged 46 percent*: Emily Glazer, "Coffee Mogul Defends Loans," *The Wall Street Journal,* May 10, 2012.

207 *A Thai monk*: Rob Williams, "Buddhist Monk Filmed Enjoying the High-Life on Private Jet Has Assets Frozen," *The Independent* (London), July 4, 2013.

214 *the U.S. Marine Corps book of strategy*: U.S. Marine Corps Staff, *Warfighting* (CreateSpace Independent Publishing Platform, 2012).

217 *Not all the Marines*: Elizabeth Stanley et al., "Mindfulness-Based Mind Fitness Training: A Case Study of a High-Stress Predeployment Military Cohort," *Cognitive and Behavioral Practice* 18 (2011): 566.

218 *"create someone less disposed to action"*: Georgetown University, "Troops' PTSD May Be Reduced With Mind Fitness," http://explore.georgetown.edu/news/?ID=52782.
   he blew a fuse: Laura Gottesdiener, "Christian Fundamentalists Freak Out Over Yoga in the Military," *Salon,* January 9, 2013.

219 *"It's a heck of a return on an investment"*: Courtney Comstock, "Ray Dalio Explains How the Beatles Inspired Him to Meditate," *Business Insider,* October 26, 2010, http://www.businessinsider.com/ray-dalio-talking-about-meditation-hedge-fund-manager-bridgewater-the-beatles-2010-10.

220 *"American life is a powerful solvent"*: Frederic Pryor, "Buddhist Economic Systems," in *Mindfulness in the Marketplace,* edited by Allan Hunt Badiner (Berkeley: Parallax Press, 2002), 163.

227 *mindfulness and McMindfulness*: Jo Confino, "Thich Nhat Hanh: Is Mindfulness Being Corrupted by Business and Finance?," *The Guardian* (London), March 28, 2014.

10. The Future in Microcosm

233 *"When I talk to Google"*: Confino, "Google Seeks Out Wisdom of Zen Master Thich Nhat Hanh."

234 *"the future in microcosm"*: Huston Smith, introduction to *Zen at Work,* by Les Kaye (New York: Random House, 1996), xiii.

241 *"The main benefits"*: Elizabeth Hayes, "Ommmmm . . . Intel Employees Use Mindfulness and Meditation to Cut Stress, Enhance Focus," *Portland Business Journal,* January 22, 2014. *"If we show people pages and pages"*: Kristine Wong, "There's No Price Tag on a Clear Mind: Intel to Launch Mindfulness Program," *The Guardian* (London), April 8, 2014.

244 *"Leadership is not an affair of the head"*: James M. Kouzes and Barry Z. Posner, *Encouraging the Heart: A Leader's Guide to Rewarding and Recognizing Others* (San Francisco: Jossey-Bass, 2003).

245 *"builds enduring greatness"*: Jim Collins, "Level 5 Leadership: The Triumph of Humility and Fierce Resolve," *Harvard Business Review,* July 2005, http://hbr.org/2005/07/level-5 -leadership-the-triumph-of-humility-and-fierce-resolve/ar/1.

Index